TQM: MANAGEMENT PROCESSES FOR QUALITY OPERATIONS

Also available from Quality Press

TQM: Leadership for the Quality Transformation
Richard S. Johnson

TQM: The Mechanics of Quality Processes
Richard S. Johnson and Lawrence E. Kazense

TQM: Quality Training Practices
Richard S. Johnson

TQM: A Step-by-Step Guide to Implementation
Charles N. Weaver, PhD

A TQM Approach to Achieving Manufacturing Excellence
A. Richard Shores

An Approach to Quality Improvement That Works, Second Edition
A. Donald Stratton

Management Excellence Through Quality
Thomas J. Barry

Total Quality Management: Performance and Cost Measures
Dorsey J. Talley

To request a complimentary catalog of publications, call 800-248-1946.

TQM: MANAGEMENT PROCESSES FOR QUALITY OPERATIONS

RICHARD S. JOHNSON

Sponsored by the ASQC
Quality Management Division

Volume II of the ASQC
Total Quality Management Series

ASQC Quality Press
Milwaukee, Wisconsin

TQM: Management Processes for Quality Operations
Richard S. Johnson

Library of Congress Cataloging-in-Publication Data

Johnson, Richard S.
    TQM: management processes for quality operations/Richard S. Johnson.
       p.   cm.—(ASQC total quality management series; v. 2)
    "Sponsored by the ASQC Quality Management Division."
    Includes bibliographical references and index.
    ISBN (invalid) 0-87389-336-7 (alk. paper)
    1. Total quality management. I. Title. II. Series.
HD62.15.J642 1993
658.5'62 — dc20   92-34009
                                          CIP

1098765432

ISBN 0-87389-226-7

Acquisitions Editor: Jeanine L. Lau
Production Editor: Mary Beth Nilles
Marketing Administrator: Susan Westergard
Set in Palatino by Linda J. Shepherd. Cover design by Wayne Dober.
Printed and bound by BookCrafters.

For a free copy of the ASQC Quality Press Publications Catalog, including ASQC membership information, call 800-248-1946.

Printed in the United States of America

   Printed on acid-free recycled paper

  ASQC
Quality Press
611 East Wisconsin Avenue
Milwaukee, Wisconsin 53202

Contents

Acknowledgments

There is an obvious debt to hundreds of authors who have provided the works I studied over the past 30 years. Their thoughts are evident throughout and credit is provided wherever possible. Many of these people are listed in the bibliographies. However, these are only a few of the many authors who have inspired my ideas over a lifetime of study. Often one cannot remember the source of an idea, but knows it came from somewhere.

An even greater debt is owed to the U.S. Navy and the men and women who serve it. I was a member of this outstanding organization for 24 years, a time spent living in a true quality- and process-oriented system with outstanding leaders. Until the Gulf War, most Americans didn't understand the dedication of military personnel nor their capability.

Many leaders and managers from corporations and the government have added to this effort. In my efforts with training and consulting activities, I am in constant contact with dedicated professionals in many organizations. Their thoughts and practices also are a part of the ideas and concepts presented herein.

Credit must be given to unknown authors whose work has appeared on the Board. Over the years I have always had a bulletin board or part of a board where people could post appropriate material. Many statements were developed as an interest grabber for upcoming training subjects. These entries are used in this text and where the entry's contributor is unknown, credit has been simply given to the Board.

Material in this book follows lesson plans developed by Quality America, Inc. of Mechanicsburg, PA. The checklists and lists are from those programs and are used with permission.

Four other people must be recognized for their contributions over a great many years. My grandmother, Maude M. Johnson, who set a fine example during tough times in difficult situations. My parents, Richard and Ada Johnson, helped develop my value system. Lastly, and the most important person in my adult life, my wife, Sandy, has put up with years without vacations, supported a never-ending string of all-night projects that resulted in this effort, typed, edited, and encouraged every effort of which I have been a part in the last 25 plus years. Thanks, Sam.

Preface

Management books pay considerable attention to topics such as planning, control, and scheduling, and devote less space to the subjects that support employee performance. Continuous process improvement begins with the workers who complete the work of each organization. Since people are all important to quality efforts, this book devotes considerable space to hiring practices, employee support structures, culture that promotes high performance, and a performance management system that produces results.

New employee roles and relationships are required to produce continuous process improvement but the current structure of many organizations doesn't support these changes. Other organizations have no formal performance management structure in place. This book provides a structure that supports the quest for excellence.

Culture is another important ingredient for total quality management because it is an organization's personality. It begins with the leaders and flows down through every level to the work floor. Most organizations require considerable cultural change in their quality efforts. Luckily, culture is usually much easier to change than structure. Structures, even the informal kind, are often difficult to change because they have become "the way we do business." Changes in the actions and displayed values of management quickly signifies changes are expected throughout the organization. Leadership by example provides the emphasis for employee changes. Employees take part in planning exercises, problem-solving evolutions, and process improvement efforts. Customer-driven performance becomes the driving force for process improvements throughout every department and operation within the organization.

Attention to the customer doesn't just happen—it is made to happen by leaders who truly emphasize the importance of internal and external customers. Every member of the organization must understand customer relationships in a quality environment, what customers need and expect, and how those expectations can best be met.

Quality processes require solid employees with the ability and desire to produce excellence at every level and department if the customer is to be satisfied. This mandates employee planning and solid hiring practices. These are other weak areas where many organizations experience considerable difficulty.

Performance appraisals are a sticky subject when discussed in terms of a total quality environment. W. Edwards Deming is noted as an opponent of appraisal systems and many managers would like to do away with them. There are reasons for this. Performance appraisal systems in general have been halfheartedly utilized and incorrectly administered. Under the abuses that exist in many systems, these appraisals are demoralizers. However, solid appraisal systems that are fairly administered have proven in practice to have a great influence on performance improvements. The superstars want their performance noticed, appraised, and recorded. Those on the other end of the performance spectrum will seldom improve unless their performance is appraised, their problems noted, and a concerted effort is made to ensure they have everything they need to improve to the required level.

Managers face considerable change as they strive to implement quality processes. Although people may not fight changes they understand and are a part of, they dislike being changed. Resistance can be expected when change is thrust on them. Employees fear the unknown and many have witnessed layoffs and job reductions because employee performance improved. Learning how to plan for quality and lead change are significant parts of the implementation process.

Teamwork is also required. Many performance improvement efforts begin with the selection of quality teams. This can be a major mistake. Groups seldom gel into teams until they are trained in team evolutions, problem solving, and quality tools. Training alone is not enough—employees must have reason to support teamwork. This requires an organizational vision where all employees benefit from the performance improvements they help create.

These management efforts all require time and effort and time is a commodity most managers find in great demand and short supply. Solid time management skills are essential. Time-wasters must be curtailed and eliminated where possible. Managers must gain control of their time in order to lead quality efforts effectively.

This implementation oriented book provides guidance in all these areas. An implementation guide and a sample quality manual provide a structural framework to tie all these concepts together into a quality system.

The book ends with a discussion of management ethics. Managers are faced with an endless supply of choices, most of which are not easy to make. There are always extenuating circumstances and a variety of pressures to make these decisions even more difficult. However, solid decisions supportive of quality are essential to long term performance improvements. This discussion should aid in that endeavor.

Chapters were developed as stand-alone topics that require little if any additional research. This allows the reader to begin where there is the highest need and progress at a pace best suited for them.

Effort was made to make this book as nonsexist as possible without resulting to the cumbersome use of he/she, him/her, and so on. Hopefully, this approach proves to be a satisfactory one for all readers.

Introduction

Volume I dealt with the total quality management (TQM) process from the perspective of leadership. Volume II provides a management study of the same process. The leader looks at leading people, vision, and the inspirational side of the program coupled with skills to carry them out. Management examines performance management, planning, implementation, quality customer service, and the other organizational systems that support the TQM process. Some of the subjects included in this volume (such as quality teams and change management) are both leadership and management functions.

CHAPTER 1

TQM—A Management Overview

Globally competitive industries have come to understand that previously acceptable quality and customer service standards are no longer tolerated. This understanding must now be transferred to all American businesses, governments, school systems, nonprofit organizations, communities, and individuals.

Sales, customer relations and satisfaction, product and service costs, profitability, market share, and even organizational survival depend directly on the value the customer receives in terms of service and product quality. Commitment to quality and ownership of organizational processes must become the way of life from the top down if Americans are to remain competitive and retain the standard of living to which they have grown accustomed.

Serious problems stand in the way. The loss of high-technology jobs to offshore entities, the enormous trade deficit, the ever-increasing tax burdens, and governments at all levels operating as if they have no plan for tomorrow compound the situation. Add the serious performance decline of U.S. secondary schools and the situation appears bleaker. Consider the lack of quality training practices of most organizations and the situation appears dismal. Stir in the short-term profit, merger situation, and questionable practices of major brokerage firms and things may seem hopeless. However, when things get really tough, Americans join together to overcome the obstacles that face them. U.S. history is full of such examples.

Evolution to a quality way of life will not just happen—it must be led. It must begin as a cultural change within every organization including the home and school. There isn't any magic to the quality process or excellence as a way of life. It is a long-term process that is planned, organized, and controlled

1

through leadership beginning at the top of each organization. The leadership structure and requirements were thoroughly covered as they pertain to TQM in Volume I.

Leadership by itself will not be enough to complete the quality job. Each organization must have a system that defines the organization, provides guidance for its operation, and supports its efforts along the journey to excellence. This volume discusses a management system that supports and guides TQM efforts.

Stop! Please read on before deciding this is another new management system that requires complete reorganization. It is not. There is no need for a completely new management system in order to implement a TQM process.

Reorganization concerns often create heartburn for managers who participated in the installation of new systems over the past several years, and well it should. These types of reorganizations often are chaotic and disrupt operations for a considerable amount of time. They also tend to fragment organizations into polls, one group for the old system, one for the new system, and one for anything but either of the systems presented.

Most organizations (and "most" is used advisedly) have management systems in place that are working to varying degrees. These systems evolved over the years as the organization progressed from birth to where it now stands. The organization is getting along under this system or it wouldn't be considering a quality process; rather it would be considering disbanding.

This volume's purpose is to present a generic management system that supports TQM and the evolution required for continuous quality improvement. It readily adapts to most systems now in place and will strengthen the management process in all organizations. It provides a model of a complete performance management system which is discussed further in Volume III.

The management system present herein evolved over a considerable time span. As new systems were presented over the years, they were carefully reviewed and incorporated where they seemed to support an evolutionary process that readily adapted to the changing needs of organizations. After this volume was completed in draft stage, the works of various quality experts were reviewed to ensure this information was compatible. This was necessary because many organizations have used parts or all of these systems with varying degrees of success, and they certainly don't want to backtrack from any successes enjoyed to begin all over again.

There is another reason. Organizations just beginning the quality journey often hire personnel who have worked in organizations with TQM programs that produced results. Many such organizations can be found with factions that support various systems because of the past successes they enjoyed through them. Should these ideas appear to be in conflict, there is quite serious disagreement over how to proceed. When the faction that supports the status quo enters the fray, disagreement replaces the cooperative teamwork required for quality and progress will be seriously hampered.

Commitment to quality must be earned and it will only happen when the work force witnesses management setting the example. This means that every person in a management position must be singing from the same sheet of music. Therefore, management training from the top down must take place so this team is in step and marching smartly before the work force will invest considerable time and effort into a process it sees headed nowhere. Instead, the work force will mark time waiting for the action to begin.

Focus must once again be concentrated on the customer. For business, this means the customer who buys the product or service; for government, this means the taxpayer and citizen who need the services; and for schools, this means the taxpayer and student. Without this customer focus there is absolutely no hope for quality improvement. Unless all Americans become concerned with and committed to quality soon, our very way of life is threatened. We could easily become a has-been nation with a downward spiraling standard of living. The beginnings of such a situation are evident. This must not be allowed to happen.

Many of our current concepts concerning the way we deal with our work force must be reviewed and changed drastically in some instances. Those things we are doing correctly must be improved. The worker is the most important ingredient in the pursuit of total quality and is not going to commit to any process where a personal benefit is not evident.

Management must be at the forefront of the quality movement, leading the way. It is a situation that cannot be delegated nor demanded—it must be led. In many organizations current management practices not only won't support quality, but actually stand in its way. These practices must be understood before quality improvement can become a way of life.

Current Management Practices

Management, in its current form, is a relatively new concept that evolved after World War II. It rapidly became the in-career accompanied by significant prestige and excellent salaries. College management curriculums exploded. Now as the twenty-first century looms on the horizon, there is every indication that management, at least as we know it, is a declining career field. Why is that?

It is important to understand the context within which management has been viewed. Major consideration was given to management as a control system used to guide progress and performance within an organization. As such, it has a valid and continuing need. After World War II, the United States was noted for having the best management systems in the world. These systems, and the people laboring in them, were the most productive on Earth. This productivity played a major part in winning the war because the capacity to build quality military equipment couldn't be matched by the opposition.

Enough is enough, but the philosophy was not applied to management. It was believed that if a little was good, more would be better. As the rest of the world applauded the United States for our management structure, we became enamored with improving it. Layers of management were added until the smallest organizational details could be controlled by attendant rules, policies, and procedures.

Managers often appeared to work themselves up through organizations by creating a staff under them which pushed them upward in salary, if not true value, to the organization's performance. As management staffs grew, so did rules, regulations, policies, and procedures—the red tape that controlled the organization. Managers moving upward tended to carry their control functions with them. Thus, if a manager had approval authority for purchases up to $10,000 and a new management staff was created under that manager, approval authority for $10,000 purchases became one more level removed from the production force.

Communications also had one more level to traverse up and down the chain. As upper management moved away from the work floor, it required more reports and information to control operations, and elaborate systems were instituted to generate this information. Paperwork tends to consume about 110 percent of the time allotted for it. With increasing levels of management in place to churn out requirements for paperwork, the resultant red tape can quickly stifle initiative and throttle performance.

System Problems

The loss of initiative and performance restrictors are two factors that create severe and rather easily recognized problems in management-heavy organizations. A larger problem lies somewhat hidden from view. As management levels grow, managers at each level become more distanced from the workplace and less familiar with the action that takes place there. Instead of continual contact with production personnel, management relies more on reports and statistics to determine what is happening. This makes managers more reactive and less proactive to the environment. They become less familiar with the work and work force, and farther removed from the realities of the production work world.

The manager who is distanced from the work area finds it much easier to ignore personnel problems and training deficiencies. The $10,000 request for new tooling is more readily turned down from farther up the chain than it is for the supervisor on the work floor who witnesses the need and must face workers struggling with archaic methods and machinery on a daily basis.

Conversely, supervisors on the work floor find it easier to pass questionable requests up the line for disapproval rather than rejecting them at their level where they would be forced to face the disgruntled requester. The disapproval can then be blamed on the "people upstairs who just don't understand our needs." Mistakes are easily made in the process when unknowing managers approve requests that should not be approved.

Performance problems in terms of either production or quality serve well as other examples of the problems encountered. Managers tend to make assumptions that may or may not be correct when they are in positions removed from the workplace and review problems through reports and statistics. Decisions are then made based on these assumptions and passed down the chain for implementation. The people in the work area look at the decisions, scoff about the head shed not knowing what is happening, and go on about their business. Few improvements are made even when those who made the decision were lucky enough to hit upon a correct solution. After all, the workers had no input on the decision and little ownership of the process. Besides, who in a position of authority is going to check on them. Heads may roll, but it probably won't be theirs.

That is a simplistic look, but it is appropriate. Allow me to share a personal example. During the described period, I became a staff manager serving a recently chosen executive who had it together. He was responsible for seven operating units spread over a 10-state area. At that time the staff included six managers (some of whom had small supporting staffs).

The operating divisions experienced problems that resulted in this executive being introduced. Problems were immediately tackled. Each staff manager developed additional controls, planning, marketing, and operational initiatives that required increased support staffs both at the headquarters and the operating units. Often workers were transferred from production positions to staff positions to meet the new administrative requirements without exceeding personnel caps.

Operating units soon complained about the increased controls that micromanaged their operations, but met with little success in changing things. Instead, the controls increased. One operating unit blew its operating budget and the other six units' funds were redistributed to cover the problem. Instead of tackling the obvious problem in the unit that was failing, new procedures and controls were placed on all units. This occurred in similar situations.

Another situation caused problems. Operating units were requested to submit various plans with little guidance for developing them. Often these were disapproved and returned for rework with minimal explanation. Operating units complained of having to guess about what was wanted instead of having clear directions while staffers wondered why they didn't know how to do their jobs.

Computer systems were installed to control paperwork and support management, but they seemed to increase it instead. Operating forces were not happy campers.

I returned to an operations management position after four years on the staff. At the time of departure, that staff had more than doubled in size. My management problems in the new operational assignment seemed to double from what they had been in a similar position four years earlier while production and quality had improved only slightly, if any. At times, controls had to be ignored to get "today's work out today."

There is a postscript to this example. The organization now is considering cost-cutting moves to meet the challenges of the 1990s. With an administrative staff that ballooned over the years in comparison to production workers, they are deliberating the elimination of operating units without considering how to reduce staff positions. Time will tell what happens.

Let's review two types of organizations that faced similar management problems: big business and government entities at both the federal and state levels during the 1960s, 1970s, and early 1980s. Both groups had hierarchal systems during that period to control their organizations. It was the accepted norm, the way it had been taught in management classes.

As American businesses faced the global competition of the 1980s, it became evident they would either make drastic changes in the way they did business or they wouldn't survive. Searching for answers, they found their improvement efforts throttled by red tape and layers of management which they had purposely created to meet previous needs. These management-heavy staffs now ate up their dwindling profit. What to do now?

Some organizations, such as GE, reacted quickly and reduced management layers beginning in the 1980s. Results were positive and evident. Costs decreased, communications became easier, red tape was reduced, performance improved, and with the exception of those white-collar workers who lost their jobs in the process, the results proved extremely rewarding.

Other large companies are just now making white-collar staff reductions to stay competitive. It is not an easy decision to make, nor is the process an easy one to carry out, but it is a reality for survival.

Government has not yet learned this lesson, possibly because it is not competing with anyone for survival. Its bloated management structures throttle initiative, restrict performance, eat up salaries unnecessarily, and restrict communications. It also makes TQM endeavors extremely difficult. After all, who gains by improving performance in a government organization?

Since management-heavy systems do not support leadership (someone out front going somewhere, perhaps rocking the boat), leadership became a lost art. After all, the system provides direction and not the people within it. The tendency becomes to make new rules rather than decisions to solve problems.

Many in career management positions didn't and perhaps still don't understand that management by itself accomplishes little. Its only function within the organization is to serve as a supporting part of that operation. This simple fact escapes many.

Within many organizations there can be found a solid textbook example of a management function that has come to act as if the line functions producing goods and services were designed to support management and not the other way around. A review of the numbers of reports, forms, information requirements, red tape, and so forth, required by management to control operating personnel provides a means to determine who is supporting whom. This must be turned around so that management is a support and service unit for the producing work force. Without the producing elements within organizations there is absolutely no need for any type of managers.

Management didn't set out to become what it is in many organizations; it evolved with the best of intentions. Eliminating management certainly isn't the answer, although flattening the structure (as GE and so many other world-competitive companies have done) supports organizational improvement and TQM. There is a necessity to redirect management focus to the guiding, planning, and serving functions, supported by the leadership actions previously discussed in Volume I. As management becomes more focused on both internal and external customers, its value to the organization will be inflated.

How this transformation will take place becomes a question that must be resolved. Fortunately, well-thought-out answers and solutions are currently available and in place within many globally competitive organizations. The task is to study these organizations, benchmark them for their quality and productivity achievements, and then adapt the lessons learned to transform our own organization into what it can and must become.

"Damn the Torpedoes, Full Speed Ahead"

Many managers realize something must be done to improve the performance of their organization, yet they hesitate. Why is this? The first problem is that the unknown can be frightening. The second problem is that they must personally change if their organization is going to become TQM. That's even more frightening.

Have heart. Most people facing this situation hold similar hesitancies. One executive was anxious about presenting a quality program to his board the following morning. The program would be a severe departure from past programs. He related he couldn't sleep and, in fact, told his wife he could get fired over the entire thing. Fortunately, although it didn't really understand all it knew about TQM, the board enthusiastically endorsed the program.

In 1864 with the Civil War raging, Admiral David G. Farragut steamed into the heavily defended Mobile Bay. His lead ship struck a mine and sank. The ships following in line stopped dead in the water waiting direction. It wasn't long coming as Farragut climbed into the rigging and thundered, "Damn the torpedoes, full speed ahead." He took action and the battle was won.

Incidentally, Farragut was in his sixties at the time and was determined to proceed ahead into the unknown and dangerous immediate future. Some dangers always face any departure from the known way of doing things. The *what-iffers* will be out in force and some members of the organization won't want to climb on board. A few individuals will openly resist installation of the quality program and others will downplay efforts behind the scenes.

A quality manager recently related that the new company president called a meeting after his initial thrusts toward TQM were resisted. He asked what the hesitancies were and when it was obvious they were more excuse then substance, he hammered the table and announced, "TQM will take place here with and through this team. Those of you who cannot support this move will be removed from the team." The word is that people decided to give it a try.

Certainly, there will be turbulent times because most senior managers grew up in directive organizations with little participation or delegation. Those who aren't familiar with TQM leadership styles will be uncomfortable with them at first. So what? We are all uncomfortable with new things until we master them. Once mastered, new methods become old hat and we wonder why others new to the particular discipline are hesitant to try them.

The old styles of management took managers away from the workplace as they gained seniority. Continuous quality improvement programs require them to return to the workplace, to see what is happening there and how it is happening, to be available to the people completing the organization's work, and to assist them in their efforts. This is another scary proposition for those who have been away from the action. However, the immediate satisfaction of being a part of the process draws them back like a magnet.

One manager remarked, "I was hesitant to go out on the production floor at first. I forced myself to go out there every morning. It wasn't long though until I enjoyed it so much I had to force myself to go to the office and complete the work that faced me there. The workers seemed to enjoy teaching me their crafts and the surprising part was performance went up while I was out there learning what I should have known all along."

Worker interest in TQM tends to rise at about the same rate as they *witness* management commitment to the program. You can't tell them, you must show them. Remember, they have been involved in other "programs that will revolutionize the way we do business" that fizzled out. Many have witnessed the demise of such programs as Benny Suggs, Zero Defects, and Quality Circles which faded away because management allowed their failure. These employees remain skeptical.

TQM Outline

As previously mentioned, TQM does not require throwing out the complete system that brought organizational success up to its current point in order to start all over. TQM ties the parts of the process together as an operating unit, brings these units together as an organizational entity, and marries them with suppliers and customers to make an operational team working together for performance improvement.

TQM requires changes in the use of the system from a way to control operations and people to a means of supporting people in their continuous process improvement efforts. This mandates that each person in the organization must develop new ways of viewing the organization, the way the organization operates, and her operational place within the organization.

TQM is a system that demands each person use solid leadership and management skills in each individual leadership/management position. Management actions deal with the support systems for TQM and leadership provides the power to use TQM. The following definition developed for use within the Department of Defense provides an excellent TQM overview.

> Total Quality Management (TQM) is a disciplined management process under the leadership of the top executive, involving everyone in the organization in a cooperative effort to achieve a quality product or service through continuous process improvement combined with continuous life cycle cost reduction to satisfy customer needs and maximize combat capability.
>
> Jack C. Strickland
> Director of Industrial Production and
> Quality in the Office of the Assistant
> Secretary of Defense for Production
> and Logistics

By this definition, factors of the TQM process include the following:

- Disciplined top-down management process.
- Leadership by a top executive.
- Every member in the organization is involved.
- It is a cooperative effort requiring teamwork.
- Continuous process improvement is required.
- Quality products or services are produced.
- Continuous life cycle cost reductions occur.

- Customer needs are satisfied.

- Combat capability is maximized.

At first, maximizing combat capability might not seem to be a factor outside the defense department. However, the competition for customers of both goods and services in the private sector can become a combat zone. Perhaps if there was more competition in the public sector, that too would become a combat zone.

Many individuals contend that competition should be introduced within the public sector. Choice-in-schooling bills under consideration of many state legislatures are an example of one such program. Another example is the recommendation to make governmental agencies compete for work against other government agencies and contractors from the private sector. These acts would force public organizations to realize the need for improved performance.

TQM strongly supports public organizations of every size and type. This process focuses organizational assets on organizational performance improvement to continually perfect customer service. It provides guiding principles for this process as organizations take the quality journey. All available performance improvement methods and techniques are used in conjunction with the human resources to improve that organization's total performance. This is done for one purpose—to meet customer need and satisfy customer want through quality goods and services.

The quality goal must become one of providing continuous improvement in terms of the quality goods and services necessary for survival and growth. Nothing less will do.

The Management Triangle

The management system presented herein is simple in theory and appears to be based on common sense. Simplicity in itself, however, does not mean that this, or a similar system, is currently in use within most organizations. Unfortunately, the work of the day and the seemingly never-ending deluge of fires that need to be put out often preclude efforts to establish a system. This work can be integrated over time as the quest for excellence continues.

Figure 1.1 presents the overview of this management system.

The Goal

Every organization has a goal that may contain several subgoals. These goals must be met or the organization's reason for existence and the capability to exist will terminate. For business, this translates to basic survival. For other organizations, this also means basic survival although the end may not be as immediate. Let's review organizational goals.

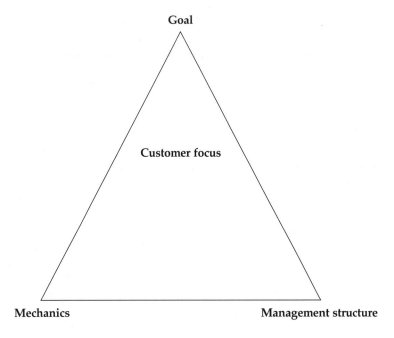

Figure 1.1   Management System Overview

Business–The goal of all business is *profitability*. Without profits, no business can survive. Quality products, superior customer service, and a quality work life for employees are extremely important subgoals, but they are of little value if the organization operates at a net loss.

Education systems–The goal of education should be to educate students so they are qualified to meet the challenges presented by careers, families, and service to others. The percentage of students who graduate and SAT scores are useful benchmarks, but the overall measurement must be, "Are these students prepared for the challenges they meet when they leave this institution?"

Government agencies–The goal of government agencies should be to provide quality services that meet the people's collective needs, which cannot or will not be provided through the private sector. Legislation and laws should support the process to provide these services economically.

Nonprofit organizations–The goal of these organizations is to meet service needs in areas that should not be provided by government and will not be provided by the private sector.

Military–The goal of the military is to win wars. Training and developing people, satisfying careers, and security are niceties, but they are not the goal.

Religious organizations–The goal of religious organizations should be to save souls. Group activities, training, and all that goes with these organizations support the goal, but are not the goal.

Customer Focus

Customer focus requires that both internal and external customer needs be met. Meeting external customer needs cannot happen if internal needs are neglected. Employees tend to treat customers exactly as their organization treats them. If they are ignored, they will ignore their customers; if they are treated with hostility, they will be hostile toward their customers; if their needs are neglected, they will neglect the customer; and if the internal system does not provide quality services, they will not provide customers with quality services. This means that *every department and operation within an organization must be engaged in the journey to excellence or results will be mediocre at best*. Workers whose pay or medical benefits are mixed up will not be excited about providing superior customer service, at least not during the period of their personal problems. Instead, they will focus on attaining their needs to the exclusion of both internal and external customers. Can one blame these employees?

Several considerations are important in the evolution to a customer-focused environment.

Define expectations–The determination must be made as to what the customer expects in the way of products and services. Several factors will be on most customers' lists: quality, competitive costs, timeliness, convenience, variety, and pleasant, supporting attitudes.

Define need–Need and expectations are not always the same. The customer might expect one product, but need something quite different. The provider must know what is expected and needed and then assist the customer in fulfilling both areas.

Define the product and/or service–This definition should be mutually arrived at and agreed on by provider and customer.

Define quality standards–Zero defects is a great goal but is not easily attained. Six sigma or 3.4 defects per million is the current goal of many organizations such as Motorola and IBM. The word *current* is used because quality is a moving target continually adjusted upward with continuous improvement successes over time.

Provide products and customer service–Products and services must meet or exceed expectations and they must be constantly improving. Solid customer relations will convey the provider's efforts to customers so that they know how important they are.

Management Structure

Management systems provide the structure through which customer focus is maintained on the way to meeting the organizational goal. These systems provide guidance, understanding, monitoring, and measurement.

Organization–Management organization provides an operational framework through the definition of roles and relationships. This framework is provided with parameters through rules, policies, and procedures.

Culture–Culture provides an environment where excellence is encouraged and continuous quality improvement moves from the realm of theory to the accepted way of doing business.

Performance management–This personnel supportive system encourages quality through continuous improvement of the work force. The level of quality will be no greater than the ability of the work force to produce it. The only way for continuous quality improvement to occur is through a continually improving work force. Volume III is devoted to the development and operation of a performance management system.

Performance standards–Each organization must develop performance standards and an audit system to monitor progress against established goals. Volume III provides the mechanics for supporting the management structure.

Mechanics

The mechanics that support management systems are contained in Volume III. They include audits, productivity, problem solving, quality tools, and statistical process control (SPC).

Summary

1. Many would say the age of the manager is over. However, the needs of TQM are such that management and leadership skills must be used in tandem to win the quality wars.

2. Organizations are now reviewing their management structures, streamlining them to make them more effective and supportive of their quality efforts.

3. TQM is a top-down process requiring leadership from the top and the effort of every individual within the organization. The focus is on continuous quality improvement through teamwork.

4. The management system can be described as a triangle that has a management structure supporting the continuous quest for customer satisfaction while meeting that organization's goals.

5. Each organization has a different goal, but meeting that goal is equally important in all organizations.

6. Customer focus requires the producing organization to define customer expectations, needs, and the required products and services. The quality standards needed to meet these three items must be determined so correct products and services are provided.

Bibliography

Bradford, D. L. and Cohen, A. R. *Managing for Excellence*, New York: John Wiley and Sons, 1984.

Drucker, P. F. *Management: Tasks—Responsibilities—Practices*, New York: Harper and Row, 1973.

———. *The Frontiers of Management: Why Tomorrow's Decisions Are Being Shaped Today*, New York: E. P. Dalton, 1986.

———. *Practice of Management*, New York: Harper and Row, 1954.

DuBrin, A. J. *Contemporary Applied Management*, Homewood, IL: BPI Irwin, 1989.

Filley, A. C. *The Complete Manager*, Champaign, IL: Research Press Company, 1978.

Harmon, F. G. *The Executive Odyssey*, New York: John Wiley and Sons, 1989.

Hitt, W. D. *Management in Action*, Columbus, OH: Battelle Press, 1985.

Hunsaker, P. L. and Alessandra, A. J. *The Art of Managing People*, Englewood Cliffs, NJ: Prentice-Hall, 1980.

Kirby, T. *The Can-Do Manager*, New York: AMACOM, 1989.

Lundborg, L. B. *The Art of Being an Executive*, New York: The Free Press, 1981.

Morgan, J. S. *Managing Change*, New York: McGraw-Hill, 1972.

Odiorne, G. S. *How Managers Make Things Happen*, Englewood Cliffs, NJ: Prentice-Hall, 1987.

Practical Management Associates. (Course) *Executive Management Program,* Canoga Park, CA.

Quick, T. L. *The Persuasive Manager,* Radnor, PA: Chilton Book Company, 1982.

Schoenberg, R. J. *The Art of Being a Boss,* Philadelphia: J. B. Lippincott, 1978.

Seidman, L. W. *The Executive's Guide to Competitiveness,* Armonk, NY: M. E. Sharp, 1989.

Sloma, R. S. *No-Nonsense Management,* New York: McMillan Publishing Company, 1977.

CHAPTER 2

Organizational Structure

Many individuals consider TQM as a revolutionary idea when virtually all of the ideas have been around for some time. The concept of putting them together, integrating them into an organization as the "way we operate," with a focus on the customer is not entirely new, either. In days past, the customer also was king to varying degrees depending on the organizations involved. What is new about TQM is that it is an evolutionary process, not revolutionary. One does not have to begin over to get started.

That is why TQM makes so much sense. Organizations and their people begin the quality road right where they are, build on their strengths, and overcome their weaknesses. Many organizational theories would replace all the elements or major segments of the structures that are in place with new concepts foreign to current ways of doing business. The odds of achieving such a changeover, while maintaining performance and customer satisfaction, are overwhelmingly against success—about the same odds as accomplishing a list of 10 New Year's resolutions. The tendency is to use part of the old system and some of the new (the parts of each which require the least effort or upheaval) and these parts may conflict in the manner in which they operate.

This does not mean change is not required—it is. These changes, however, are instituted over time, concentrating on the areas of most immediate need with the greatest long-term payoff. In Chapter 1 an overview of a TQM system was provided. This chapter provides the next step, which is the development of an understanding of the changing roles, relationships, and administrative structure necessary for a quality environment.

A Structural Overview

Organizational structure provides order, enabling members to understand their roles, relationships, and responsibilities. It defines how the organization will operate, provides role and relationship guidance so necessary for teamwork, and provides the rules by which the game is played and a way to keep score. Goals can be established and assets allotted through this framework. Work teams provide identity for the players through common objectives. The structure also provides a communication system.

TQM requires some immediate structural change in almost all organizations. Performance and customer service improvements will not occur unless the organizational structure which supports the work force also changes. Employees tend to perform and treat customers exactly as they perceive their supervisor performs and as the organization treats them. A brief review of the way the work force operates internally provides a solid overview of how the customer is treated and where the first changes should occur.

To have good employees, an organization must begin with employees who *fit* the organization. Solid citizens who do not blend in with organizational need and philosophy will produce the same performance problems as those who cannot do the work. After the correct employees are chosen, they must be trained and their performance must be managed correctly.

Note: Performance is managed, not the people. People will not be managed.

A model performance management system is presented in this book and a training system is provided in Volume IV. The presentation order was determined because it is believed that culture and structure must be understood in terms of quality before people are hired or their performance is appraised.

Roles and Relationships

Every organization consists of a framework containing a system of individual roles which provide behavioral guidelines. These roles provide guidance which should assist individuals in the execution of their duties. As the vision and mission of an organization changes, these roles also must change. Too often this does not happen. The role becomes a rigid prison, rather than a flexible guide to help the people who fill these roles.

Relationships determine who reports to whom, who works through whom, and who provides support to whom. The quest for quality demands new types of relationships for success. Managers must get out with their charges and establish credibility as it concerns the quality process. Groups must become working teams, and these teams must work with other teams to spread quality throughout the operation.

Rules, Policies, and Procedures

Rules are statements that tell individuals exactly what they can and cannot do. Policies provide boundaries within which individuals can use some discretion to accomplish the day's work. Procedures are standards that guide work performance to ensure processes are completed the same way each time.

Rules, policies, and procedures serve as guidance that prevent the continual need for supervisory instruction and decision. They specify ways of acting, provide guidance on the action that should be taken, and establish the parameters for that action. Managers are then freed up to complete their assigned duties.

"The Way We Do It"

In most organizations rules, policies, and procedures do not keep up with process evolution, and the people develop a system for completing the work at hand. Audits often reveal systems that are alien to the written rules, policies, and procedures.

The problem is not with the makeup of these unwritten systems; they develop over time as a necessary means to accomplish the process in the correct manner. The problem is that the formal written structure is not updated to indicate the way the system evolves. As a result people are trained and their performance is appraised according to a written structure that is no longer used. It is easy to understand why some people are trained outside the work area only to return to the "that's nice, but it isn't the way we do it here" attitude.

Performance Management

Personnel seldom are chosen at random although it might appear that way when auditing operations at a later date. Each organization has a maze through which people must pass to become employees. The junctions in the maze have one leg that acts as a deselect path while the other progresses to another junction the applicant must get through. Some junctions include the resumé, application form, screening interview, employment tests, interview, and background screens.

Some applicants successfully weave their way through this system and become employees because they understand the system and know how to manipulate it. This is in contrast to those who possess a solid track record of accomplishment, work ethic, teamwork, and attitude that is in line with organizational need. Obviously, the first type of individual spells trouble with a capital "T," while the second spells long-term team performance, the basis for continuous quality improvement.

Personnel selection, whether through advancement or introduction of new employees into the organization, must be considered one of the organization's most important functions. Long-term excellence begins here.

Training is the second step. Few people have all the skills and knowledge required of them in a new position. A blend of coaching, on-the-job, and formal training is required to bring them up to speed.

When it is determined that the employee has the required knowledge and skills, application of these fundamentals must be evaluated against the job's positional needs. Performance appraisal and the corrective/improvement processes that follow ensure continued performance improvement. The performance management system and training are covered in detail in separate volumes.

Controls

Controls provide a means of standardizing process and operations by monitoring performance and taking actions to improve the organization based on the results achieved.

Roles

Roles can be regarded as different hats people wear. Every person plays many different roles. Specific roles guide supervisory activities, team efforts, management meetings, and other organizational activities. An individual often has supervisory, subordinate, and peer roles along with the attendant relationships.

There are family roles, church roles, and roles required in recreational activities, such as bowling and golf. Membership in various community and service organizations provide other role requirements. Occasionally, the various roles support each other while at other times they are in direct conflict.

Individuals have many different sources of on-the-job roles. Task roles are associated with the efforts to accomplish the assigned duties on time and with quality. Team roles involve the efforts associated with team activities. Personal roles are those associated with the individual's attempts to meet her personal needs, such as job satisfaction and promotion.

Roles have prescribed behaviors that are expected of people within those groups. These behaviors change as one progresses up through an organization because job requirements define associated roles and behaviors. Contrary to popular belief, the higher one progresses up through an organization, the more dominating the roles become, limiting freedom and choice. Many executives find it difficult to separate themselves from their career roles.

Legal ramifications, safety requirements, and union agreements may further define roles. At times these roles may be narrowly defined and in other areas there may be considerable latitude. Skill level, knowledge, and track record generally affect the width of latitude allowed.

Solid performance requires that employees know exactly what role has been assigned to them. There can be no uncertainty as to what the expectations and responsibilities are that attend that role. Supervisors have the responsibility to ensure roles are understood and carried out correctly.

The role intention of the supervisor must be properly communicated to the subordinate and that subordinate must understand it as it was communicated. Misunderstanding concerning roles and the attendant responsibility, authority, and accountability is a major source of conflict which prevents success in many organizations.

Role Assignments

The role assigned to those on the work floor consists of the technical requirements to accomplish the day's work. This will be added to quality team roles and perhaps training roles or roles within groups (such as a union). Many of these workers will have roles that are associated with meeting the customer's needs and expectations.

Foremen and first-line supervisors have other roles. Their main role is the leadership/management role. Roles descending through the chain of command are determined by the subordinates' needs and the supervisory duties they are assigned. Their roles are further defined by the needs and expectations of their supervisors. Quality team leader duties and liaison with other operations produce other roles they must fill, including negotiator, communicator, and salesperson for ideas, concepts, assets, and assistance. Many quality team leaders will have roles associated with meeting the needs of the customer similar to those of the workers they supervise.

The various levels of management have leadership roles associated with their positions and team responsibilities. Management roles are similar to those associated with line manager positions even though their role responsibilities increase as they progress up the ladder. Managers will hold quality team roles and some will have roles associated with the quality council. Some managers will have various roles associated with serving the customer.

Executive-level managers have roles in addition to those they share with the managers below them. These roles are relegated to them because they are in a position to view the entire picture within which the organization operates. The visionary leadership role is crucial in the quality journey. The vision developed at this level must be believable by every layer of the organization. It must be exciting enough to move the team to action, attainable so they do not lose spirit, provide for continuous quality improvement, keep the customer in focus, and provide direction toward the goal.

Executives have the additional role of providing organizational culture. The way they support immediate subordinates, provide for their welfare, and promote their personal improvement efforts sets the tone for every succeeding level of the organization. It also will have a significant affect on the way they are viewed by those below them, which can considerably influence the pursuit of quality.

Executives also hold many ceremonial roles. They serve as guest speakers for all types of internal and external functions, represent their organizations at various events, and head rewards ceremonies. They may also maintain promotional roles such as Lee Iaccoca at Chrysler.

As one progresses up through the chain, the job's technical aspects become less important and the leadership/managerial role becomes greater. The manager cannot afford to allow the technical side to slip away entirely, although it becomes less important. This knowledge will help considerably when making decisions concerning processes and operations. It also is necessary in dealing with the organization's lower levels. Management must be able to speak the language if they are to understand the inner workings of their organization.

Another role concept is important. The various levels of the organization view the organization differently, often as if it were an entirely different operation. For example, we were discussing a potential training effort at a factory that was part of a major corporation. The manufacturing manager was new and had invited us to the site. He took us through the plant and his knowledge of operations was considerable, prompting substantial notes.

Our organization received a contract and after developing the technical program, we presented a pilot program. This involved two separate sessions. Between sessions, the production manager came into the training facility and offered to take me on a plant tour. His tour was considerably different than the one provided by the manufacturing manager. At the time, I attributed that to the fact that he had been on site for a considerable amount of time.

We received an extension contract to complete additional training at that plant. One afternoon I had finished a session with the day shift and was waiting for people on second shift to arrive. While I waited I read some of their marketing material and was quite impressed with it. The day shift supervisor dropped in to say that he had received several favorable comments from people who attended the session. He added that people thought we were employees because the material had been tailored specifically to their organization. Although it wasn't intended, it made us feel good to know we understood their language.

The supervisor then asked if I would like a tour of the place. I almost declined, but decided to go along. It was an exciting time. The man was the third generation of his family employed at that plant. He had started at the bottom and quickly worked up through several different operations. He made the plant come alive as he explained things in technical terms and then applied management requirements so that I could understand how things worked from both a technical and managerial view.

He also knew the workers and their jobs. He made mental notes as we went through so that he could go back and work with people on several aspects of production. New processes were being installed and several people were hanging on to old ways of doing things. He was particularly careful not to discuss things in front of me unless people asked for advice.

I took a fourth tour of the plant on a subsequent visit, this one was a repeat with the manufacturing manager. He was now an old pro in the place, knew the people and the operation, explained changes that were occurring, and plans they had for future changes. It was amazing how much he knew about the operation in the short time he had been there. It was as though he too had worked there previously.

Since then I have given considerable thought to these tours and discussed them with a few individuals. Each of these managers saw a different operation based on their backgrounds and the roles they held. As the manufacturing manager seasoned in the job, however, it was evident he had made a special effort to learn the technical aspects of the job and many of the process innovations were his.

We have since discussed this different factory concept away from the job site. The manufacturing manager explained that his previous efforts in both quality management and manufacturing management positions at other sites made him aware of the necessity of getting out on the shop floor and learning what was happening, not superficially but a genuine working knowledge. He related that when people were swinging sledgehammers on a previous job trying to fix a problem, he took a turn too; when they were thinking through process problems, he stopped and listened, helping where he could. It provided the background to work in new process ideas with the people and because he was interested and knowledgeable, they willingly gave his new ideas a try. Over time he earned their respect and enjoyed himself thoroughly.

He considered one other factor extremely important. He knew the people and how valuable they were to the operation. He knew their capabilities and shortcomings and was able to help them use their strengths and improve weak areas. Most of all, because he knew the operation, he owned a large part of it, too; it was his. This ownership is crucial to success in the quality evolution.

The Firefighter

There is one role that should be called out for what it is—the firefighter. The firefighter exists in most organizations. Many individuals are so busy fighting the fire of the day they never have time to improve performance and prevent the problems that cause the fires.

Firefighters tend to enjoy this method of operation. Why shouldn't they? They receive considerable attention because they face one raging inferno after another, overcome them to some degree for a period of time, and then receive considerable attention for their efforts. This encourages more of the same.

Organizational firefighters can be likened to the arsonists who occasionally set fires so they can return to fight them in their role as a member of the fire department. Fighting fires is much more exciting, and in most organizations more rewarding, than being a solid citizen who continually improves the process in order to avoid the problems. These solid citizens who are so important to continuous improvement are often overlooked in the organization. After all, anyone can do their jobs because nothing ever goes wrong.

TQM demands that the role of the firefighter be eliminated so people can work on problem prevention rather than problem correction. Those people who are noted for being firefighters should be carefully monitored to find out where they are going astray in order to help them through this problem. Only when we all recognize the harm firefighters inflict on our operations will we work to put them out of business.

Role Conflict

Role conflict occurs when a person is faced with conflicting choices because of the various roles people have. They understand the role requirements, but for one reason or another they cannot comply with all the roles. This can be a stressful situation at best.

Role conflict can occur between role requirements of the family and the workplace. The choice of working late to ensure a project is completed correctly, on time, vice attending a son's or daughter's play-off game is an example.

Workplace role conflict can occur between intergroup team activities and responsibilities to subordinates. Another source of conflict is when an individual is given an impossible assignment. This could occur when the person is required to complete a project with uncooperative people who do not work for him. Another case is an assignment to acquire information that is not available or that other groups refuse to share. There are a number of catch-22 situations in most organizations that employees can quickly point out as examples.

Still another type of conflict occurs when a person receives conflicting orders from several different sources. This can be further complicated when those orders are in conflict with the requirements of one's assigned role.

Continuous role conflict caused by role overload can devastate employees, reducing their effectiveness and hampering performance. Employees noted for performance often receive considerable additional tasking above the level normally assigned to people in similar positions. This sort of conflict, which employees cannot prevent, often is a source of the decision to change jobs. To prevent these problems, the supervisor must continuously monitor performance, ensuring selected individuals are not continually assigned additional duties just because they will complete them at all costs. The problem can occur quite innocently. Supervisors who make assignments without checking subordinate workloads often are guilty of this overload and are not even aware of it. The situation is compounded when performance is not monitored which precludes recognition for superior performance. Employees generally read the problem as an uncaring supervisor rather than an unknowing one.

Role Assumption

Managers must be aware of another situation that can impact negatively or positively on performance. Hard-charging employees often are prone to assuming roles that have not been assigned them. For example, an employee might assume the role as group spokesperson for a work group. This can be a positive action when that employee has the best interests of the organization in mind and is experienced enough to handle such a role. In this case, the employee may coordinate improvement efforts, communicate needs to supervisors, and warn supervisors of potential problems.

Problems can occur when the individual is self-serving and uses the assumed role for personal gain or to disrupt the organization. Ongoing monitoring is a supervisor necessity in this situation.

Relationships

Successful relationships are extremely important in any organization bent on performance improvements. Changes require new relationships which carry new responsibilities. Each of these must be understood and mastered for correct job performance.

Job Relations

Managers at all levels must change the way they carry out their duties. Attention to detail becomes important because performance improvements come through correction of all aspects of the process. This requires in-depth knowledge of both the processes and the people who complete them. Managers must devote more time to the workplace where the products and services are created. One cannot effectively improve an operation that is not understood.

Performance must be continually monitored, measured, and recorded. This information is then graphed and posted so that work teams have continuous feedback on their efforts. This feedback provides instantaneous reward for successes and encourages continuous efforts.

Subordinate Relationships

Managers must know their subordinates in terms of skills, knowledge, level of commitment, and what makes them tick. Each person has strengths that must be successfully utilized and weaknesses to overcome. Payoff actions in improvement efforts occur mainly in participative and delegative situations which require a deep knowledge of every person on the work team so they can be correctly employed.

This knowledge is valuable in other ways. Training must accompany continuous improvement efforts. As managers spend more time with the troops, they discover areas that require additional training efforts, and they can provide it in a timely manner. Successes also will be readily visible, and these can be recognized as they occur.

Managers will feel more secure and be able to depend on subordinates because they know their capabilities. As managers allow them to make more decisions, their confidence increases along with their commitment to the quality effort. Their successes will prove motivational and fuel the efforts. This encourages them to assume additional responsibilities which permits the supervisor to work on other critical tasking.

Boss Relationships

Required assets, support, success, recognition, and more depend on one's relationships with superiors. Because bosses are also responsible for the success of the organization, they must be involved in all aspects of performance improvement. This requires ongoing communications to keep them abreast of efforts and the results achieved.

Subordinates headed up the success ladder will find ways to assist their bosses with their duties. This is a training step for the subordinate while it frees the boss up for more pressing duties. Simultaneously, it allows the subordinate to demonstrate ability and initiative, prime factors for promotion.

Peer Relationships

Peer relationships change significantly in a quality organization as workers become members of interdepartmental teams. Nothing drives these changes more than the realization that every person has internal customers who must be satisfied.

As people progress in their team efforts, interdependency creates a different type of organization. People begin to understand they are all in this together and that the gains and losses of one part of the team are felt by all members of the organization in one way or another. Cooperation improves, usually dramatically. Much of this is driven by the increased presence of managers working with their work teams. These same managers are being forced to work closely with the managers of other departments in their quality team efforts at other levels. Often, executives are working members of various teams. And who wants to stand out negatively in front of the person responsible for evaluation and promotion?

These multilevel, interdepartmental teams broaden every player's horizon as they begin to understand the operation in its total instead of the small, fragmented parts they knew before TQM. The more people know about the operation, the greater the degree of ownership they feel, and that is the real performance enhancer.

External Customer Relationships

TQM is customer-focused. As the working climate improves internally, people see their external customers in an improved light. Customers and suppliers often become part of problem-solving teams, working jointly to improve end products and services. This draws them closer together, and they find they have a lot more in common than they previously thought. People working together toward joint goals that benefit all parties cement relationships thus improving performance for all who are contributors to the process.

Level of contribution tends to be the deciding factor. One cannot expect more out of an effort than is put into it. However, few people can become part of these teams without getting caught up in the action. It just doesn't happen that way.

Developing Productive Relationships

In the past, managers were judged almost entirely on productivity, and in turn, subordinates, were evaluated on the same criterion. TQM adds quality and customer service to this equation which makes productive relationships increasingly important.

The first rule for productive relationships is the golden rule, "Do unto others as you would have them do unto you." People will react to you in much the same manner as they perceive you acting toward them. This means team players and leaders must be sensitive to the needs of others.

The second rule is, "Do not let competition get in the way of teamwork." Quality cannot occur unless solid teamwork exists at every level, and teamwork won't occur in a competitive environment where people attempt to promote themselves or their team to the disadvantage of others. Friendly team competition can spur on quality improvement as long as one team doesn't win at the expense of others.

It matters not how talented or ambitious you are if you don't develop productive relationships. Quality initiatives thrive where cooperative teams labor and fail where cooperation is replaced with conflict.

Rules

Rules are specific statements that tell an employee exactly what can and cannot be done in terms of the types of behaviors that are required and those that are prohibited. They leave no room for discretion, decision, or judgment.

Rules provide individuals with the direction they need to function within the organization. Without rules there would be utter chaos and more time would be spent arguing about what should be done than would be invested in doing it.

Rules also restrict performance and that is where problems begin. Within long-established organizations, many of the rules were enacted to support operations in periods quite different from the current situations. They carry over and detract from performance improvement in many ways.

Any time a group wants to engage in a work slowdown to protest something, all it generally has to do is follow the rules. Were the rules reviewed and changed on a regular basis to support the organization and its employees, this problem would not occur.

The manner in which many rules are created causes much of the problem. People serving in leadership roles encounter people causing various problems. Instead of correcting the problem with that individual, they develop new rules that cover all employees.

We worked with an organization that had flex time. The vast majority of the people conscientiously obeyed the established rules. One person, however, tended to arrive late and sign in for a previous time which cheated the company out of 10 or 15 minutes each day. Other employees noticed and talked with the guilty party who ignored their concerns. The matter was reported to the manager who witnessed the matter over several days. It was quite easy because the sign-in sheet was just outside his office.

Each day the supervisor checked this sheet after the person signed in and noted the actual time. At the end of the week he held a meeting and provided new rules for sign-in and prescribed penalties for nonconformance which affected everybody. You can guess what the results were. Morale dropped, but the solid citizens complied with the new rules. The person who caused the problem continued to thwart the system and the organization was the loser because people checked in and out exactly on time as a means of quiet protest.

Rules are approached in various ways. I had lunch with a group that included an Air Force officer who had flown with the Navy during the Vietnam War as part of an exchange program. He contrasted the Navy and Air Force rules governing flight operations thusly: "The Air Force teaches you to fly and then guides your performance with rules which specify what you can do with the bird. The Navy teaches you to fly, checks you out, and then tells you what you can't do. The difference is there is a lot more room for discretion when your guidelines say what you can't do and leaves the rest up to you." This may not be exactly true, but it serves as a good example for the concept.

One of the first steps management should undertake in any program of excellence is a review of the rules. In all probability, rules will be discovered which are broken every workday by workers who do so to get the day's work out. No one notices because the system runs along quite well this way until new people come on the job, try to follow the rules, and find it next to impossible.

Rules that no longer apply should be discarded. Rules that negatively impact on performance should be studied for reason and if there is no solid reason, the rule should be changed so that it is supportive. This may require review with the union and/or work teams. These groups, however, generally support rule changes that improve operations without a great deal of negative impact on them. In some cases compromises will be necessary, but this is understandable.

Also, rules should be sufficient to cover the situation and no more. A lot can be said in a few words, as witnessed by the golden rule, the Ten Commandments, and the Gettysburg Address. Rules tend to be made to cover every possible eventuality and they become so mammoth that no one bothers to read them to see what they say. In most cases it is much better to have short, concise rules and cover special exceptions as they occur.

Procedures

Procedures are formalized processes that define the steps that are to be taken in order to complete specific jobs correctly. They are designed to standardize work efforts. They outline specific steps that are taken to complete designated tasks.

For example, tellers in a bank process all checks in prespecified steps. As a customer, I witness some of the steps. They check to make sure the check is correct and signed. They compare that information with your personal identification and initial the check, sometimes adding other information. The check is then processed, dividing the money among the accounts as directed with the difference provided in cash. Often they require you to sign for any cash you receive. Finally, customers are thanked for their patronage. At our bank the process is always the same regardless of which teller waits on you.

Quality improvement demands that all processes follow established procedures until improvements are made. These new procedures are then changed to reflect the improved method of doing business. The new procedures are followed until further improvement and change. Process problems are difficult and sometimes impossible to detect if there is variance in the way jobs are accomplished from one time to the next. Continuous quality improvement depends on correct problem identification and diagnosis. Without that, any quality program is dead in the water.

Policies

Policies are similar to rules in that they provide employee direction. Unlike rules, however, policies provide parameters within which employees can make decisions. They permit employees some level of discretion whereas there is no discretion allowed in rules.

As many organizations journey through TQM, they are finding cause to change rules into policy statements. Employees have enough guidance to keep them from feeling as though they are operating out on the limb, yet they still have the discretion to adapt to changing requirements. As an example, wage and salary administration manuals usually provide salary ranges. This allows salaries to be tailored to experience, value to the organization, and the location of that particular operation. The verbiage may declare that a competitive wage will be paid that falls within the specified range.

Not all policies are written. This can be good or bad, depending on the circumstances. Some managers are known for having unwritten policies which they bend to suit the circumstances and their personal desires. In such situations, employees become disgruntled and tend to distrust both management and the organization.

Some policies are written, but they are superseded by word-of-mouth policies or accepted ways of doing things. This is another area that causes ongoing conflict and occasional disaster. A rule of thumb is that policies should be written, reflect the best way of doing things, changed as required, and followed within the established parameters.

Other policies will never be written, but often are evident. Preferential treatment for family members, hiring biases, and promotion restrictions not based on performance are a few examples of such policies. Other policies that will remain unwritten are those that verge on unethical or illegal practices.

Rituals

All kinds of organizations have rituals. The Masons, Elks, Moose, Navy Chief Petty Officers, college fraternities and sororities all have rituals as a membership rite of passage.

Companies have rituals for employees who start at lower-level positions and are watched until such time as they demonstrate their value, loyalty, ability, and worth. It is called "paying your dues" by some, but it is a ritual, nonetheless. There are other rituals such as IBM's fondness for white shirts. Understanding and following organizational rituals may have a lot to do with the successes enjoyed within an organization.

Controls

Controls often are discussed after topics such as planning, organizing, and scheduling. This was not done here for two reasons: controls support the current discussion of structure, and planning is covered as a stand-alone topic in Chapter 7.

Controls are put in place to ensure that rules, policies, procedures, and processes are carried out as they are intended. They ensure standardization, thus precluding many human errors which would occur without controls. They also support participative and delegative leadership styles by providing a means to monitor project progress without being continually involved in the project.

Controls should focus on the important aspects of the operation. A few key variables usually drive performance. These variables are important to the operation's success and are difficult to measure. They can change quickly, often for reasons divorced from the controlling person's span of control. For instance, an operator cannot control the characteristics of the metal received in a metal fabrication center, but these characteristics can greatly affect the operation. Prompt action is required when there is a change in these variables. Most operators are gaining the authority to stop production lines, computer operations, and so forth when a problem is detected that requires action.

Internal and external controls are necessary. Internal controls are self-controls that occur in the workplace through the actions of the employees completing the effort. External controls are controls produced by rules and regulations or acts of supervisors. As the move to quality increases, it is hoped that controls move away from external control and toward internal control as a method of operation. Quality increases are much more pronounced when internal controls are the dominant controlling factor.

This discussion of control assumes the organization has a plan, knows where it needs and wants to go, and is in the process of getting there. Without plans, people and organizations do not know where they are headed and they have nothing to control. Controls are made up of four components: performance standards, performance measurement, comparison of performance against the standard, and the action required based on the comparison's results.

Many achieve the first three steps and stop. It must be understood that control has not taken place until the action step has been satisfactorily completed. This step must occur for true performance improvements to take place. The improvement or action plan as the vehicle for corrective action is recommended.

Standards

Standards are based on established objectives and provide a yardstick for performance measurement. Standards are utilized for soft measurement areas such as customer service, conformance to rules, regulations, policies and procedures, employee turnover, efficient asset utilization, and hiring efficiency. They also measure hard subjects such as productivity, quality, on-time deliveries, and various costs.

Electronics test equipment calibration labs provide an example of the way procedures and standards interact. Each kind and model of test equipment has an exact calibration procedure that must be followed during the calibration process. Exact standards are used to ensure the test equipment meets specifications at established steps of the procedure. When the calibration procedure is complete, the equipment is certified to meet the designated standard. The test equipment can then be used to tune and adjust other equipment correctly. Standards are discussed in greater detail in Chapter 4.

Measurement

Measurements are taken to determine the actual performance that has occurred. The measurements are taken against organizational plans and the standards they present. Controls should be developed for all parts of the plans, even aspects that appear difficult or impossible to measure.

The periodicity of these measurements is determined by the criticality of the process and the potential for variation. For example, crystal-controlled clocks would not require comparison with a standard time nearly as often as the older models that are timed through pendulums.

It is important to understand that measurements can be subjective, as are most other actions when humans are involved. Let's see why.

Most people have studied the Hawthorne experiments of Western Electric. This experiment involved measurement of the effect lighting had on production workers. The magnitude of light was increased in their workplace and production shot up. Researchers thought there was a direct correlation between light and productivity. They did further research and found that increasing the light again further increased performance. They decided to see how much productivity was lost when the light was decreased from this now optimal level. To their amazement, decreased light increased production. From this experiment it was determined that control of the available light was not the factor; it was a function of the attention paid the people.

From this we can see that control is subjective. Singling out these people for observation changed the environment and thus biased the control system. Systems are biased because a human being is an observer who is naturally biased by events, people, and one's own background. The very nature of controls makes them conducive to setting goals. This was discussed earlier when it was noted that people automatically rank themselves and move away from the bottom when controls are established.

Comparison

Once measurements are completed, the results are compared against the standard. Three possibilities emerge: the results can meet the standard, the result may fail to meet the standard, or the result may be better than the standard requires.

The Action Step

Some type of action is required for all three possible outcomes. No immediate action is required when standards are met. However, the process should be continually analyzed for improvements that have the capability to improve performance.

Immediate action is required when performance does not meet standards. The trend is toward allowing operators to stop the production line until the problem is corrected. Longer periods of time are required for problems in which a higher level of human involvement is concerned. The teaching profession provides an example. A teacher could be having problems that show up in the form of an increased number of students failing. This teacher's classroom performance would then be monitored over some period of time along with other corrective measures to determine the problem's cause.

Action also should be taken when performance is better than expected. It should be determined why it is better and how can it be maintained at that level. Such performance improvements should not be taken for granted, they should be investigated so they will continue.

Control Guidance

Some guidance is appropriate for establishing rules, policies, procedures, standards, and controls. The following are directed to controls, but are applicable to all of these factors.

Necessary–If controls aren't required to ensure performance, don't waste time establishing them.

Simple–Controls must be easily understood by all participants.

Timely–The time period for the control should meet the circumstances at hand. Hourly measurement of processes noted for long-term stability are a waste.

Appropriate–The control covers problem areas or areas of high cost, customer concern, safety, and so forth.

Focused–The control is applied to the part of the process where control is possible. It cannot occur after the product is completed.

A Structural Checklist

The following checklist provides questions that should be answered when determining how well the organization supports TQM.

_____ 1. After careful review, the overall structure supports the TQM process.

_____ 2. The roles assumed by the various levels of management are supportive of TQM.

_____ 3. The relationships between various levels of the organization and the interdepartmental relationships support the quest for continuous quality improvement.

_____ 4. Managers from different work centers work closely together to coordinate work and quality efforts.

_____ 5. Interdepartmental teams are easily formed to tackle problems as they arise.

_____ 6. Rules support quality initiatives without restricting performance improvement.

_____ 7. Procedures accurately define how each process should be handled.

_____ 8. Rules, procedures, and standards are updated as required when process improvements are achieved.

_____ 9. The structure focuses emphasis on both internal and external customer satisfaction.

_____ 10. Controls are in place for each process so employees can measure performance against a standard and take actions to correct deficiencies.

Summary

1. Organizational structure defines how the organization works, guides the players in their roles and relationships, provides parameters to work within, and standards to measure performance.

2. The people at each level of an organization are assigned roles with prescribed behaviors. Employees must understand these roles and carry them out in order for the organization to function correctly.

3. The firefighter role is evident in most organizations. Those who fill this role must be searched out, trained on techniques to prevent the need for firefighting, and monitored so they get out of the habit of waiting until the fires are raging before they act.

4. At times there are role conflicts that seriously hamper the performance of individuals and produce considerable stress which impacts performance.

5. TQM requires supportive relationships up and down the chain and between the departments and work centers.

6. Rules tell employees what can and cannot be done. They become problems when they are unnecessarily restrictive or out of date.

7. Procedures explain the steps of a process that must be accomplished to ensure quality products and services. Standards accompany these procedures and form the basis for determining success.

8. Policies are like rules in that they provide parameters to work within. Unlike rules, they allow some level of discretion.

9. Controls provide a performance standard, a means to measure performance, a way to compare performance achieved against the standard, and the action to take for the results that were achieved.

10. A checklist provides questions managers can use in their determination of how well their organization supports TQM and the quest for continuous quality improvement.

Bibliography

Athos, A. G. *Behavior in Organizations: A Multidimensional View,* Englewood Cliffs, NJ: Prentice-Hall, 1968.

Costly, D. L. and Todd, R. *Human Relations in Organizations*, New York: West Publishing Company, 1983.

Drucker, P. F. *Management: Tasks—Responsibilities—Practices*, New York: Harper and Row, 1974.

Elbing, A. O. *Behavioral Decisions in Organizations*, Glenview, IL: Scott, Foresman and Company, 1970.

Hunsaker, P. L. and Alessandra, A. J. *The Art of Managing People*, Englewood Cliffs, NJ: Prentice-Hall, 1980.

Schermerhorn, J. R., Hunt, J. G., and Osborn, R. N. *Managing Organizational Behavior*, New York: John Wiley and Sons, 1982.

Scott, W. G. and Hart, D. K. *Organizational America*, Boston: Houghton Mifflin, 1979.

CHAPTER 3

The Quality Culture

Organizational culture is a personality of sorts that defines the way business is conducted internally and externally. The definition for quality-conscious organizations generally contains concern for employee well-being and customer service. The degree to which these needs are served often is a measure of how successful that organization will be over the long term regardless of what measurement standard is applied—production, quality, profit, customer service, or some other applicable gauge.

The culture in each organization tends to have distinctive properties that make it different from other organizations. The list of such characteristics for an organization with known quality would include the following and the magnitude of each would provide organizational shape.

1. *Top-down leadership*–Leaders know where they are going, and they are taking their people with them.

2. *Vision*–A clear image is provided depicting exactly where the organization is going, what plans, objectives, and goals are required to get there, and the benefits employees can expect when goals are achieved.

3. *Customer focus*–Satisfying both internal and external customers is a primary part of all mission considerations.

4. *Employee well-being*–Employee well-being is considered in the decision-making processes and efforts are made to strike a positive balance between this and other important factors.

5. *Performance management system*–Employees are selected for quality, trained, appraised against a standard, and recognized for their achievements.

6. *Rewards system*–Employees are rewarded based on accomplishments rather than seniority, longevity, or a subjective standard.

7. *Communications system*–Communications are open and employees know what is occurring and why.

8. *Roles and relationships*–Roles are supportive rather than directive, where possible, and relationships up and down the chain are designed to encourage teamwork rather than conflict.

9. *Structure*–The structure is discretionary allowing more employee input into operations and process improvement.

10. *Teamwork*–Lone Rangers are out and teams are in. The rewards system supports team efforts.

The founder(s) of an organization has much to do with the surrounding culture that develops. Christ in Christianity, Thomas Watson at IBM, Henry Ford at Ford, and your company's founder all impacted significantly on the way organizations initially operated.

As time passes and the leadership changes, much of an organization's culture moves toward the beliefs, actions, ethics, and characteristics of the person at the top. Subordinates emulate and try to please the boss, often subconsciously. Organization structure impacts heavily on the culture that develops. Red tape, burdensome rules, and restrictive policies promote a culture that is anything but supportive of continuous process improvement.

People joining the operation generally have little immediate impact on an organization's culture unless they are at the top. Their immediate energy is devoted to assimilation into the current structure and not to changing it. Those who join an organization bent on immediately changing it before they know how it is supposed to operate are viewed with a jaundiced eye, as well they should be. How can you improve a process you don't fully understand? There is an exception to this rule—the person hired as a change agent will hit the deck ready to make changes, but these proposed changes usually are the reason that person was hired.

The type of operation also affects culture. A research and development center tend to have a different culture than a sales distribution center, blue-collar and white-collar operations differ, headquarters differ from operational sites, and battleships differ from destroyers. Cultural differences also stem from the location (for example, Boston vs. Appalachia).

All of these differences impact on the culture which develops, but nothing impacts so heavily as does leadership. Strong leaders who show concern for employee well-being and customer service will spawn a culture supportive of quality, and those who take a different approach will have decidedly different results.

The Culture Pyramid

Broad cultural changes must occur in many organizations before TQM and the accompanying continuous improvement can become a way of life. These changes include the way we view quality from detecting defects to prevention practices. Change also must occur in the way workers are viewed, from simple production assets to valued team members who are the only people in the organization who can ensure the TQM process will produce quality goods and services.

Most importantly, managers must become quality leaders from the top down through the organization. Quality concern emanates from the top and flows down through an organization—it cannot begin on the work floor and push up through the chain of command. Organizational gravity will not permit quality flow in this direction. Besides, who has more at stake in survival through quality than the people at the top of the organization?

The quality culture pyramid exhibited as Figure 3.1 illustrates the steps which must occur in the quest for quality. It is entirely possible that other steps will be added to your organizational pyramid, but these provide a framework for culture change.

Each step of the pyramid serves basic purposes that should be recognized. Many additional purposes are also served but only the principal ones are recognized.

1. Top-down leadership–power and energy
2. Vision, mission, objectives, and goals–direction
3. Quality philosophy–reasons why
4. Quality policy–course of action
5. Process understanding–knowledge of the operation
6. Quality work environment–support
7. Awareness, involvement, and commitment–conviction
8. Continuous "how to" training–skills and ability
9. Quality action–confidence and pride
10. Process ownership–possession

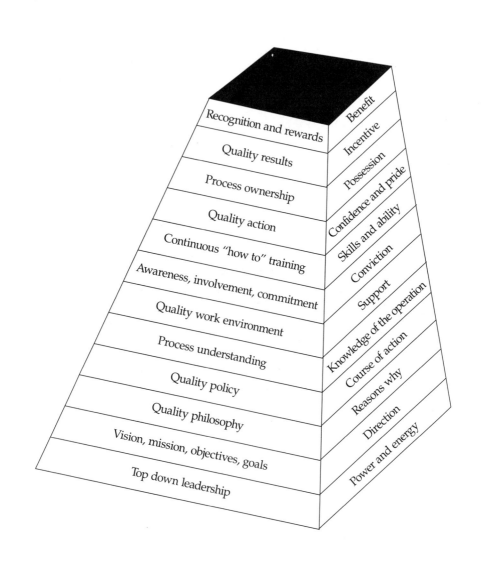

Figure 3.1 Culture Pyramid

11. Quality results–incentive

12. Recognition and reward–benefit

As previously mentioned, your culture pyramid may have more steps than this example. However, without these basic steps it may be difficult, if not impossible, to bring about culture change. For example, if top-down leadership doesn't exist, the TQM process won't begin; if vision, mission, objectives, and goals are missing, there won't be direction to guide the process; and so forth.

Developing a Quality Culture

Understanding organizational culture and developing culture within an organization are different processes. One requires a certain amount of studying, the other requires a lot of hard work over time by all of the members in the organization's management team.

The task of creating a quality culture is much easier when the organization already has a positive work environment that supports the work force. Without that environment, the task is considerably more difficult, but not impossible. Volume I, Chapter 15 outlines a process for creating a quality environment. This process supports the development of a quality culture.

The first step in developing a quality culture is to determine exactly what the current culture is. Once this is defined, it can be compared against what the culture should be. Each organization must discover itself, which may require considerable soul searching. The characteristics of a quality culture presented earlier in this chapter and the steps of the culture pyramid provide guides for determining what the culture should be, but the organization should make the determination.

The second step requires a management chain that supports the evolution to the quality culture that has been selected. Many managers will not immediately support such a change without prodding. The status quo is comfortable and they are getting along fine the way things are. "Hey, what's wrong with the system the way it is? We aren't exactly shrinking violets in this industry and are holding our customer base. TQM and people orientation—for what? I climbed up through the system the way it is and I made it. Why should things suddenly be given to the newbies who have yet to prove themselves? They can earn their parking space and toilet key the same way everybody else did."

This attitude is prevalent in some corners within most organizations. Is it any wonder that change requires considerable time and effort? Telling employees the change is being made won't do it, they must see the change in terms of long-term specific actions beginning with management. Only then will they believe.

Loyalty to Employees

Loyalty is the first element in a quality culture and it begins with the organization. Expecting loyalty from the people while showing marginal loyalty to them is like sitting by a wood stove waiting for heat without putting wood in it. It won't happen.

Many people contend there is no case for loyalty in an organization. Workers are expected to go to work each and every day, put forth their best efforts according to their ability, and be as productive as possible. For this they will be provided the agreed upon compensation package. That should be the limit of loyalty in an organization.

That scenario would be great if TQM would occur in that situation, but it won't. People do what they get rewarded for doing and they don't consider the basic paycheck as a reward; they consider that as their just due. Generally, they won't contribute more than they are rewarded for and continuous improvement demands extra effort.

The organization must be loyal to its people and exhibit it through a caring attitude that says, "You're the most important part of this operation." Saying it and exhibiting it, however, are different animals. Employees who are told they are valuable only to be laid off every year over the Christmas holidays so the annual profit margin is retained are at best skeptical of their true value to the organization. Workers requested to take pay cuts or to delay raises because of economic reasons who then see executives getting bonuses on top of their six-, seven-, or eight-figure incomes generally aren't all that excited to go above and beyond the minimum effort required to survive.

The organization with a history of labor unrest, high employee turnover, poor quality, and poor customer service has not earned employee loyalty. Moving from that position to a quality culture will take time, the length of which will be determined by the depth of the organization's efforts in this area. The efforts are necessary, worthwhile, and rewarding. TQM won't occur without loyalty, and people will treat customers no better than they are treated by their organization.

Consider this scene. The head of the sales/marketing team, Ms. Brown, is supposed to be meeting with a major customer over a proposed contract. Even though everyone else is in the conference room waiting her arrival, she is standing with hat in hand in front of Mr. Big's desk. She was summoned at the last moment about a point paper she had submitted the previous week. Mr. Big has been reading her the riot act for some time about the suggestions she had made concerning changes to a rule which impacted unnecessarily on production and customer satisfaction. Mr. Big's final comments go something like this, "Miss Brown, your job around here is to follow rules not make them. Should changes be required, I'll know that and make them without your help or interference. Things ran quite well before you came and they'll run after you leave. Now, if I'm not mistaken, you belong in the conference room selling Acme on the value of the contract we proposed. I expect a signed contract delivered to my office when Acme leaves today. If you can't deliver, we'll find someone who can."

This may seem quite harsh to some, but many of you can recall similar situations of which you were a part. A senior technician who worked under me developed an inexpensive change which prevented an expensive malfunction that had plagued that equipment wherever it was used. He had procured the components and made the change himself and it worked. Only when it was noticed that there were no recent failures did he admit what had been done. The suggested field change was then written up and submitted to the appropriate level of that organization. The word that came back was not recognition for a job well done. Instead, it was a reprimand for making unauthorized equipment changes with the further comment that our job was to maintain and repair equipment and not engineer it. I never revealed the outcome to the person who made that suggestion. He really didn't need to know.

A discussion of how loyalty can be created is not necessary here. Each organization must sit down and decide for itself what it will take and how they can achieve those things they can afford. Two key people items should be discussed at such a meeting: respect for the individual and promotion from within. These items, more than others, seem to send positive signals to the work force.

Loyalty to the Organization

Employee loyalty to the organization, and in turn their fellow employees, is the other half of the loyalty equation. Reciprocal action is almost a certainty when employees find the organization loyal to them and considerate of their needs.

Loyalty is absolutely mandatory before employees will become involved in the quality improvement process, let alone commit to it. Once the organization has this loyalty, teamwork becomes a way of life and there is virtually no limit to what can be achieved.

People-Builders

Excellence begins with the work force. Each organization must develop solid hiring practices and realistic appraisal systems so the proper employees are hired and retained. These subjects will be covered in detail in later chapters.

Additionally, the people in the work force must be developed in order to reach their fullest potential. Some companies have internal training programs designed to train their people for performance and promotion. One group we work with developed an apprenticeship program to train people, thus providing upward mobility. It is now approved by federal and state governments. This program, by itself, increases employee value to the organization. Continual training, personal goals, ever increasing responsibility, and so forth, prepares people for upward mobility and most promotions come from within. Low employee turnover rates and continuous performance improvement readily testify to the program's success.

Many companies now offer employee retraining programs when jobs are phased out due to technology changes. Both the organization and the employee benefit. The employee maintains employment and the employer retains a successful employee on the payroll.

The number of organizations encouraging work force participation continues to increase. Workers are taught to troubleshoot processes, solve problems, make decisions; they are encouraged to use these skills to improve their work areas. Delegated responsibilities also are used to prepare people for promotion, which in turn frees up their managers for greater responsibilities.

Some organizations now permit and encourage workers to make many process improvements without waiting for permission. This responsibility encourages workers and raises morale. Other important issues are tackled. Threatening situations are sought out and removed. Finger-pointing and blame are replaced with problem-solving efforts. Employees are encouraged to help each other, and creative efforts are advocated and supported. Although cost-control measures must continue, the emphasis is switched to quality improvement.

Each of these could be "how to" topics for discussion here. However, a great deal more will be accomplished by taking each of these topics and using them as the subject of brainstorming sessions with employees. They know their processes and will produce great ideas. Best of all, it will encourage ownership of their processes.

None of these ideas costs much, especially in comparison to the return. They all mean a great deal to the employees and add to the quality culture.

Supporting the Quality Culture

I have been a part of quality cultures and visited many others. The ideas expressed here come from those places with the exception of a comment about Motorola, which is noted for its quality culture.

I recently went to a retirement ceremony at an organization with which I worked previously. It was a well-attended affair; there were appropriate gifts and a retirement cake. It was a sad time for the recipient because she had invested greatly toward that organization's significant successes over the years and hated to leave. The presence of her many friends and family made it easier.

Retirement, reward, and recognition ceremonies add a great deal to the development of a supportive culture. Thank-you notes recognizing special contributions, and especially those sent to the home, add a great deal to this culture.

One plant we worked with recently sponsored lunchtime pizza and sub parties for all employees at the end of each month in which they produced performance increases from previous months. The spirit that was evident certainly exceeded the cost of the party, and it set the stage for performance improvements the following month.

Another organization has a Christmas party and a summer picnic. There are all kinds of fun activities at each of these, and they prove to be significant morale boosters. Management and the work force lose their identities at these functions. The positive effects last long after the parties as people post pictures on the bulletin boards, discuss the fun they had, and so forth.

I once worked with an executive who maintained an index file on the people in the organization. When he visited various operations, which was a regular routine, he knew the people and something about them. He also took spouses to lunch with their mate when they had made some special contribution. Those men and women would do anything for him because they knew he cared.

Another organization I worked with had a policy of sending cards to workers' homes on special occasions. It cost the company little because the people all chipped into what they called the sunshine fund to pay for the cards and postage and the office manager addressed them on her own time.

One executive sends personal Christmas cards to every employee who worked under him, complete with a note thanking him or her for their efforts on behalf of the company that year. He also sends thank-you notes to their homes for their special achievements. Nothing else he does contributes more to the positive way he is perceived by the work force.

A site manager with about 100 employees takes the time to hand out paychecks personally each payday at a short training meeting. Employees are personally thanked for their contributions and hands are shaken when they receive the check. It means a lot to both the manager and the employees.

Much is written about the lifetime employment practices of the Japanese. Although these practices are misunderstood by most Americans, they are morale boosters where practiced.

The Japanese aren't the only people who do this. Motorola sponsors the Motorola Service Club. Employees become members after 10 years of service. Once a member, they cannot be released without permission of the chairman of the board. To enact such a program successfully, an organization must have sound hiring, training, appraisal, and retention programs.

Honesty, respect, and fairness are commodities that play an active part in all of these, and they are necessities for the emergence of a quality culture. The executives who lead and the employees completing the organization's work must respect each other and be honest and fair in their dealings if TQM is to work.

The Culture Changes

Employees expect change whenever the organization decides on a new course of action. In fact, they will be disillusioned if they don't see change occurring.

Change is more readily made when the organization is undergoing a transition of major consequences, such as new executive leadership, a merger, or the company is sold. People expect it because they know what can happen in these situations.

Culture change requires alterations in the way quality, personnel, and customers are viewed and understood. Old ways are ingrained and must be driven out so that we can assimilate the new quality concepts required in the TQM process.

Changing the Approach to People

This section does not push the idea that "we're all equals in this and we're going to make decisions on that basis." Those kinds of theories haven't worked nor will they. People depend on leaders with vision. Leaders require followers to carry out the organization's effort. Hopefully, many of these followers aspire to leadership roles as they progress in an organization, but there is a role for everyone who wants to be a constructive force within a quality-driven, customer-focused organization.

The way organizations and their leaders view the people who carry out the work must change if employees are going to support the changes and invest the efforts required for the necessary improvements.

Organization vs. personnel orientation–Task-dominated approaches guided most organizations previously. Mission was the focus without much consideration for the people who were to make that mission successful. The organizational goal remains prime, but the methods of reaching it change. Leaders interact with all layers of the organization to create plans to reach the ultimate goal whether it be profit, economical service, educated students, or whatever. Employees become partners in progress instead of assets who carry out assignments. This requires leaders to become counselors, team players, and supporters.

Directive vs. supportive–There is a time for directive leadership, but it is not the dominant style used in all situations. Coaching, participative, and delegative styles must become the way of doing business when they are appropriate. Volume I thoroughly discusses these concepts.

Rule dominance vs. development of commitment–Organizations that force compliance through endless rules, heavy-handedness, and fear are headed for a rough time on the journey to excellence. Personnel development produces commitment and that is where the quality journey reaches payoff territory. Committed employees who feel organizational ownership produce quality products and services with customer satisfaction both internally and externally.

Status quo vs. well-planned change–"Talk is cheap; it takes money to buy whiskey." I don't know the origin of this comment, but one person who said it used it to describe a situation where a branch of government was talking quality, but contracting by a lowest salary structure bid. Quality can't be discussed as a way of life without considering the required changes necessary to bring it about. Employees must see examples of this change emanating from the top that requires those individuals to change their way of doing business before they will become serious about quality. Expecting employees to change without changing the way of doing business at the top is hope against hope—it won't happen.

These concepts are not radical, nor are they new. They simply haven't been practiced in many organizations. Some organizations delude themselves into thinking they are people-oriented when in fact the people perceive they are strictly goal-oriented. Perception is important. It requires employees who perceive themselves as team members going after a mutually beneficial goal before performance improvement progress will become a viable force. When employees become valued problem-solvers and decision-makers committed to improvement, that progress will be evident and ongoing.

Changing the Concepts of Quality

New direction is required in the way American organizations conduct business in order to implement the TQM process. We must move away from choosing suppliers and vendors on the singular basis of initial cost. Life cycle costs that are a factor of designed quality are a much better indicator. This also means movement away from multiple sources for similar items. Too often competition does not drive overall costs down for several reasons. Like products may not be identical in many ways and adapting them to internal need can be expensive. The suppliers often can give bigger discounts when they are the only supplier because they have larger volume, and if the quality remains high they may secure long-term customers. In this regard, the Department of Defense multiple source contracting scenario is at cross-purposes with the TQM initiatives it is taking.

Working relations must be developed with suppliers and customers so that this unit becomes a working team. Development costs decrease for everyone and the end product becomes more user friendly with higher quality and lower costs. Suppliers should not be told how to do their job, but what product is required in terms of product performance. Vendor performance would be a driving factor in the selection process. It is wise to make sure suppliers have their own TQM process in place so that they, too, are continuously improving. Thus, suppliers would have incentive to continually improve their performance in terms of both quality and production.

Contracts must not tie contractors to strict technical regimens because improvements become virtually impossible and are not cost-effective. The process should be dynamic with changes allowed when the supplier can demonstrate technical and/or cost benefits. Flexibility in contract requirements promotes a cost-effective program which benefits everyone.

The outmoded, inspection-dominant concept of quality in organizations and operations of all types must switch from inspecting-in to building-in quality. Do away with sorting good from bad. The focus changes from:

- Quality perceptions that some level of defects is permissible to zero defects.

- Changing from selection of suppliers based on cost and tolerating their scrap or rework to zero tolerance, and from inspecting-in quality to process control.

- Switching from total inspection of incoming materials to vendor certification of quality.

- Changing from what the end user will accept to conformance to customer requirements.

- Moving from the production of less expensive initial cost products that are of inferior quality to providing cost-competitive, quality products that are less expensive over their useful life cycle.

- Transforming from the minimum service it takes to stay in business to the quality service it takes to increase business—from survival to tough competitor.

This requires change in thoughts and attitude on quality from top management down through everyone in the work force. No operation, process, or individual within an organization should be excused from the TQM process. Those individuals who make the greatest case for not being involved usually are the ones with the most need. Every function from executive management to janitorial services is vital for survival and requires continuous improvement. TQM is viewed as a way of life rather than a short-term project. It requires commitment to total quality beginning at the top and enthusiastically supported with energy and focus through all levels.

There must be responsibility for TQM with commitment beginning with the CEO, government executive, or school and hospital administrator, down through managers and supervisors, to workers at the lowest levels. All vendors must share the same responsibility. It also is wise to bring the consumer into the TQM process. Their education supports both sales and overall customer satisfaction.

The reasons for quality are many and varied. Quality bears heavily on product investment for both purchase and support costs. Product performance is extremely important to the customer and the people who supply them. Customers become upset with poor quality, which affects sales in many ways and impacts negatively on organization costs for repair and recall.

Morale suffers within any organization whose quality is less than its potential to produce quality goods and services. Recruiting efforts are made more difficult for all organizations where there is a perception that their way of doing business and the products and services they produce suffer in quality. Retention is another factor. People want to remain with a quality team while they leave poor quality organizations like rats leaving a sinking ship.

Customer Concepts

The way customers are viewed and the way they are treated, becomes important in this quest for quality. Internal and external customers must have their needs and expectations met. This subject is discussed in some detail later in this volume in Chapters 12 and 13.

Training Changes

Customer focus, with continuous drive to increase user satisfaction, is vital in the drive for excellence. Long-term training programs are central to TQM and benefit the organization and each employee. Where possible, it is an excellent idea to train supplier and customer personnel at the same time as internal training. This builds teamwork and supports everyone playing from the same sheet of music.

Considerable precedence has been set in this area. Many manufacturers are expanding distributor training beyond product knowledge to include sales, marketing, bidding, and negotiation training. Organizations implementing quality programs provide excess training capacity as seats to their customers and vendors. Each of these ideas supports the vendors and customers which improves business relationships at little real cost.

This necessitates training changes in many areas. Surveys show that virtually no supervisor receives training on how to be a supervisor prior to promotion to a supervisory position. Less than 25 percent of all supervisors receive training in management techniques and practices within the first two years of becoming a supervisor. Seldom does one outside the sales/marketing force receive customer relations training, yet all of us have customers. Quality training systems have been academic, rather than grass roots, hands-on programs from the work floor up. Training generally does not emphasize team strategies and concepts. Most organizations have no quality management training programs, and initiatives are lacking for individual self-training.

Once again, research and development must become a high priority. It costs money, but it is necessary to compete in the world market. The practice of exporting high technology to our competitors must be questioned. How long can America continue to provide competitors with technology that they improve slightly, use to protect the internal market for their manufacturers, and drive U. S. companies out of business? Autos, semiconductors, and the swept-wing aircraft technology (to name a few) are examples of this process. The result is that commercial industry in the United States is no longer able to provide certain products of key importance to our defense industry (such as some semiconductors for defense systems, machine tools, and high-grade jeweled bearings). Relying on overseas sources contains a risk to all Americans, the defense of our country, and American security.

American business and industry is faced with ever-increasing offshore competition. This is partially attributable to consumer awareness of quality and the desire for that quality. Survival is paramount. We cannot allow the continued degradation of our manufacturing base and maintain our quality of life. Poor quality breeds employee dissatisfaction. Who wants to work for a low-quality organization?

Money and assets are almost always tight in any organization. There never seems to be enough to go around. At the same time, when solid training programs are not in place, marginal performance is a given. People cannot work to a higher standard than that to which they have been trained. We need to change the total concept of the way we do business if we truly decide to get our standard of living and our organization performance back on the march upward again.

Roadblocks to Change

There are roadblocks to the TQM process that begin with the misconceptions about TQM. Let's examine some of them for identification purposes. Many of them probably exist in your operation.

- TQM is just another management program.
- TQM is a quick fix.
- TQM is free.
- TQM requires little effort once it is in place.
- TQM, quality assurance, and quality control are virtually the same concept.

Cultural change is required to overcome these misconceptions which can be quite difficult in organizations that have no basis in quality. The TQM philosophy must replace existing cultures that have become the way the organization does business, and in turn considers itself as an operating entity. Participative and delegative leadership styles must replace the old autocratic ways.

Many organizations have no central structure capable of leading or administering TQM initiatives. Standardization, development time, and implementation costs are allowed to be major obstacles to TQM. Often there has been questionable success on previous quality type programs. The promised quality in advertisements, proposals, and during research and development phases often does not translate to superior performance once the product or service has been provided to the customer.

However, all is not lost. The long-range forecast appears good. The United States is headed in the quality direction. Many organizations are now operating superbly and are strong forces in global competition. Dedication to the concepts of TQM with quality goods and services will ensure the United States leads the way in quality, productivity, research, and innovative use of technology.

Aiding the March to Quality

As stated, many organizations have excellent systems already in place. The executive leadership has developed a solid vision of where the organization should go and an excellent mission statement that supports this vision. Strategic plans with great potential have been developed at considerable time and expense. Goals and objectives include quality, productivity, safety, and customer service. When carried out, these goals would see the vision come true. Active training programs are in place and functioning, providing employees with the training they want. The reward and recognition system stands ready to support the program. An organization such as this should really be humming along on the quality journey—right?

Maybe and maybe not. There could be major disconnects between the vision, plans, goals, training, and customer requirements as viewed at the executive level, and what the producing elements of the organization regard as the direction they should be headed in each area. The best system is of little use if it is not supporting the work force in their continuous improvement efforts. How can the visions, plans, and systems be made TQM supportive?

Certainly, each organization must have strategic plans based on the vision and mission of the organization. Strategic plans are the basis for business, marketing, quality, and training plans, which are used to develop a working budget that supports these plans.

The training plan must have two parts: the strategic function, which supports the organization's strategic plan; and a working or annual function, which outlines the annual training program in order to meet long-range goals. This program must be need-based and customer-focused. Need says that employees must be allowed to work on performance improvement with training provided to assist with these efforts. Training must be tracked and evaluated to determine to what degree training objectives are met. A solid indicator is the degree to which employees are able to meet the established performance goals and objectives.

Let's assume that these plans and goals are completed. How do you communicate all of this to the work force in a simple manner they can and will easily digest? It sounds impossible. After all, the various plans and goals are immense and the people who should closely follow them often don't. Why would people on the work floor bother? The answer is that they won't in most cases.

How about a simple pictorial that schematically communicates the plan on a simple sheet of paper? It could then be posted throughout the organization so every person has access to the organization's vision, mission, plans, and goals. Employees would see it everyday, it would become a topic of discussion in training, meetings, and so forth, and employees would assimilate it into their work life.

This sounds easy to discuss, but difficult to achieve. During a recent visit to GPU Nuclear's Three-Mile Island plant, I witnessed just such a schematic. It is well-done in color, understandable, and posted throughout their operation. This poster is accompanied by a pocket-size trifold with the same goals and is available for employees. Can it serve as a model for your organization?

Summary

1. Organizations have personalities that define the way they do business. This culture has distinctive properties that sets it apart from other organizations.

2. This culture is explained through the use of a quality culture pyramid. This pyramid provides specific steps that will support the quality culture. Each step meets a cultural need.

3. Loyalty and people builders are discussed as they pertain to the development of a quality culture. Other supporting factors also are covered as they have been viewed in organizations successfully traveling the quality road.

4. Changing culture is achieved through attention to change in important areas. The way employees, quality in general, and customers are viewed must undergo change in those organizations pursuing excellence.

5. There are many reasons for quality and just as many obstacles in the way of quality improvement. TQM provides a process for continuous improvement which overcomes the obstacles within each work environment.

6. The different parts of the TQM process would fill volumes. Vision, mission, goals, and objectives, however, are important requirements all employees must understand and be aware of in the drive for quality.

Bibliography

Bradford, D. L. and Cohen, A. R. *Managing for Excellence,* New York: John Wiley and Sons, 1984.

Drucker, P. F. *The Frontiers of Management: Why Tomorrow's Decisions Are Being Shaped Today,* New York: E. P. Dalton, 1986.

———. *Management: Tasks—Responsibilities—Practices,* New York: Harper and Row, 1973.

———. *Practice of Management,* New York: Harper and Row, 1954.

DuBrin, A. J. *Contemporary Applied Management,* Homewood, IL: BPI Irwin, 1989.

Filley, A. C. *The Complete Manager,* Champaign, IL: Research Press Company, 1978.

Harmon, F. G. *The Executive Odyssey,* New York: John Wiley and Sons, 1989.

Hitt, W. D. *Management in Action,* Columbus, OH: Battelle Press, 1985.

Hunsaker, P. L. and Alessandra, A. J. *The Art of Managing People,* Englewood Cliffs, NJ: Prentice-Hall, 1980.

Kirby, T. *The Can-Do Manager,* New York: AMACOM, 1989.

Lundborg, L. B. *The Art of Being an Executive,* New York: The Free Press, 1981.

Morgan, J. S. *Managing Change,* New York: McGraw-Hill, 1972.

Odiorne, G. S. *How Managers Make Things Happen,* Englewood Cliffs, NJ: Prentice-Hall, 1987.

Practical Management Associates. (Course) *Executive Management Program,* Canoga Park, CA.

Quick, T. L. *The Persuasive Manager,* Radnor, PA: Chilton Book Company, 1982.

Schoenberg, R. J. *The Art of Being a Boss,* Philadelphia: J. B. Lippincott, 1978.

Seidman, L. W. *The Executive's Guide to Competitiveness,* Armonk, NY: M. E. Sharpe, 1989.

Sloma, R. S. *No-Nonsense Management,* New York: McMillan Publishing Company, 1977.

CHAPTER 4

Performance Management

The study of leadership in Volume I began with a discussion of the differences between leadership and management. There it was determined that you lead people and manage processes. Many people question how you can improve performance if you don't manage people. This chapter answers that question with an outline of a performance management system and discusses the system in its entirety. A few key areas receive additional discussion in subsequent chapters.

Good enough is never good enough in a quality environment. Since continuous improvement will not happen by itself, some system must be in place to support this effort. Performance management (PM) is a manager–employee process used to determine the work that must be accomplished, the type of person required to complete such work, the training which is required to meet expected results, how accomplishments will be evaluated, and the means to ensure continuing performance improvement becomes a working part of the TQM process. This turns performance into a management process rather than a once-a-year appraisal of what occurred. Everyone benefits from a well-run PM system.

It is necessary to outline the complete PM system although some parts of this discussion will receive only a cursory review in this chapter.

The organization–The organization benefits from continuous performance improvement, payoff training based on proven need, and a personnel management system that features a system for hiring quality people and produces verifiable data upon which to base promotions, salary increases, recognition, rewards, discipline, and terminations.

Management–Supervisors develop a much deeper understanding of their people in terms of their job and personal needs. They are able to assist with personnel development at a higher level with verifiable need-based training. This provides a considerable savings in time and dollars and ensures people receive the training they need. They also know their people and their abilities which enables the use of participative and delegative leadership styles that are so important to the TQM process.

Individuals–Individuals enjoy a much deeper understanding of the organization and its needs. They have immediate input to performance standards and goals, and their performance appraisal is based on standards they helped create. They are an integral part of the system and are able to communicate ideas, needs, and concerns to their supervisor. They have confidence in the system because they are a part of that system which in turn promotes organization ownership. They also gain security through the continuous performance improvements. Most importantly, they are recognized and rewarded for their achievements.

Figure 4.1 provides a graphic overview of a PM system and how each portion of that system interacts.

System Overview

Organizations manage or attempt to manage performance for many reasons. Basic objectives in a TQM process include the following:

1. Create understanding of the work to be accomplished.

2. Create understanding of the quality level expected.

3. Develop a mutual manager–employee plan to accomplish the designated work with quality.

4. Determine if performance met the agreed upon level.

5. Determine how performance can be improved.

6. Provide recognition and reward for achievement.

This system allows management to plan work and quality requirements, appraise work, and develop a new plan. It must be understood that employees can accomplish outstanding work and have it noted in a process where there is room for improvement. Process must be evaluated against agreed upon goals, not what the process potential might be.

Some steps of this system receive only a cursory overview because they are beyond the scope of this program. Job analysis and job descriptions are covered as a basis for the performance appraisal process, but additional work is required to develop them from scratch. This discussion provides the

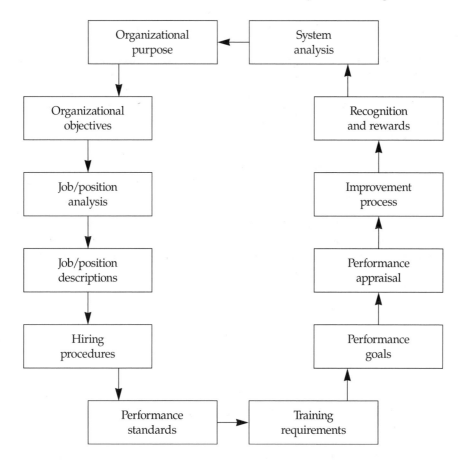

Figure 4.1 Performance Management System

information required to analyze the job description program to ascertain if there is room for improvement. Some parts of the PM system will be fully developed in this chapter and other parts will be discussed in stand-alone chapters.

Organizational Purpose

Each organization has a purpose or reason for existence that must be understood by the organization's members. This purpose should be outlined in a written purpose statement which provides the means to communicate ideas about the organization and may contain implications concerning how the organization will function.

Two basic questions must be answered to determine purpose: who are we and what do we do? Answers to these questions form the basis for planning, budgeting, and performance management. To accomplish this, the statement covers areas such as why we are in this particular business, who our customers are, and how we will serve those customers. A sample statement follows.

> The purpose of Acme Electric is to serve our customers in the building trades industry and our employees by producing quality products that meet customer need.

Much can be said about purpose, but it is something that should be a part of the initial decision to form the organization and not expounded on in a quality manual. If you have progressed to this point without a prepared purpose statement, it is time to develop one.

Goals and Objectives

Organizational goals and objectives provide guidance for where the organization is going. Vision, a topic thoroughly discussed in Volume I, provides the foundation for this step. Goals outline a desired outcome or result as an achievement target for completion by members of that organization. They provide a guide for making decisions and form the basis for planning work objectives on an annual or some other such basis. Goals are thoroughly explored in Volume III. A goal statement follows.

> To increase product and service quality to best serve the needs of our customers . . . .

Objective statements specify measurable results the organization meets over some specific time period in order to accomplish the determined goals. Objectives are divided into subobjectives which provide result requirements for each part of the operation or process in order to meet objectives. An objective statement follows.

> To increase product quality by 10 percent and reduce service complaints by 15 percent during 199__ . . . .

Job and Position Analysis and Descriptions

Once visions, goals, objectives and plans are determined, it becomes possible to analyze the jobs and positions required to meet these plans. This requires a survey and analysis of the workplace. The details of this process are outlined later in this chapter.

Job descriptions serve in the development of the salary structure, recruiting, hiring, performance appraisal, training, and more. Although they will not solve management incompetencies, they do support management in the efforts to manage and improve performance. This process is outlined in more detail later in this chapter.

Hiring Practices

Hiring practices are thoroughly discussed as a stand-alone subject in Chapter 5. The steps of the PM chain developed up to this point support the hiring process and every evolution after that. Suffice it to say, the personnel hired must be limited to those who have the potential to meet performance standards.

On the surface this would seem a rather elementary observation. However, given the fact that many people complete their formal education process without the foggiest idea of what they are going to do for a living, selection appears more complicated. If people are not sure what they really want in terms of a career, how are they going to package their credentials so those responsible for hiring them know they match organizational requirements?

Performance Standards

Performance standards provide the basis for appraising performance. They are a means to gauge performance based on predetermined quantifying factors. Standards are more fully developed later in this chapter.

Training Requirements

Three types of training must be considered in the PM process. The first is PM training to ensure understanding of the PM process. The level of success that can be expected from any process cannot be greater than the knowledge level of the people employing that system. No organization would consider installing automated machinery or advanced computer systems without training the people who will use them. The same must be considered for the PM process. This chapter provides the basis for training on the PM system.

The second training consideration is the development of initial training sequences that ensures employees have the ability to perform to the level outlined for performance standards. This will be an evolutionary process because PM is a system designed to be compatible with TQM and ongoing process improvement. As processes are improved, training requirements must be reevaluated to ensure people have the capability to further improve the system.

The third training consideration is that which develops employees beyond the immediate needs of their current position, then assists with their preparation for promotion and ensures they possess the skills and knowledge required to support the long-term journey for excellence. Training is deemed so important to the TQM process that an entire book, Volume IV, is provided to cover the subject.

Performance Goals

Performance goals are established between a supervisor and an employee. These become the targets against which performance is appraised. This area is explored in more detail in Chapter 6.

Performance Appraisal

Performance appraisal is the step taken by the supervisor to rate to what extent the employee met the performance goals. This subject is explored in Chapter 6.

Improvement Process

Improvement requirements are formulated after performance attainments have been appraised. Depending on the individual, there may be rewards for exemplary performance accompanied by new targets. There could be a requirement for more training, continual coaching, or even disciplinary action. The results of the appraisal determine what steps are taken in the improvement process. More on this subject in Chapter 6.

Recognition and Rewards

Recognition is an extremely important part of performance management and all performance is recognized. Performance that meets or exceeds established goals is recognized and reviewed for potential reward. The various media receive notice of achievements, formal ceremonies are held to recognize participants, and other kinds of thank-yous are provided.

Poor performance also is recognized. Training sessions are planned and held to correct knowledge or skill deficiencies, counseling sessions work on other aspects of performance problems, and ongoing coaching efforts assist employees in their efforts to improve.

Outstanding efforts must be rewarded in some manner. Team rewards or awards are most supportive of the TQM effort. Personal awards, however, also are appropriate for those singular efforts that are above and beyond.

Recognition and rewards cannot be overdone if they are handled correctly. Positive recognition and rewards must be earned. They are provided for *performance improvement* and not the status quo. There is little benefit for anyone whose performance remains static. To do so is to go backward in comparison to everyone else. Both recognition and rewards should be timely; they should be provided as soon as possible after the improvement action takes place. Recognition must be appropriate for the circumstances. Employees won't be thrilled about $10 gift certificates for a process improvement that saves the organization millions of dollars.

This subject is developed more fully in Volume I.

System Analysis

After each round of performance appraisals, the system must be analyzed for strengths and weaknesses. Hiring processes are analyzed in terms of the performance received by newly hired employees. Training is continually monitored to ensure that it is paying off in terms of improved employee performance. As each area is analyzed, the results are fed back into the system to improve that area.

All parts of the system are affected by performance improvements. The purpose of the organization may change to take advantage of new markets or to produce new products as its employees' performance makes these available. Job descriptions will change to take advantage of new technology and manufacturing techniques, additional product requirements, and more. This requires changes in hiring processes, training requirements, and so forth. As each round continues, performance improves, improving processes and requiring reevaluation and changes to the system in an upward spiraling performance improvement process.

Job/Position Analysis

Job analysis and the resulting job descriptions are crucial activities. Recruiting, training, performance, and performance evaluation depend on proper job descriptions. There also are significant legal ramifications that attend job descriptions so they must be accurate and nonbiased.

Perhaps the place to start is with a definition of jobs and positions as they generally apply to an organization. Although they often are used interchangeably, there is a difference in the terms. A *job* is the work in terms of the various tasks performed by a person in a particular occupation. A *position* is a particular assignment within the organization. For example, the job of machinist generally has people engaged in various activities associated with machining metals. Although they are not all the same activities, they are all associated with the machinist job. There could be positions such as lathe, milling machine, and grinder operators. Similarly, consider the computer programmer as a job. Computer programmers could all have the same job description with the same requirements, yet be performing different activities associated with their programming positions.

The terms (position and job) have other connotations in job analysis and description efforts. Position descriptions generally are reserved for management-level employees and professionals where there is only one personnel manager, manufacturing manager, site manager, or training manager. Job descriptions usually refer to lower level personnel such as machinists, data processors, and clerks where there can be hundreds of people performing the same basic task.

Job analysis is the process of gathering, documenting, and analyzing jobs in terms of content, requirements, and conditions. Job content describes activities, duties, and tasks. The level to which they are defined is determined by factors such as complexity, safety, and so forth.

Job requirements identify skills, knowledge, experience, and training needed to complete the job satisfactorily. Physical characteristics may be identified, but these must be able to stand certain tests in order to be used. They cannot be used to discriminate against any particular group. At times, education, professional licenses, certificates, and similar credentials also may be listed as requirements if they are necessary to complete the job correctly in most cases.

Special attention should be paid to skills and knowledge requirements, such as process control, problem solving, quality tools, and similar performance improvement subjects as they pertain to each particular job. This keys both the person holding a job and the supervisor on those requirements and the training needs required to keep the person current in that area.

The conditions of the job include the job's purpose, level of supervision required, reporting requirements, relationships with other positions, responsibilities, and other such guidelines.

There are many sources of information for the job analysis. Any analysis that does not include physical observation, however, may be on shaky ground in court and not readily accepted by the employees. Questionnaires, logs, and personal interviews are other ways of gathering information, but it is best if those items are used to support actual observations of the work being performed.

Who Should Gather the Information?

Immediate supervisors or managers should gather initial information. They know the type of work that is performed and often completed the effort themselves prior to promotion. Their efforts can then be corroborated with personnel specialists to ensure all bases are covered.

Some organizations designate an individual to complete all job analysis and job descriptions. Others hire outside consultants for these efforts. However, there are concerns with these methods. There can be considerable misunderstanding, including how the work process is completed in its entirety, how each job fits into the process as a whole, or the processes that take place to complete a single operation. Erroneous conclusions can then be drawn that will impact on every subsequent step of the performance management process. It also can impact on salary determinations.

One organization hired an outside consultant to prepare job descriptions for the entire organization. The consultant was a skilled professional who conscientiously worked through the process. When salaries were derived from the analysis, however, noticeable inequities immediately surfaced.

Since the consultant did not have a thorough knowledge of all jobs, she was forced to rely on descriptions prepared by supervisors. Some supervisors prepared more thorough descriptions, others had better writing skills, or indepth knowledge of the job analysis/job description process and how salaries were derived from the information. This skewed the information received by the consultant, biasing it toward the detail-minded supervisors who could write well. A few supervisors intentionally puffed up minor aspects of the jobs to make them sound more important than they were.

The organization then had to invest considerable additional time and effort to correct the problems which had been created. They rectified the situation by holding training for the supervisors and then having the personnel department work through the analysis writeups with these supervisors. The consultant used this information to construct new descriptions which proved satisfactory. The organization, however, could have completed the process themselves given their level of involvement with the second analysis.

Who Should Be Surveyed?

Technically, all job incumbents should be surveyed, but time, cost, and work schedules may preclude this even though the level of participation could significantly improve results and worker commitment to the process. One way to survey large operations with many similar jobs is to sample selected individuals who are noted for job knowledge and quality performance.

Results of the analysis should be reviewed with management prior to beginning the task of writing job descriptions. They may know of future upgrades for the positions, a dumbing-down process that is in the works to cover the less educated people available in the workplace, and so forth. Once agreed upon, the process of developing descriptions can begin.

Job/Position Descriptions

This overview of job descriptions provides knowledge that assists with a determination concerning the quality of current job descriptions within your organization. For those who do not have job descriptions, it provides an overview that exhibits how they support the performance management process.

There are costs involved with the job description process. Development takes time and money. It also costs to maintain and update the descriptions in order to keep them current. Unless they remain current, job descriptions soon are outdated and of little use in the quest for performance improvement.

Many different kinds of job descriptions have been outlined. Excellent books are available in most libraries to assist with this task. Some have complete descriptions ready to personalize for any organization's use. Several such sources are listed in the Bibliography at the end of this chapter.

Generic descriptions are written in broad terms after several jobs are analyzed for common denominators. Using the machinist as an example, the description would include the areas of expertise expected of one holding the title "machinist." It would not include precise to the level of specific job descriptions written to cover lathe operators, surface grinders, milling machine operators, and so forth.

Some organizations use generic descriptions to get them up and running. In this context, they assist efforts such as recruiting, training, planning, salary determinations, and the development of performance standards. Once developed, generic job descriptions tend to remain in effect over the long term.

Specific job descriptions detail particular or individual jobs. They provide detailed information on reporting procedures, inspection requirements, quality standards, performance expectations, and so forth. Organizational need is a criterion used to determine which type of description should be followed. Time, asset availability, and cost become factors in this decision.

A sample job description format and job description are provided to exhibit how they are developed and the ways in which they support a PM system (Figures 4.2 to 4.4). These examples illustrate a method to compare your job descriptions with others and perhaps discover ways that your system can be beefed up to support PM.

For those organizations without job descriptions, these examples will not provide all the information required to develop such a program. It will exhibit the beneficial aspects of solid job descriptions as a basis to improve employee performance.

Although these samples provide for performance standards, most job/position descriptions do not. Provision for these standards on this common form supports the entire PM process and they are included for that reason.

Job/position title:

Organizational unit: (Department, section, process, etc.)

Reports to: (Title of the person to whom this job reports.)

Supervises: (Titles of the people this person supervises.)

Liaisons with: (Titles of the people outside the work group or the organization with whom this person must work to accomplish the mission.)

Job function: (A short description of the mission or purpose of this job which includes the range and scope of operations.)

Responsibilities: (Statements identifying the significant ongoing tasks and responsibilities for supervisory, technical, administrative, and other appropriate areas. These statements should show depth of responsibility and frequency of requirements.)

Performance criteria: (Specific quality, production, and customer service specifications or standards peculiar to this job.)

Prepared by:

Approved by:

Effective date:

Figure 4.2   Sample Job Description Format

Job title: Computer Operator

Organizational unit: Computer Center

Reports to: Computer Center Supervisor

Liaisons with: Assists personnel within the computer center and customers from other departments to accomplish the mission of the center and ACME Company.

Job function: Provides computer-centered services for all departments within the company.

Responsibilities:

Operates computer hardware and software utilized within the computer center.

Ensures all assigned projects are completed on time and completion information is entered in the daily log.

(Figure 4.3 continued on next page)

Assists customers in their efforts to define projects and determine completion schedules.

Maintains equipment in a clean and safe condition.

Maintains accurate logs of equipment malfunctions and reports malfunctions to the appropriate person.

Maintains an inventory of computer processing supplies and reorder as required.

Performance criteria:
Correctly operates all designated hardware and software.

Ensures agreed upon customer requirements are fully met.

Produces work to the agreed-upon standard achieved during performance goaling sessions.

Requirements:
High school degree or general equivalency degree (GED) with two years of related experience. Experience may be substituted by appropriate education above the high school level.

Prepared by: A. Searfoss

Approved by: T. Quinn

Effective date: November 1992

Figure 4.3   Sample Job Description

Position title: Production Control Manager

Organizational unit: Manufacturing

Reports to: Manufacturing Manager

Supervises: Quality Assurance Supervisor and Production Control supervisors in stamping, fabrication, paint shop, electrical, and final test.

Liaisons with: Procurement, marketing, engineering, shipping, aftermarket sales, and training.

Job function: Responsible for manufacturing quality, on-time production, and continuous improvement processes of all computer-controlled units produced at the Hartford, Connecticut, facilities.

Responsibilities:
Manages production and quality supervisors and monitor such activities as manufacturing planning, production scheduling, inventory control, and quality assurance.

Directs activities required for effective work flow schedules that meet customer requirement dates.

(Figure 4.4 continued on next page)

Monitors quality checks throughout the process and the results obtained at final test.

Reviews all customer survey sheets and product action plans where applicable for performance improvements.

Selects appropriate personnel for job openings in order to maintain excellence in the performance management process.

Ensures personnel training to meet performance requirements and support the internal promotion systems.

Performance criteria:
Monitors final test and ensure that all shipped equipment meets performance specifications to 100 percent.

Monitors production schedules and ensure that customer delivery dates are met within the production process.

Monitors quality team performance and ensure their efforts are both productive and rewarded.

Prepared by: A. Searfoss

Approved by: T. Quinn

Effective date: December 1992

Figure 4.4   Sample Position Description

These position and job descriptions serve only as an example. There are several performance areas that would need to be fleshed out to be organizational specific. Performance criteria would cover several other areas that address waste, inventory, and so forth. The description serves as a guide.

Requirements are not listed for the position of production control manager. Requirements could be designated if so desired, but these positions generally are filled through internal promotion based on proven credentials. Even when filling these positions from external sources, it may be wise to determine specific requirements at the time hiring is planned. After all, continuous improvements could change the requirements since they were last updated. Some flexibility may be necessary because the perfect candidate seldom appears.

No further effort is included for job descriptions. If your organization doesn't have them, it will be difficult to develop sound hiring practices and performance appraisals. In that event, it would be wise to invest the time to develop a job description program to support the PM process.

Performance Standards

Performance standards and the goaling procedure covered in Chapter 5 provide the foundation for continuous performance improvement. They provide guidance for performance appraisal by describing how well a job must be done to be considered acceptable performance. Some individuals would argue that acceptable is not good enough; it takes a well-done job to be competitive in the global economy.

However, TQM states that quality is a moving target that constantly moves upward. What is acceptable one year may not be the next, as process improvements are completed, performance improves, and new, higher goals and standards are established.

The next step is determining acceptable performance. A control chart in Figure 4.5 serves as an example. Figure 4.5 was selected from an automobile engine head foundry.

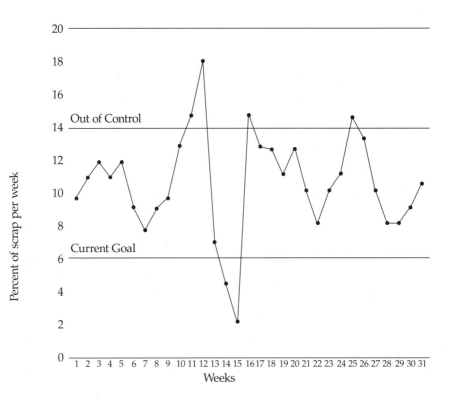

Figure 4.5   Percent of Scrap per Week for a 30-Week Period

The foundry had a low-scrap bonus plan in effect for any month in which scrap was below 8 percent every week for the month. The bonus was seldom awarded even though scrap averaged about 11.5 percent with the lowest record amount being 2 percent for one week and the highest being 19 percent one week. The 19 percent was clearly out of limits and the 2 percent was achieved only once. The chart depicts scrap recorded per week over a 30-week period.

Studying Figure 4.5, at what point is performance acceptable? There are possibilities between 2 percent and 19 percent scrap rates which were achieved over the 30-week period. Some would say 2 percent because it was possible to hit that scrap level. The odds, however, are strongly against any supervisor being found acceptable if that rate was immediately established as the target. Others would say 14 percent because that is the control line between acceptable and out-of-control-performance. Another possibility would be 8 percent, the scrap level at or below which a bonus is paid. That rate, however, was attained only four times in 30 weeks and would be extremely difficult to achieve. If people have not attained it to make the bonus, how likely is it that level of performance will be achieved to meet the needs of the PM process?

All of these answers are possibilities. We believe that since 11.5 percent scrap has been the approximate average, that number or a slightly lower one should be the new acceptable performance standard for the coming year. That figure should be agreed on by management, the supervisor, and the work force. This number is realistic because it has been achieved over a lengthy period. There is an excellent opportunity for the supervisor to get below the new target and since the new standard is realistic there is ample incentive for the employees to do better than the target and receive recognition for excellent performance.

The goal for scrap percentage rate should be lowered from this standard each succeeding period by an amount the concerned parties believe is achievable. This amount becomes the goal against which performance will be appraised for the following year.

Some considerations should be mentioned at this point. Managers must be careful when appraising performance, and it should be agreed upon ahead of time whether the acceptable/unacceptable line is the performance standard or the goal. If it is the standard, then every supervisor's performance will be rated against a common mark that has been proven attainable over some period of time. If the goal becomes the line between acceptable and unacceptable, there is a disincentive for supervisors to make their goal anything other than the standard.

Another area should be considered. As work teams improve performance and reduce the average scrap rate, there may be a tendency to lower the mark at which the scrap bonus is paid. Caution should be exercised here, also. If the scrap bonus rate becomes a moving target always just out of reach it will be a turnoff that precludes team efforts to reach it.

It is recommended that the scrap bonus rate line remain the same as performance improves until such time as management and work teams can agree that it should be lowered. Actions that could trigger the movement to lower this line include market conditions, installation of new equipment, significant process improvements, or the necessity to remain competitive. Employees should participate in the discussions concerning such a movement even when management reserves the right to final decision.

In actual practice, a manufacturing facility, such as the one described, discovered that by tracking scrap to the individuals producing it and posting these results in individual work centers, scrap dropped dramatically. Those who produced high levels of scrap were singled out for remedial training and performance appraisal. In most cases, they did not like their name associated with high scrap levels and their performances greatly improved. The people with low scrap rates didn't like to be prevented from receiving the low scrap bonus and placed additional pressure on those who produced it. These frontrunners assisted poorer performers in their efforts to improve and actively competed with other high performers to become the best of the best, which further improved performance.

Everyone became winners. Company production, quality, and profits increased. The scrap bonus became a regular part of the paycheck as performance improved and there were other attendant benefits as well.

Once the performance standard is established, performance is unsatisfactory if this standard is not met. Previous standards no longer count for anything other than a record to show how far and fast the organization is improving.

The established standard cannot become unattainable or it takes away the incentive for continuous improvement. Neither can the monetary incentive (in the form of a scrap bonus in this case) be made unattainable. Another situation to be aware of is that performance could become so good that people work themselves out of a job. Any of these events become immediate signals for work force slowdown to protect themselves, thus the quest for performance improvement by affected employees will cease.

Criteria for Standards

1. *Established for the job*–The performance standard should be the same regardless of who occupies the job or position. Although there may be as many different goals or targets as there are people on the job, the actual standard is the same for all.

2. *Standards must be understood*–All concerned managers, supervisors, and employees must understand the exact standard.

3. *Agreement is required*–All parties must agree that the standard is a fair one. A standard that allows the employee to make the bonus but bankrupts the operation is of little value to anyone, nor will an impossible to meet standard serve as an incentive to employees.

4. *Realistic, specific, and measurable*–The standard must be one that is possible for *all* employees to attain. A major premise of the PM system is that all personnel must be trainable to complete the job requirements. The standards should be coached in quantifying terms so that the specifics are readily apparent and can be measured.

5. *Time specific*–The time requirements of each standard must be specified.

6. *Written but changeable*–Standards are written to ensure everyone knows exactly what is required. At the same time, they are not chiseled in granite precluding change. The PM process supports continuous process improvement so the standards must be changeable to reflect these improvements. Standards that specify "as agreed upon during performance goaling sessions" provide flexibility for the system.

Establishing Standards

Performance standards could be developed in a number of ways. The boss could review requirements, the job descriptions, and arbitrarily establish standards. He could establish the standards and allow for employee review and comment before making them law. The boss could allow subordinates to establish standards, review them, make necessary changes, and then make those law. A consultant could be hired to develop standards for the entire operation. The boss and employees could develop standards separately, compare them, and then use the results to develop mutually agreeable standards.

As in most evolutions of this nature, it generally proves best if both parties develop standards after thinking through the process, and then working through the evolution together to combine standards into a workable document at an agreeable level. This makes all parties think about what should take place and come to a mutual agreement as to what is the best for all involved.

The second aspect of the development processes that must be addressed concerns the number of standards. There is no set number of standards that are appropriate for all jobs because standards are job dependent. Some jobs require more than others. Perhaps the best way to determine the number of necessary standards is to take the number required to qualify and quantify the position's expectations. It is better to have a few too many standards on the initial go-round than to not have enough because it provides direction and makes it easier for the employee to do an acceptable job. However, as soon as it is discovered that a standard is not required, it should be eliminated.

Summary

1. PM is a structured manager–employee system that provides a means for continuous performance improvement.

2. A PM system creates understanding of the work and the quality level that is expected. It develops a mutual manager–employee plan to accomplish these factors, provides a means to measure performance, determines how performance can be improved, and provides recognition and rewards for achievement.

3. Job and position analysis are required to outline the exact parameters of each job. This requires gathering information that describes each job and the type of people necessary to complete that job.

4. Job descriptions result when the assembled information is put into a formal format which describes that job in terms of title, organizational unit, function, responsibilities, and performance criteria.

5. Performance standards are developed for each position. They serve as the basis for performance appraisal by describing how well the job must be done.

Bibliography

Alexander Hamilton Institute. *How to Develop a Job Description Program*, New York: Modern Business Reports, 1980.

Baird, L. S., Beatty, R. S., and Schneier, C. E. *The Performance Appraisal Sourcebook*, Amherst, MA: Human Resource Development Press, 1982.

Bemis, S. E., Belenky, A. H., and Soder, D. A. *Job Analysis—An Effective Management Tool*, Washington, D.C.: The Bureau of National Affairs, 1983.

Dailey, C. A. and Madsen, A. M. *How to Evaluate People in Business*, New York: McGraw-Hill, 1980.

Famularo, J. J. (editor in chief) *Handbook of Human Resources Administration*, New York: McGraw-Hill, 1986.

Fear, R. A. *The Evaluation Interview*, New York: McGraw-Hill, 1984.

Ghorpade, J. V. *Job Analysis—A Handbook for the Human Resource Director*, Englewood Cliffs, NJ: Prentice-Hall, 1988.

Grant, P. C. *Multiple Use Job Descriptions*, New York: Quorum Books, 1989.

Johnson, R. J. *The Appraisal Interview Guide*, New York: AMACOM, 1979.

King, P. *Performance Planning and Appraisal*, New York: McGraw-Hill, 1984.

Kirkpatrick, D. L. *How to Improve Performance Through Appraisal and Coaching*, New York: AMACOM, 1982.

Landy, F. J. and Farr, J. L. *The Measurement of Work Performance*, New York: Academic Press, 1983.

Maddux, R. B. *Quality Interviewing*, Los Altos, CA: Crisp Publications, 1986.

Mager, R. F. and Pipe, P. *Analyzing Performance Problems or You Really Oughta Wanna*, Belmont, CA: Fearon Pitman Publishers, 1970.

Maier, N. R. F. *The Appraisal Interview: Three Basic Approaches*, La Jolla, CA: University Associates, 1976.

Mohrmand, Jr., A. M. and Resnick-West, S. M. *Designing Performance Appraisal Systems*, San Francisco: Jossey-Bass Publishers, 1989.

Morf, M. *Optimizing Work Performance—A Look Beyond the Bottom Line*, New York: Quorum Books, 1986.

Morrisey, G. L. *Performance Appraisal for Business and Industry*, Reading, MA: Addison-Wesley, 1983.

Plachy, R. J. and Plachy, S. J. *Performance Management—Getting Results from Your Performance Planning and Appraisal Systems*, New York: AMACOM, 1988.

Rae, L. *The Skills of Interviewing*, New York: Nichols Publishing, 1988.

Wolff, R. H. *The Complete Portfolio of Prewritten Job Descriptions*, Brentwood, NY: Asher-Gallant Press, 1988.

CHAPTER 5

Work Force Quality—Hiring Correctly

The connection between a quality high-performance work force and TQM process success should be quite obvious. The importance of hiring cannot be overstated. It takes quality people to produce quality products in terms of goods and services. Quality work life is dependent on quality people in the workplace. People must get along or they cannot become team members and team players concerned about the organization, the customer, fellow workers, and quality, each of which are necessities for TQM. This requires that the organization pay considerable attention to hiring procedures and policies.

Incorrect hiring practices can be disastrous and far too many people are hired for the wrong reasons. Many are hired strictly on their interview performance. An executive I once worked for discussed interview problems this way, "The convincing liar generally does better in most interviews than the person with solid credentials."

Credentials also can be deceiving. In 1990, the city of Harrisburg, capital of Pennsylvania, fired the city water chief. The man was hired approximately one year earlier after an interview with the city mayor. He had a strong resumé which stated he was an engineer, had a Ph.D., owned a public relations consulting firm in Texas, served as a captain in Air Force intelligence, and worked as an executive for Proctor and Gamble. It is reported the mayor was highly impressed with the applicant when he read recommendation letters from President Reagan, J. Edgar Hoover, Senator Lloyd Benson of Texas, and Edwin Meese III. The person also accepted a part-time job with Harrisburg's Polyclinic Medical Center after an extensive interview.

Problems arose when a college from which this person had supposedly graduated notified the city that his degree had been revoked. An investigation followed which produced evidence that everything was a hoax. All of the recommendation letters were forged. In fact, the letter from J. Edgar Hoover was dated after Hoover's death. There were no valid degrees, most of the jobs were bogus but had been used previously to fool several Fortune 500 companies. Other hospitals also had bitten prior to this point. The only thing that seemed remotely based in truth was that he had been a member of the Air Force, not as a captain as claimed, but as a private who had been dishonorably discharged after three court martials.

Another problem area is hiring people on the basis of their looks or personality. Personality is important for interpersonal relationships, but interview personality may not equate to the person's work personality. People may be hired because of their particular college or discriminatory reasons such as race, color, sex, age, or religion. All of these can cause serious problems.

Some people are hired who just don't meet job requirements. When this occurs there is little chance the work will be accomplished with quality. The person who lacks the skills necessary for high performance often becomes a dissatisfied employee, especially when there is little hope for promotion since performance always is marginal.

There is a high cost that accompanies poor hiring practices. Firing is much more difficult and time consuming than hiring. Often the things that caused the firing were evident in the information available when the person was hired. It is estimated that U. S. organizations lose $100 billion annually through hiring mistakes. This does not take into account the lost business because of the poor customer service these people provide. Mis-hires cost an estimated two to four times the dollar amount to terminate as they receive in annual salaries.

Employee Planning

A sound employment plan is paramount for a successful TQM process because employee commitment to quality is one third of the TQM process. Certainly commitment to quality begins at the top, but without quality employees it is doomed to failure.

The major problem with employee planning is that there usually isn't an employment plan. When times are good, people are hired quickly with little consideration about the future. When times are good for one organization, they usually are good for others. Quality employees may be hard to find at this point. Too often performance problems are handled by hiring additional employees to sort out the junk, check and recheck paperwork, or to increase production in some way. When the quality or production problems are corrected, these people continue to fill positions that are no longer necessary. They often hinder performance. The real glitch comes when times get lean. In American organizations, personnel cuts through layoffs and similar procedures often are the first measures taken to fatten the bottom line. Quality performance seldom is the measure by which people are determined to stay or leave. Internal employee rules, union regulations, organizational politics, and other policies affect the layoff decision. What is worse, management often isn't even certain which employees are quality performers and which ones are not. It doesn't end there because layoffs do not breed organizational loyalty with those who remain.

When there is an employment plan, it is often a stand-alone document divorced from the strategic business plan. The optimum employment plan would contain required personnel by job categories for a range of performance figures. Temps (temporary employees) are a part of this plan. They provide an excellent shock absorber for short-term buildups. A second part of this situation is that handbooks, personnel manuals, and other documents are not checked and upgraded to conform to the needs of an employment plan.

Recruiters, interviewers, managers, and others who are part of the employment team may not be trained as a team. As a team, they need to know exact employment needs—what the organization needs in terms of a total work force. These needs should be based on position descriptions, the organizational policies, and the contents of personnel manuals, handbooks, and other pertinent documents. Training must include techniques for effective interviewing, including how to listen, effective questioning, and analysis of answers.

Six major rules for employment planning follow.

1. Ensure there is a correct description available for each position that is to be filled. These should spell out minimum requirements. There may be other rules and everyone must understand this.

2. Define expected performance in terms of production and quality. These are the final determinants for success.

3. Keep the position description and performance criteria logical, yet simple.

4. Designate a list of requirements to be checked against resumés, job applications, and screening interviews. These include education, experience, training, acquired skills, production and quality orientation, technical and interpersonal skills, and personality.

5. Develop logical questions to determine to what degree applicants meet the established criteria.

6. Hire only people who can meet employment expectations. I know an executive whose favorite personnel-related statement is, "If you want someone

bad, that's exactly what you'll get, someone bad." He was obviously burned by a personnel decision.

No one is immune to poor hiring decisions. The February 1988 issue of *INC* magazine featured an article about a hiring mistake made by quality guru Philip Crosby. He hired a director of finance for his international unit in 1985 after what appeared to be a reasonable interviewing process and background checks. In a period spanning less than two years, this director of finance directed most of a million dollars to personal needs. When the heat was on, he disappeared. Although the current status of this case is unknown, it serves as a grim warning of what can happen with personnel hires.

One of my previous management positions was as a leader of a substantial number of recruiting personnel located in offices throughout the Northeast. Personnel were continually trained on interviewing techniques covering the common mistakes that people who are involved with the employee selection process are prone to make. Interviewers tend to make the human mistake of first impressions. The error is that first impressions are made during the icebreaker stage and not after sufficient job-related information is acquired.

Many job interviewers perceive their ability to select the correct applicant as much higher than it really is. Perhaps the personnel responsible for interviews should be assigned duties as a representative of the organization when people are fired. This can be a trying experience from which interviewers are too often sheltered. The information gathered at these exit interviews can be valuable in the interview process.

Most interviewers do not have a structured interview process. This leads to wasted time and precludes gaining the information necessary for a second interview. Too many interviewers do not precisely identify the organization's needs prior to interview, and therefore it is impossible to match applicant credentials with organizational needs.

Often interviewers do not use the *whole person* interview theory. Seldom does an applicant meet every selection criteria to the level the organization would like. Often the criteria is inflated well above need and applicable salary limits. The problem is worsened by the tendency to place much greater emphasis on negative information than positive information, whether or not the information is position-related. Most people are nervous during interviews, and the interviewer must help them relax so they can present themselves properly.

Structure for Applicant Requirements

There is a tendency to wing it in too many hiring decisions. To prevent this, structure must be given to the hiring process. The following format provides such structure and can be copied for in-house use. It would be completed prior to the active recruitment of personnel.

Performance Expectations

List five key performance requirements that are expected for the position, more if that is appropriate. These should include performance standards as measured by production and quality, leadership and management requirements, and interpersonal skills and needs. Examples could include the following:

- Improve quality by reducing rejects by 75 percent over the next 12 months.

- Improve performance by increasing shipped units by 50 percent through reduced rejects and reworks by 60 percent each.

- Increase customer satisfaction by developing an equipment training program and presenting it to all equipment purchases beginning "Date."

- Improve education by raising SAT scores by ___ percent in all areas and decreasing dropout rates by ___ percent.

Performance expectations

1. _____

_____

2. _____

_____

3. _____

_____

4. _____

_____

5. _____

_____

Main Requirements

List the realistic requirements for the position. Do not understate or inflate them. If the job requires a four-year degree, don't request a masters degree. Will tradeoffs (such as exceptional experience) be accepted in place of some of the educational requirements? The ideal candidate may not be forthcoming. Thus, the choice becomes one of leaving the position open or selecting someone below the desired requirements level. Examples might include the following:

- Three years of experience as a TQM leader in a departmental position.
- A four-year business degree from an accredited college.
- Five years of supervisory experience in a manufacturing environment. Knowledge of robotics would be helpful.

Education requirements: (Minimum expected requirements)

1. _____

   _____

2. _____

   _____

Experience: (Specific type and amount of experience)

1. _____

   _____

2. _____

   _____

3. _____

   _____

Skills: (Specific interpersonal and task skills)

1. _____

   _____

2. _____

   _____

3. _____

   _____

4. _____

   _____

5. _____

   _____

Personal traits: (Specific personality traits demanded by the position)

1. _____

   _____

2. _____

_____

3. _____

_____

4. _____

_____

A one-page sample Applicant Requirements Form is provided as Figure 5.1.

Recruiting

The goal of recruiting is to secure qualified personnel to interview. Every organization must attract quality people to survive. Too often, the person hired is the best of the interviewees, not necessarily the ideal candidate.

There are four basic rules for successful recruiting for quality personnel.

1. *Always recruit in-house first*–Promotion from within tells employees there is a future in the organization. It encourages high performance because people who see internal promotions become motivated for increased responsibility. People are loyal to organizations that show loyalty to them. There are benefits for the organization in addition to motivated members. Internal promotions provide a person–job fit that is known. The person's skills, traits, training, and work habits are common knowledge.

   Remember, people from the outside may not be what they appear during the interview. The organization can ensure the internally promoted person can start with the training needed for the new position.

2. *Employee referrals*–The second best source for most positions is employee referrals from high-performing employees. Birds of a feather flock together. Those potential hires referred by in-house people generally belong to professional associations and organizations where people with similar qualifications are also members. People talk. Solid employees will not recommend someone unless they believe that person will perform. If the opening is caused by a resignation, ask the person resigning for referrals before they depart. If that person has been treated correctly during their stay, they usually will try to help you out. They also know the marketplace and may have knowledge of people who interviewed for the position they accepted.

Performance expectations:

1. _____

2. _____

3. _____

4. _____

Educational requirements: (Minimum expected requirements)

1. _____

2. _____

Experience: (Specific type and amount of experience)

1. _____

2. _____

3. _____

Skills: (Specific task and interpersonal skills)

1. _____

2. _____

3. _____

4. _____

Personal traits: (Personality traits)

1. _____

2. _____

3. _____

Figure 5.1   Sample Applicant Requirements

3. *Recruit a substantial number of applicants*–Always try to attract a reasonable number of qualified applicants for interview. Too few applicants limits selection while too many can make the process a nightmare. Compare the applicant requirements to make sure it matches the ad you are placing. If it doesn't, there isn't much chance of having the correct applicants reply.

4. *There are differences in recruiting*–Remember, there are differences between recruiting for technical and nontechnical positions and exempt and nonexempt positions.

Unsolicited resumés	Internal posting
Employee referrals	Newspaper ads
College placement offices	Public agencies
Job fairs	Private agencies
Professional journals	Technical schools
Professional meetings	Community colleges
Headhunters	High schools
Executive search firms	Walk-ins
Networking	Open house

Figure 5.2   Sources of Applicants

Preparing a Recruiting Campaign

Complete the applicant requirements form with the help of the hiring manager. Define current and long-term goals. These are important in the attraction of quality applicants and designing questions for the interview.

Design an aggressive marketing campaign. Successfully attracting the correct applicants is every bit as important as marketing the organization's goods and services. Figure 5.2 provides an outline for selecting potential recruiting sources that match applicant openings. There are many other sources of applicants.

- Trucking companies advertise on the backs of their rigs.
- Companies advertise on their marquees.
- Some companies place ads on buses, taxis, etc.

The first two sources considered should be internal posting and employee referrals. Successful training programs generally have several employees in the pipeline for each potential opening. This provides incentive for potential promotees to produce to their peak ability. It allows training to be held in areas that match the requirements of positions of increased responsibility. Management can delegate projects to people under promotion consideration which provides the opportunity for management to monitor performance as it pertains to handling additional responsibility.

Posting should be at all applicable sites within the organization. Referrals should be requested informally at employee meetings. It is especially important to seek referrals from employees active in the quality program.

Get the word out on the network and to recruiting agencies. Be as specific with these as you are in the ads. Also contact the public job placement services. Often they have wire services to advertise openings. Visit the resumé file. Many companies discard resumés after some period, such as 90 days. It may be wise to hold resumés longer for managers, engineers, quality specialists, and other critical, hard-to-fill positions.

Prepare both external and internal recruiters. They can provide input throughout the preparation phase for recruiting. They know the market in which they must work and often have contacts who can immediately begin the search.

Developing Ads

It helps to maintain a file of applicable ads from newspapers and trade journals. Learn the lingo used in the ads. Review the applicant requirements sheet and compare this information with ads from media sources. Rough out an advertisement and review it with the hiring manager. Once there is agreement here, review the ad with representatives from the media. They can provide many tips on methods that are currently working. They can also provide you with an ad layout to consider with the hiring manager.

The next step is to design the ad campaign. The following factors should be considered.

- Nature of the job and responsibilities.
- Skills, education, experience, and other required qualifications.
- Potential career possibilities.
- Salary range.

- Benefits package
- Benefits of working for your organization:
    a. Quality program
    b. Technology
    c. Career growth potential
    d. Prestige of the organization
    e. Visibility
    f. Promotion potential

Some cautions and suggestions are in order.

1. *Blind ads to unidentified box number*–You may receive larger quantities of responses, but not the quality desired. Many of the best people will not bother. After all, it could be their own company who might then discover the respondent is looking and make them expendable.

2. *Requests for salary history*–The immediate thought that comes to my mind is, "Are you determining value based on past salaries or potential value to your organization?"

3. *Phone calls*–Many high-quality people are not actively searching for new jobs. Their resumé would need to be updated which is a time-consuming effort. These people generally want more information before they apply, and the phone is the easiest way for them to obtain it.

4. *Designate someone to accept calls*–Provide them with the details they can pass on to potential respondents and areas to avoid.

5. *Letters of introduction might be acceptable in lieu of resumés*–The resume will be mandatory for interview, but it is not always necessary for introduction.

Resumé Review

Some resumés may not be initially available. For example, the ad might have allowed introductory letters. Applicants whose introductory letters appeared promising should be requested to submit resumés. At some point, it becomes necessary to review resumés.

Often resumés can be checked initially by an assistant. The assistant would screen out obviously unqualified applicants and prepare a rejection letter for signature. The assistant also can order the other resumés in three piles: highly qualified, qualified, and marginally qualified. This assists in the resumé review phase. It is a good idea to review all qualified resumés. Sometimes assistants may miss something that catches your attention.

Resumés selected for initial interview should be reviewed a second time. The applicants should then be contacted for a screening interview. Applicants should be given a list of other items that they should have available at interview. It is a good idea to forward applications to those people selected for interview along with a self-addressed envelope. These can be returned prior to the first interview.

The resumé and application are then reviewed and compared. From these documents, a list of questions is developed for the interview. Together, these two items present a solid picture of the applicant. The interview process will build the rest of the story. Some holes may be evident. Interview questions should be designed to fill in the gaps.

1. Does the information in the resumé track with the application?

2. Do the applicant's credentials portray the same person who is needed on the job requirement sheet?

3. If there are shortcomings, are there any pluses that would overcome these negatives?

4. Is the person overqualified? Overqualified people may become dissatisfied when the position doesn't fully utilize their potential.

The Interview

Interview preparation is extremely important. You must decide what you want to know ahead of time and then develop questions to gain the desired information. Open-ended questions provide the most insight into the applicant, their perceptions, and their attitudes because they encourage thoughtful answers. Open-ended questions might include the following:

1. What did you like about your last job?

2. What are your career goals?

3. What kind of supervisor do you now have?

4. How do you feel about quality–performance–customer service?

Closed-ended questions may provide information but require little thought. Some closed ended questions might include:

1. How many years did you work at your last job?

2. Did you like your last job?

3. Do you have career plans?

The interviewer must be a practiced listener. You already know what you know. The objective is to find out what the applicant knows or does not know. Use the pregnant pause and never answer your own questions.

Caution is in order. The example presented at the beginning of this chapter demonstrates why it is necessary to exercise care. Fraud and misrepresentation are not uncommon. This occurs in many ways. Puffing is one problem. Relatively small and insignificant bits of information are puffed up to make it appear as if they were major contributions or accomplishments. Missing information is another situation that must be guarded against. What isn't said on a resumé can sometimes be more important than what is said.

Experts estimate that at least 75 percent of the resumes presented contained misleading information about employment history and over 25 percent of them misrepresented or fabricated academic credentials. Most people in the field believe that this tendency is increasing, often due to employers who are not checking as closely as they once did.

Potential Trouble Areas

The following resumé problems occur more often than others.

1. *Holes in the work history*–These may not show when the applicant uses the year only instead of month and year. Some holes are expected, but they should be discussed.

2. *Extending periods of employment* in some areas that improve qualification for a new position.

3. *Puffing job responsibilities*–All leadership and training duties should be listed. These must be discussed at interview to determine the actual depth of experience. The same is true of other areas of responsibilities.

4. *Job title exaggeration* also is fairly common. Applicants from some organizations may describe their title in terms other than those used within their organization. This is acceptable when a previous title, such as those used within the military, would not describe the person's duties. It is incumbent, however, to determine how the level of responsibility listed on the interview relates to the job responsibilities of the job being filled. Military service can be equally difficult to substantiate. Many supervisors cannot be located. With the continual transfer of military personnel, it may be difficult to find people who signed reference letters and awards. Recent laws make it difficult to ascertain the quality of service from discharge or separation documents. Anything other than a straight honorable discharge should signify a need for clarification.

5. *Salary histories* often are different than they appear. Salary histories aren't that important because you aren't hiring for past organizations, you are hiring for your organization. What people earned elsewhere often has little to do with what they should earn in the position applied

for with you. It could be either higher or lower depending on duties, responsibilities, potential, and performance. However, if you use salary history, ascertain if the salary listed is base salary or base salary plus other amounts such as bonuses, expense accounts, and additional benefits. Some people may even list potential raises, hoped for bonuses, and other compensation.

6. *Academic credentials* often are complete fabrications. Applicants know that a low percentage of employers check these credentials. One high-level manager had listed an engineering degree from one of the finest engineering schools and an MBA from a top business university although he had never attended either. The corporate officers didn't discover this deception until the man departed, although many employees were aware of the fraud. A quick call to the college registrar will generally resolve the issue quickly. There also are institutions that sell bogus degrees for little or no effort. U. S. Senator Claude Pepper purchased one from an organization as a test. He had to read three poems for his degree. Two bogus medical schools in the Dominican Republic were selling medical degrees and these bogus doctors were practicing in the United States.

7. *Awards, honors, and memberships* often are inflated. Awards can be easily made to seem more than they are. This inflation is hard to detect on a resumé. The interview usually reveals the exact nature of the award. Honors are of the same nature. Ask to see copies of both. Memberships often are so much fluff. Many people are professional joiners. There is a big difference between the person who serves as a working officer and one who joins, but whose only real affiliation is picking the monthly newsletter out of the mail.

8. *Letters of recommendation* are to be questioned. Look for objectivity and factual data. Many employers fearing lawsuits say little in these letters of recommendation. Some applicants fabricate these letters themselves or solicit them from an internal person such as a secretary. Check them out. Call the person who signed them.

9. *Publication* is another area for caution. When the person claims to have been published, ask to see copies of the articles, books, whatever.

There are many reasons for fraudulent credentials. "The kids have to eat" is a substantial motivator. Some people believe they need an edge. Many actually believe no one will check and all too often they are correct. Others just want to be more than they are to the point that some suffer serious delusions. Many believe some resumé services may actually suggest some level of misrepresentation. Regardless of reason, all spell trouble for the unsuspecting organization.

Questions can create problems for the interviewer who does not exercise extreme care. It is easy to enter areas that are or appear to be discriminatory. It is hard to believe there is anyone who doesn't realize the repercussions that can arise from reckless questioning techniques. The following outline provides guidance in this area.

1. The following questions are acceptable:

   a. Name

   b. Dates

   c. Present home address

   d. Phone number

   e. Position applied for

   f. How the person found out about the position

   g. Whether the person is employed

   h. Whether the employer can be contacted

   i. Potential starting date

   j. Whether the person had applied previously for work with this organization

   k. Names and addresses of previous employment, position held, responsibilities, and reasons for leaving

   l. Education which includes name and addresses of schools, courses taken, graduation, and research activities

2. The following questions are absolutely taboo:

   a. Age

   b. Race

   c. Sex or sexual preference

   d. Marital and family status

   e. National origins

   f. Religion

   g. Personal traits

   h. Extracurricular activities that may provide answers to the above

Stick with prepared questions. These questions should be designed specifically for job requirements and no more. There is real danger in asking questions that are not job related. Beware of asking *why* questions. *Don't be nosey.*

Testing Criteria

Various tests can support the hiring evolution. However, care must be exercised because of the lawsuits which occur because of biased testing procedures. The following guidelines should help.

1. The first criterion is that the test must measure applicants for the job that is offered. Applicants cannot be given tests that do not pertain to specific job requirements. If it even appears that there is bias toward women and minorities, there can be trouble. The term for this situation is *adverse impact*. Adverse impact is selection from one group that is 80 percent of the selection rate for another group, all other things being equal. The organization may be required to prove discrimination has not taken place.

2. Results of tests must be applied equally to all applicants.

3. Applicants should know what role tests (such as typing tests) play prior to their administration.

4. Tests must be EEO-validated to ensure they test what they are intended to test.

Selection Instruments

Virtually anything that is used to make a selection determination must be considered a test or selection instrument. Calls to people who may know the applicant can be considered a part of the selection. Casual questions over lunch with the applicants also are considered part of the selection process. The requirements for what can and cannot be asked pertain to lunch sessions just as much as they do during the formal interview. Be on guard. Errors could have grave consequences.

The Interview Process

The interview process is important. A great deal of information must change hands in a relatively short period of time. Each party has responsibilities, but the responsibility to ensure quality people are hired is the sole responsibility of the interviewer.

The recommended order begins with an icebreaker which generally lasts a few minutes. Smile and shake hands. Offer something to drink such as coffee, water, or tea. Engage in small talk to help the applicant relax. Small talk topics should be kept simple. Be careful of first impressions developed during the ice-breaker because most people are nervous and it generally shows.

The actual interview process begins when you announce the purpose of the interview. It establishes the stage for the tone of the meeting and prepares the applicant for what will follow. It permits the interviewer to sell the applicant on the benefit of providing honest, no-fluff answers. The interviewer can make the applicant aware of the importance of a positional match for both parties.

A potential opening might be:

Jean, we want to thank you for taking the time to respond to our need. We appreciate your coming today. This meeting will give us an opportunity to know each other better. Our people are a strong, productive team, so it is important that we achieve a match with our applicants. If we both believe that match is achieved, the interview information and the reference checks will help us prepare a smooth transition into our organization. It also allows us to plan a development program. This meeting is for our mutual benefit. I'll take notes and recommend you do the same so we can ensure all questions are answered. We want to allow you all the time needed to interview us concerning the organization and available opportunities. How does this sound?

Most applicants are enthusiastic about this approach. It lets them know there are mutual benefits for the meeting. It tells the applicant that the organization is a sound team where employees are valuable. It also is an exhibit that shows the organization helps its members develop. Caution is in order. Only the parts of this presentation that are true should be used. These items, however, are team-builders that should become part of every organization.

The interviewer should develop a process guideline. The session should begin by asking the interviewee if she minds if you take notes while she talks. It gives you ideas for questions and keeps you busy so she can talk.Remember, what you have to say is not nearly as important as what the interviewee has to say. An outline of other suggestions follows:

1. *Maintain eye contact.*

2. *Maintain professionalism.*

3. *Take notes*–A standard pocket file can hold notepaper and questions. Permit the applicant to take notes if she desires.

   a. Notes, if not overdone, make the applicant feel comfortable and ensure that you are sincere about the process.

   b. Notes help clarify questions.

   c. Notes are excellent for review after the meeting.

   d. Use a key word outline. Too much attention to notes can be upsetting to the applicant.

4. *Stay focused*–Use the questions developed to maintain focus and fill in all of them. They will guide the interview. Be careful of ad libs as they can get you in trouble.

5. *Listen*–Hear what applicants are telling you. You owe them the respect and you owe your organization a solid employee. If you don't listen carefully, you may end up with something different than the person you thought you saw at interview.

6. *Watch body signals*–You don't have to be an expert to detect problem areas.

7. *Remain empathetic*–Take breaks during long interviews.

8. *Watch for fraud, deception, and puffing.* These will be discussed further later on.

Gathering Selection Information

Unless the job is an entry-level position, work history and position responsibilities generally take precedence over education in most interviews.

1. *Work history*–This area is of great importance. Jobs of 15 years ago may reveal truths about the person's attitudes and fitness for current positions. Some time should be used to cover all employment and all periods of nonemployment. Trends may become evident that deselect the applicant. Some of these may include:

   a. "All my bosses have been stupid. "

   b. "The people at the other organizations were all lazy, backstabbers, druggies, or whatever."

   c. "I quit because of _____."

   d. This answer may be more fitting of a quality employee. "I hate to leave. I enjoy the organization and people, but couldn't pass up the opportunity."

A short introduction will get the ball rolling and save time. It puts the applicant at ease while it places the burden of discussing previous job history where it belongs, on the applicant. You can sit back and listen while watching for holes. A sample introduction is:

We would like to begin by discussing your work history. There are several things we would like you to tell us about each position. We would like to know the employer, address, titles, and employment dates. We would like to know what you expected from each job and how these expectations were met. Please tell us about the challenges you faced and how you met them, what you enjoyed about the job and what you didn't, what your supervisor and the organization were like, and what your supervisor would say your strengths and weaknesses were. We would also like to know why you left that job. Let's begin with this first position.

Watch for trends in the following areas:

- a. Applicants usually know what they can expect from each position. Their expectations should generally be met. There may be some unmet areas, but watch for positive trends.

- b. Every job should have positive work-related challenges if the employee is trying to stretch herself.

- c. There are likes and dislikes with every position. The positive thinking employee will find more likes.

- d. Most supervisors are good people. Solid employees who are productive usually see it that way.

- e. Most organizations have more positive than negative attributes. The people who earn their keep generally see it this way.

- f. There should be both positive and negative reasons for leaving a job. If it is all negative, beware.

The answers to these questions will establish patterns that signal what type employee the person will be. There is little chance that the person will be any different, good or bad, in your organization. In each case, ask where the supervisor is now and if that supervisor can be contacted. The answers to these questions can be revealing.

2. *Leadership and training experience*–People do not necessarily have to be managers to be leaders. Discuss all leadership positions. Ask the person to rate himself as a leader. Training is becoming increasingly important. Ascertain if the applicant has training experience or aptitude.

3. *Technical skills*–Every job requires technical skills of some sort. Ask the applicant to discuss all technical skills and how they might be applied at your organization. Try to ascertain if the applicant is improving technical skills over time.

4. *Work habits*–You may have a feeling about the person's work habits by this time. Clear up any questions. Ask the applicant to describe his work habits.

5. *Education*–High school may be somewhat removed from the present. If it is, you may simply ask the applicant to describe the high school years. More recent attendance should be thoroughly discussed. The following topics can provide relevant insights into high school years:

   a. Tell me about your high school, the curriculum you took, any activities you participated in, and any awards you received.

   b. Please give me your thoughts about high school.

   c. Were there any events that affected later career decisions?

   d. Were you employed during high school?

   e. What were your plans upon leaving high school?

   College undergraduate studies are next. Questions for this area follow:

   a. Please tell me about your college, why you chose it, and if it met your expectations.

   b. Can you tell me what your college years were like?

   c. With what campus activities were you involved? Were you an officer in any of these?

   d. You list a ___ GPA. How does this relate to your abilities?

   e. What factors influenced your career decisions?

   f. Were you employed during college? Please tell me about it.

   g. Please tell me about the high and low points of your college experience.

   Graduate school questions follow:

   a. Why did you select this school and degree?

   b. What were your career thoughts at this time?

   c. What were the high and low points of this educational experience?

   Other relevant training experience:
   Many people take other significant training programs. These should be discussed using the approximate format for college undergraduate studies. Previous employers may have provided in-house training programs. Discuss these and how they might be of value for the position being discussed. Discuss seminars, night schools, and other training

the applicant may have attended. Find out if they were applicant- or organization-sponsored programs.

6. *Interpersonal skills*–Does this person get along with fellow employees? The best trained, hardest worker is of little use if no one wants to work with her.

7. *Career goals*–This section will determine if a match is possible. The most talented candidate may be a poor choice if his goals and career expectations cannot be met in the position being offered. Watch for words such as performance, production, quality, and customer service. The following questions will guide the discussion.

   a. What are you looking for in your next job?

   b. How have you prepared yourself for the position you are seeking?

   c. Where do you see yourself five years from now? Ten years from now?

   d. What do you see the advantages are for joining our organization?

   e. What drawbacks would you see with our organization?

   f. What other job possibilities are you looking at and what potential do you see for employment?

The Benefits of Your Organization

This section may be brief if the person is a sure nonselect at this point. For all of you still in the hunt, a corporate overview should sell the applicant on the benefits of being a member of the organization. Some discussed topics include:

1. Overview of the organization, its values, and how this position ties in with the organization.

2. The organization's stands on quality, performance, people, and quality of work life.

3. Training programs.

4. Benefits package. Be thorough; have these written down. Don't exaggerate, but never sell yourself short, either. It could be the deciding point of a great candidate.

5. Ask if there are any questions. Answer any that are posed.

Close the Interview

A short wrap-up speech is in order: "Well, that about does it. Do you have anything else you would like to add?" If there is, listen to the addition. If not, thank them for their time. Tell them when you will get back to them *after checking references.* Ensure all applicants know you owe it to them and their success to check references.

Here is an optional idea that can support your hiring efforts. At one company, we paired those in the running with people in the same category within the organization, usually within the work center the applicant would be attached to if they were hired. They were given a private room where they could discuss anything but salaries and classified information. They were then brought back to clear up any questions. The applicant could get an honest feel for the organization to help make her decision. Our employee got a feel for working with this person, how she felt about quality and productivity, and if they would be a team player. Sound performers do not desire to bring nonperformers into their work center. This practice served us well.

This procedure also gives you time to review the interview notes to see if there are any other questions. When they return, you can clear up questions and then escort him to the door, reception area, or whatever. Thank him and allow him to leave.

Reference Checks

The applicant should know from the beginning of the interview that reference checks are in order and will be made. This will help keep the information factual. The applicant may even begin by starting with a confession about some part of their resumé or application form.

Begin checking the most important information first. When that is college, call the registrar's office and confirm all educational achievements. Some applicants may provide you with transcripts or offer to have them sent to you from other institutions. Accept transcripts received directly from the college. Call previous employees and supervisors. You can at least confirm employment in most cases. Some supervisors and organizations will not provide any other information on the phone. These may answer specific questions forwarded to them by mail.

A surprisingly large number of people will answer some or most questions. Their answers will provide great insight into the applicant's value. Sometimes their nonanswers provide even more information.

If the applicant requests you do not contact current employers, the request must be respected. It is best to let the person know any job offer will be contingent upon talking with the employer once the official job offer has been made. There can be problems when you agree not to contact the current employer. One applicant was a continuous problem where he was and had filed a nuisance suit for discrimination against that current employer. The previous employer would not answer any questions other than the period of employment. Luckily, he didn't stack up well in other areas.

Call the listed references. Often they provide an insight the applicant would not believe. It may say something about choices for reference. When in order, check with credit bureaus, police departments, court records, and other such organizations. You may question the importance of reference checks. Judges are increasingly holding employers responsible for making poor hiring choices.

Make the reference calls. A format is important in this area in order to gain any measure of success. You must sound professional. A sample follows:

Good morning. My name is _____ and I represent XYZ organization. Thank you for taking this call. We interviewed Sue Peters for a position with us as a _____. We are considering hiring her and are seeking information for a final decision. Could I ask you a few questions? The answers will be very helpful to Ms. Peters and me.

Anything we discuss will be held in strictest confidentiality. Could you tell me about her strengths, areas for improvement, and potential?

What exactly were Ms. Peters responsibilities? How would you rate her in these responsibilities? How do you rate her technical skills? People skills? What about work habits? Emotional stability? Leadership ability? Training skills? Communications skills?

Clear up all questions from the interview. It is important to have these listed before each call.

The Decision

The hiring manager must be a partner in this procedure. There will be further discussion on this matter later.

Putting the Puzzle Together

Review the applicant requirements form. Analyze the following to see how this information fits the applicant requirements form:

1. Resumé

2. Job application

3. Interview information

4. Reference checks

5. Tests

6. Information from other sources

Answer the following questions:

1. Were all prepared questions answered?
2. Were all holes in the information satisfactorily filled?
3. Have you operated within the law?
4. Can you identify patterns? Work habits? Motivation? Interpersonal relations?
5. Were your first impressions substantiated by hard evidence?

Does more than one candidate stand out? Whether they do or not, it is best to schedule follow-up interviews with the top candidates. I have discovered that some people do much better on second interviews. They have more courage because they see themselves in the running where they might not have at first. At times, third choices rose to first choices in a second interview.

Additional interviews must be scheduled when more than one person stands out for a position. This should be routine for all positions of any consequence. The following recommendations will assist with follow-up interviews.

1. The hiring manager should be a part of these sessions. It is important that the applicant is a total match for the manager's team needs.
2. Questions are fine tuned. With the information now available, details and specifics can be addressed. Their questions should be designed to determine:
   a. Facts from assumption
   b. How strong are strengths
   c. How weak are weaknesses
3. Leadership, technical skills, quality management experience, and goals should be deeply explored. Interpersonal relationship also should be weighted heavily in all team environments.
4. Charts can be developed that list important categories down the left side and names across the top. The various categories can be graded and a relative score developed. Caution is in order. A person can score highly on less important items and lower on critical ones and come out better than the more qualified person.

In-depth analysis is important. Remember, gut feeling is not enough. As mentioned earlier, the convincing liar can have a leg up on the highly qualified applicant. It is necessary to sort out the modest, highly qualified applicant who plays down significant accomplishments from the modestly qualified person who plays up meager accomplishments.

Evidence of team play is a strong positive. Look for the person who uses "we," "our team," "our group," and so on in conversations. That individual scores much higher as a team player and leader than the person who slaps you with "I did this" in every sentence.

Tips

1. Remember that when you want someone real bad, that is what you'll probably get—someone real bad.

2. *Never* hire the best of the bad. It is better to leave the position open than it is to hire a problem. When you don't have a match, keep searching. You may need to change advertising strategy. The applicant requirements may be out of line with need or interviewing techniques. The refinements in this area may take some effort, but they will payoff in the long run. Hiring for expediency pays poorly. Take your time.

3. Beware of the perfect applicant. He may have spent considerable time and resources preparing his resumé and interview so they make him appear as the perfect candidate. The obviously overqualified person may be another problem. She may get bored quickly if she doesn't have to stretch to fill the position. The choice isn't easy. Make it wisely.

4. Watch for the whole person. The person who does not meet all the specified requirements may be the best applicant overall. The specifications may be off.

5. Don't ask questions and then feed the applicant the correct answers before they can answer. One manager who sat in on interviews had this habit. He became uncomfortable when applicants searched for information and provided the answers for them. Silence can be golden. The pregnant pause works.

6. Never ask questions that are none of your business, would involve proprietary information from another organization, or could be interpreted as discriminatory. Regardless of whether the applicant opens the areas, they are *taboo*.

7. Remember your notes. The shortest pencil is more accurate than the longest memory.

8. Never tip the applicants off as to why certain questions were asked. That should be considered classified information.

9. Watch for signals that spell caution. They may not always be negative because some people will get on a soapbox for a positive cause when their go button is tripped.

    a. Sudden stalling

    b. Incomplete answers or answers that do not match the questions that were asked

    c. Overly complete answers

    d. Broken eye contact

    e. Blushing

    f. Sudden voice changes

    g. Nervous movement

    h. Sudden perspiration

    i. Inconsistency between verbal and nonverbal communications

    j. Use of humor in nonhumorous situations

10. Recap the highlights of the interview.

The Rejection Letter

1. The first rule is that all rejections should be by letter. Even when you know the person is a nonselect, the applicants should be thanked for their time and told you will contact them. They should then be notified in a reasonable amount of time.

2. Personal rejections can lead to endless questions, unfounded accusations, crying spells, and requests for another chance. Letters can be checked for legality, correctness, and empathy prior to their mailing. People seldom respond to a letter unless it is favorable.

3. There is another reason for rejection letters. In one case, a technical position was being filled. The choice came down to two finalists of whom one was selected. By the end of that week, the rejection letter was prepared. Another spot opened, however, and the rejected applicant was hired. He is still performing superbly after five years and several promotions.

The Letter of Offer

The offer letter should spell out the details of the offer as agreed upon. If the offer involves an hourly wage, it should be so stated. It could be a mistake to note the annual salary that can be expected at this wage. This could easily be interpreted as the intention to pay this salary for a one year period. The letter should contain a place for date and signature, a no-later-than date, and a return, stamped, self-addressed envelope.

Indoctrination

The indoctrination after the hiring process should support the interview and serve as the foundation to launch a successful career. Topics should include:

1. A position and organization recap.
2. Offer letter clarification.
3. Recap of salary and benefits.
4. Importance of quality and teamwork.
5. Interpersonal relationships.
6. Reporting procedures.
7. Administrative details.
8. Importance of the position.
9. Introduction to key people and work center personnel.

Summary

1. Quality people are paramount for the quality program. This quality team begins the solid hiring practices.
2. A sound employment plan is the foundation of a successful hiring plan. This plan should support the strategic business plan and quality plans.
3. Performance expectations should be outlined on an applicant requirement form. The main requirements are also listed: education, experience, skills, and personal traits.
4. Sound recruiting practices are required to produce an ample number of respondents for the positions that are open. It is important to recruit in-house first, followed by referrals and other recruiting efforts.
5. Resumés are an important part of the screening process. An initial screen can be handled by a secretary who has been trained for this effort.
6. Interview preparation generates much smoother sessions. During the interview it is important to watch for fraud, misrepresentation, and missing information. Some questions are taboo. These are outlined along with the criteria for testing.
7. References always should be checked. A considerable amount of solid information is collected via this process.
8. The hiring decision is one that should not be easily made. It should be made in conjunction with the manager who has the need for personnel. Never settle for the best of the bad. It is better to leave the position open.

Bibliography

Genua, R. L. *The Employer's Guide to Interviewing*, Englewood Cliffs, NJ: Prentice-Hall, 1979.

Greco, B. *How to Get the Job That's Right for You*, Homewood, IL: Dow Jones-Irwin, 1975.

Hariton, T. *Interview! The Executive's Guide to Selecting the Right Personnel*, New York: Hastings House Publishers, 1970.

Jackson, T. and Mayleas, D. *The Hidden Job Market*, New York: Quadrangle/The New York Times Book Company, 1976.

Smart, B. D. *The Smart Interviewer*, New York: John Wiley and Sons, 1989.

Ungerson, B. (editor) *Recruiting and Selecting Personnel*, Toronto, Canada: Coles Publishing Company Limited, 1980.

CHAPTER 6

Performance Improvement

Performance improvement is a part of the PM system. It also is the most important people-related topic in this or any other book. It requires knowledgeable people bent on improving performance to make the TQM process work. Without such people with those intentions, TQM is just another buzzword destined to go the way of so many other failed performance improvement initiatives.

A quick review and summary of the subjects covered thus far should clarify the system as it is presented.

TQM was defined in terms of a management structure focused on customer needs and expectations concentrating all its efforts toward reaching and exceeding the goals of that organization.

Organizational structure provides understanding of the human elements and the administrative/management structure in terms of their interrelations in order to support the TQM process.

The quality culture discusses organizational personality and outlines the type of culture required to support the drive for continuous performance improvement.

A performance management system provided the overview of a method to turn performance expectations into performance reality on a continually improving basis.

An employee hiring process provides a systematic way to ensure that quality people required to meet organizational TQM goals are hired while those who don't measure up are rejected.

This chapter provides a system to utilize all employees correctly in a manner that supports their needs and guarantees continuous performance improvement. Guarantee might appear to be a strong word to the reader, but experience over the last 25 years has supported this system.

In one form or another, the performance improvement system has been around for many years. Its effectiveness, however, has been mixed and the success or failure of it was determined not by the system, but by the supervisors who used it. Organizations led by managers who were devoted to reaching the goal with and through people achieved outstanding success. Those who pushed and threatened, using the system only because they were forced to, met with limited success at best. Most of those in the second group never stopped long enough to understand performance management in terms of the support individuals require to produce successful performance. Had this occurred, more supervisors would become performance managers instead of people drivers.

Figure 6.1 provides graphical display of the performance improvement cycle. Some of the steps are combined because they occur at the same time in the cycle. They will be broken out and discussed individually during this presentation.

Performance Goals

The performance goal-setting evolution is important in many ways. As a supervisor/employee exercise, it provides for continuous employee input into the PM process. This encourages the more capable employees to establish

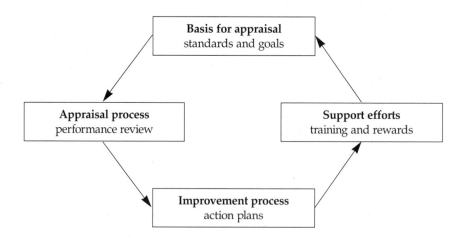

Figure 6.1   Performance Improvement Cycle

higher goals. Because they have ownership of the goals, there is much more reason to believe they will meet or exceed them.

Goals provide much needed flexibility in the process. Since quality is a target moving away from us, some flexibility must be added. If there is no flexibility, goals which are not achievable in the early stages of TQM would soon provide no incentive at all. If goals were established early with a difficulty factor applicable downstream, they would be out of reach in the early stages, thus providing a barrier many could not overlook. Making goal establishment a precursor to appraisal allows for flexibility on the same scheduled intervals as performance appraisal. After one period's performance is appraised, goals are established for the next period, which then become the basis for the following appraisal.

The goaling process is well developed in Volume III, but some criteria are important to this discussion. In this example, goals are paired up to provide another perspective of establishing goals.

*Specific and measurable–*The goals must be spelled out in definite terms of quality and quantity in order to have meaning. Vague statements such as "Improve customer service" are impossible to measure and therefore have little meaning. Once spelled out, measurement becomes mechanical.

*Challenging yet realistic–*Goals must provide challenge, or interest is lost. At the same time, they must be seen as realistic and attainable for those who must meet them or they won't pursue them over time. Agreed, it is a fine line that separates realistic and challenging, but it is a line all parties must consider. It is better to aim for excellence and achieve satisfactory performance, than it is to aim for satisfactory and fail.

*Written–*Once agreed upon, the goals must be written down and copies produced for all participants. Goals that are not written down tend to become hazy over time and lose effectiveness. They also provide for considerable disagreement as time passes. A copy of the goals posted in the workplace provides an added incentive to meet them. It is easy to drift away from goals that are not posted as an ongoing reminder of what everyone agreed upon as the target.

*Attainable as a group–*Goals may be realistic and attainable as individual items, but when examined as a group they become mutually exclusive. For example, one goal might be to increase production by some percentage and another might be to reduce overtime hours by some percentage. Considered alone, either of these goals may be attainable, but combined they might not be possible.

*Ownership–*Goals must provide ownership for all who are involved in the process. This means the goals of individuals must meet the needs of that individual, management, and the organization. Ownership at all levels occurs only after these needs are met.

Goal Responsibility

The supervisor has a guiding responsibility in the goal-establishment process. Optimists must be able to defend the height of their goals. Unrealistically high goals and mutually exclusive goals cannot go unchallenged. If they aren't confronted, the people who established them can become seriously disenchanted when they discover the odds against meeting these targets. Neither the pessimist nor the middle-of-the-roader can be allowed to establish unchallenging goals that help neither the individual nor the organization. Many attempt to do this because they realize additional effort is required to achieve performance improvement, and they are working as hard as they choose at the present time. Supervisors are not immune to this practice. They, too, realize their performance will be appraised against the agreed-upon goals, and they may want all the cushion they can get. After all, promotions, salary increases, and rewards ride on how well they do against established goals. These attempts also must be challenged.

Over the years I have been privy to both of these situations. I have heard the optimist trying to back out of original goals with the most inventive of excuses. Sales that could have been completed one month are carried over into the next month or year as a cushion against increased goals. Production is slowed at the end of a period so the system is full beginning the next cycle. The list of what can happen to cover tails is endless.

Pessimists are equally guilty of these sales and product carryover schemes especially when it is time to negotiate new goals. Excuses, carryovers, and similar problems hinder performance improvement and must be searched out and eliminated.

Level of experience has much to do with the level of the goals which are established. More should be expected from the seasoned employee than the beginning novice. As time passes, more can and should be expected of the novice.

The process of establishing goals is the windup to the performance appraisal interview in most cases. It is placed here in the cycle because appraisal measures the performance over the cycle that occurred since the last appraisal against the standard that was developed at the last goal-setting session which concluded that session.

The supervisor has another responsibility before this meeting ends—communicating the necessity of reaching these performance goals. Several steps are important here.

1. *Ask for the required level of performance*–Summarize the goals that were established and explain how important it is to attain them. Then ask the employees to meet those goals and to come to you immediately if any problems arise.

2. *Provide parting encouragement*–Recognize their previous performance which indicates these are realistic and obtainable goals. Thank them for these achievements and ensure them that these past accomplishments are the foundation for achieving the newly established goals.

3. *Offer support*–Reiterate that it is a supervisory responsibility to ensure employees have all the tools required to meet these goals. Ask if there are any known needs that were not brought forward during this session.

4. *Model your expectations*–Set a stage of urgency as a departing measure and then model that urgency in everyday efforts. Your actions must show employees you are serious about performance improvement and excellence.

5. *Thank them* and allow them to leave.

Performance Appraisal

Performance appraisal is a realistic review of performance achieved over a specific period against an agreed upon standard of performance. This is a legitimate process because the employer has a right to expect a certain level of performance for the compensation offered and the employee has a right to know how the employer is going to evaluate performance. Legitimacy does not make it a necessarily fair system or one that is easily utilized. Let's see why it is not always a fair system.

Problems

Problems are associated with most performance appraisal programs. Major problems occur when the appraising supervisor does not consider what the employee expects out of the review. The individual wants to know the following:

1. How did I do?
2. What is expected of me during the next cycle?
3. How do I have to improve to meet these expectations?
4. How will my performance be measured during that period?
5. What will the supervisor do to help me reach these goals?
6. Will I receive additional training during the next cycle?

7. Is there an opportunity for advancement, and if so, what will it take to get it?

8. What can be expected in the way of salary increases?

9. How is the organization doing in the way of performance improvement?

10. What changes does the future hold that might impact on me?

These questions satisfy the basic supervisor checklist. Although it is recommended that promotion and salary questions be separated from performance appraisal, the supervisor must be prepared to answer those questions.

Appraisal systems continually undergo review and change, but the perfect system is still forthcoming. Problems continue in the best-designed systems, most of which are caused by the human factor. People are imperfect and find ways to misuse, abuse, or thwart even the best designs. Some of the ways they do this follow.

Time–Supervisors are short of time in most organizations. When allowed, the majority will postpone appraisals because of the associated difficulties.

Avoidance–People do not like to sit in judgment of others, face hostile people, or confront poor performance. This causes many to avoid the appraisal process for as long as possible.

Poor design–Many appraisal forms are so general they are of little use or they may contain subjective areas that reduce their validity. Some forms attempt to measure too many things, often for the wrong reasons. Another common problem is trying to provide too many measurement steps. One common appraisal form ranges from top 1 percent, 5 percent, 10 percent, 30 percent, 50 percent to bottom 50 percent, 30 percent, 10 percent, 5 percent, and 1 percent. This forces the appraiser to be judgmental.

Subjective categories–A common tendency is to evaluate personnel in areas such as attitude. The best evaluation is a subjective judgment in such cases. What determines a bad attitude? Would this demeanor seem inappropriate to all who viewed it? Or is it caused by an overbearing supervisor who deserves nothing better? Such areas are better left off the appraisal form. Performance, not personality should be evaluated.

Poor preparation–Neither the supervisor nor the employee is correctly prepared for the appraisal process. The system presented here will do much to alleviate that situation. Training should be provided for all participants within the system so they understand how appraisal works and the benefits it provides.

Inaccurate measurements–Often the system is slanted by well-meaning supervisors who want the best for their people. They give their subordinates a break in every area for whatever reason. Others have bosses who are perfectionists and superb achievers who rate subordinate performance against their own. This is a problem in itself, but some supervisors rate their subordinate's performance against the highest level of performance they ever achieved. This really skews the appraisal in a negative direction. These may seem of little consequence until it is remembered that appraisals also become the basis for promotion, pay raises, or placement in other positions. At this point inaccurate measurements can wreak havoc on all who are involved.

Halo effect–The halo effect may cause good performance in one area, production for example, to have a positive yet undeserved effect in another area such as quality or customer service. The opposite also can be true. Poor performance in one area may cause detrimental reductions in other areas as well. The appraiser must always strive to ensure each area is accurately reflected by performance in that area and not affected by performance in other areas.

Purpose is misunderstood–Many employees do not understand the performance appraisal system or what is at stake for all concerned. Employees must realize it is an information exchange that searches for ways to improve personal and organizational performance. It provides recognition for past performance and produces a supportive plan for future improvements.

Incorrect expectations–Subordinates often come away from appraisals expecting things that will not be forthcoming. This can be caused by incorrect communications, a supervisor who does not face up to situations that come up within the appraisal interview, or any number of other factors.

Interview lacks focus–Many questions help focus appraisal interviews. Some which should be answered are: what was accomplished against what was planned? What should have been accomplished but wasn't? What achievements deserve additional recognition? What didn't the supervisor do that he should have? What did the employee accomplish in the area of self development? What did the employee do to improve customer relations? and What did the employee do that significantly added to the work teams?

Appraisal system is used to justify dismissal rather than improve performance–Every person deserves a fair and equitable appraisal that is no different than those conducted for any other employee within the organization. The end result may be a recommendation for dismissal when all else fails, but the purpose of appraisal must be performance improvement.

Because of these and other problems, many employees are against appraisals of any kind. This is unfortunate because neither the outstanding nor the poor performer receive due recognition without appraisal. Others believe appraisal should take place between a supervisor and a subordinate and no one else should be privy to the information. Written appraisals can be poorly prepared and subject to misinterpretation by others who might have access to them.

All of these notions have some validity, but the problems can be overcome. Those people who produce superior performance want to be appraised and recognized for their efforts. Even those people who are solid team players want the personal recognition that results from their efforts above and beyond expected levels.

System Overview

The basic system provided in Figure 6.2 is an overview of this chapter's direction.

Quantifying Appraisals

Some standard must be established to rate performance. An example was previously provided which had 10 separate divisions in its scale. This allows the appraiser to judge the degree to which the person being appraised has met the job standards. It drastically increases the difficulty of making impartial decisions as to the degree of performance. The fewer grading steps there are, the easier grading becomes and the more impartial it is.

Grade creep is a problem that continually occurs in all systems with many different rating increments. Military systems continually face this problem. They develop one method after another to make these complicated systems work without grade creep, but it continues to occur. Many supervisors do not like to be judgmental and tend to give their people a break. Then along comes a tough guy who uses the system as it was intended and throws everything out of whack. His outstanding performers do not stack up against people in other groups.

Another situation sometimes occurs that is demoralizing to high producers. An appraisal form for a school system serves as an example. It lists two categories for unsatisfactory performance (*needs work* and *unsatisfactory*), and one for *satisfactory* work. The question that must be asked is if it is impossible to do better than satisfactory why produce to any level above that. The form precludes recognition of superior efforts.

Although it is agreed that three increments are enough, one positive and two negative do not support performance improvement because there is no recognition for excellence. Three categories work well when they include outstanding, satisfactory, and unsatisfactory. The appraiser has two decisions to make: (1) Was performance in that category satisfactory or unsatisfactory? and (2) If performance was satisfactory, was it good enough to be considered

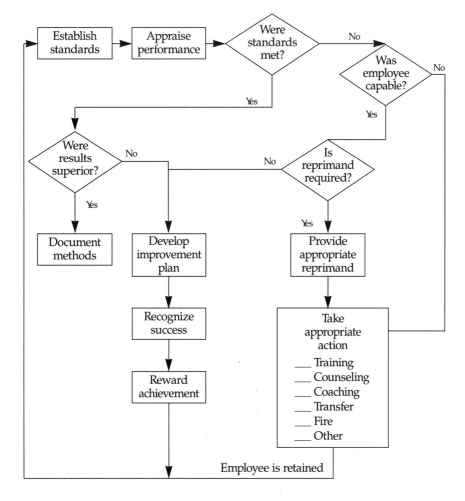

Figure 6.2   Appraisal System Overview

outstanding? This system removes much of the judgment from the appraisal process.

Figure 6.3 is provided as a sample of a performance appraisal form with three performance rating categories and several rating elements that are common to most jobs in which the organization is engaged in transforming itself to the quality life. Important concepts include the following:

*Performance measurement–*Performance is measured rather than personality.

*Meaningful–*They measure factors that are important to performance improvement.

*Relevant–*Factors are relevant to the job and quality performance.

*Realistic–*The factors are capable of accurate measurement by all supervisors in work settings.

Other Considerations

Gathering information– Information must be gathered over the entire appraisal period. The supervisor should make entries concerning achieved performance at the end of every month. Noteworthy achievements should be recognized and recorded as they occur. Performance problems also should be addressed and noted when they occur. This prevents the evaluation covering only the last few months of the period.

At times, subordinates with less-than-satisfactory performance do little about improving it until just before the appraisal, even though it is repeatedly brought to their attention. Some people even have action plans which they ignore. Just prior to the appraisal, they improve performance and some supervisors then rate them satisfactory for the entire period. It becomes a game and after appraisal their performance once again deteriorates to a marginal level.

The opposite situation can also occur when records are not kept. A person can have a few relatively minor incidents near the end of an appraisal period and be rated unsatisfactory for the entire period. Continual progress evaluation prevents both situations.

Many supervisors believe they don't have to keep records. However, a fair and impartial record of achievements and problems is required because memories are not reliable regardless of the number of people supervised. It also provides substantiating material should a disgruntled employee challenge an appraisal.

A simple notebook will suffice to keep this record. It should be kept privy from everybody except you, the individual, and your supervisor when circumstances warrant.

*No surprises–*Surprise at an appraisal is indicative of poor supervision. Employees should know what they are receiving through continuous feedback. Each journal entry should be discussed with the employee. Achievements deserve on-the-spot recognition so they will continue. Problem areas should be discussed, action plans developed, and training held as needed so the problem can be corrected.

People are not mind readers. Those who don't know they are doing well may look for a position elsewhere where they will feel appreciated. No one

| Name _____ | Department _____ |
| Supervisor _____ | Date _____ |
| Job Title _____ |

Rating Elements	Performance Rating		
	Outstanding	Satisfactory	Unsatisfactory
Quality of Work			
Quantity of Work			
Customer Service			
Job Knowledge			
Self-Development			
Team Efforts			
Initiative			
Dependability			

Comments:

Recommendations:

Employee Signature_____ Date _____

Supervisor Signature _____

Figure 6.3   Sample Performance Appraisal Form

will believe their performance is unsatisfactory if it is not discussed with them. Nor will they improve their performance any significant amount if the supervisor complains once in a while and doesn't follow through. After all, supervisors could complain because they were having a bad day or some equally poor reason.

Supervisors should have examples of both achievements or poor performance that will be discussed. People often won't believe there are performance problems when the supervisor doesn't have substantiating examples. It also is difficult to repeat solid performance if the supervisor cannot describe it.

Scheduling appraisals–The time, date, and place of upcoming appraisals should be published well ahead of time. This allows both supervisor and subordinate to be prepared. Each employee deserves enough time set aside to discuss performance, establish new goals, and seek help if required.

Prevent interruptions–The supervisor must plan for a sufficient, uninterrupted period to complete the appraisal. There should be nothing on the schedule that would rush the sessions, calls should be held, and unscheduled visitors advised to either return at a later time or wait until the interview is completed.

Neutral territory–A neutral office is best for both parties. If this is impossible, however, the supervisor should leave her desk for the interview because it can seem oppressive and prevent subordinate input. A table appears less oppressive, and it should be cleared of unnecessary material. Chairs should be comfortable for both parties. It is important that participants be in a relaxed atmosphere that does not adversely impact on the appraisal.

Salary increases and promotions–The appraising supervisor should discuss these possibilities with the manager who can approve them prior to the interview. Discussion of these topics should be kept separate from the appraisal itself. It is best to discuss them at separate meetings, but should that be impossible they must be discussed after performance. People who receive raises or promotions hear little after that, and those who don't aren't interested in discussing performance improvements. When discussing these subjects, it should always be made clear that raises and promotions are earned by the employee and not given by management. The onus is on the individual to earn them.

The future–Career path discussions are important ingredients of appraisal reviews. The supervisor must be prepared to discuss the employee's future in terms of where the employee can go, what the individual must do to reach the established goals, what the supervisor will do in the way of support, and what the organization can and will do.

Preparing for Different Types of Employees

Preparation must focus on the different types of employees who will be encountered. A review of Chapter 17 in Volume I is a good preparation exercise. It also is important to break people out in groups according to performance and advancement opportunities.

Superstars know their status and often want a little more than others. After all, they earned it through performance. However, just because one has superior performance does not mean they cannot improve. It is important to follow the same script and discuss potential improvements and new goals with these folks, too. Be prepared to discuss salary increases, promotion possibilities, and rewards that may have been earned.

Average employees generally are satisfied with their performance as it is. However, continuous improvement is the name of the game and often the person won't have to do too much to improve. Time must be taken to develop an improvement plan to ensure employees receive the required support to reach their capabilities. When performance is appraised against ability, which is the comparison that should be made, there is always room for improvement. This question should always be asked in every performance appraisal situation: "how do you rate your performance in comparison to the skills and abilities you have?" Virtually every person points out areas where there is room to improve.

Poor performers must be challenged to do more. Steps to take for poor performance are discussed later in the chapter.

Plateaued performers who have peaked out in their current position cannot be ignored. Performance can be improved here. Alternate career paths may be a discussion item. Potential awards and recognition are recommended discussion items. When these people are supervisors, discussing ways to improve subordinates' performance often spurs their performance, too.

Interview Guidelines

Icebreakers are used to begin an interview. The supervisor is warm and friendly in order to build rapport. The purpose of the interview should be stated in positive terms, and the subordinate should be encouraged to freely discuss all areas of the process.

As stated earlier, performance, not personality, is the topic of discussion. The best-intentioned supervisor will lose the battle when personality traits are judged. Avoid confrontation and open disagreements where possible. One way to achieve this is to ask questions rather than make declarative statements. Open-ended questions such as, "Can you tell me more about so and so?" elicit more input. It is difficult for anyone to argue when you are seeking information to clarify issues. Be careful of "why" questions because they can be finger-pointers. "Why did you do that?" does not seek information, it points blame.

Be an active and attentive listener. Sit up, lean forward, and pay attention to what is said. Nod agreement when you agree, restate statements to ensure you have the correct idea, and ask for more information when it is appropriate: "That sounds good; tell me more."

Begin with areas where the person did the best work. This establishes a positive tone for the meeting and makes any negative points more acceptable. Cover satisfactory work, followed next by areas where performance was unsatisfactory. Be prepared. Whenever poor performance is discussed use examples to back up your statements. Have recommendations ready for improvement, discuss how you can help, and ask the individual if other assistance is required for performance improvement. Have your performance journal ready to go over previous discussions on the topic. End with an overall summary of performance.

Use past performance to establish a future focus and discuss areas where performance can be improved. It is important to learn from the past, but care must be exercised so it serves as a basis to build the future. Make sure subordinate strengths are discussed in terms of how they support performance improvements.

Always ask employees how they can improve performance before making suggestions. People are always more committed to their own ideas than they are those of another. Often solid question techniques can lead them to their own solutions.

Practice phrasing statements in positive terms. The way something is expressed has a great deal to do with how it will be taken. The idea is not to attack them personally, but to discuss performance problems. A reminder—watch how you word questions and comments. "Can't you do anything right?" or "How could you make such stupid mistakes?" are personal slams and not problem-fixers. Turn these around to specific performance problems, "As you know Bill, the last three proposals you prepared required considerable rework," or "Mary, we have discussed the mistakes on your correspondence over the past three months. How are you using the information from the correspondence course you attended?"

Seek agreement on your perceptions of the performance. If that becomes impossible as it sometimes will, provide examples, and should that fail, you can believe concurrence is not possible. At times, employees will become angry and disagreeable. Don't allow outbursts to sway your judgment when you know it is correct and well-founded. The journal will support you when things get rough as they sometimes will.

Discuss comments you believe are appropriate for the appraisal form and then write them down. It is best to do this after performance is discussed and concurrence is gained. Write short bullets making sure both problems and achievements are noted.

Ask employees to sign the form, and then sign and date it yourself. At this point it is time to wrap up the session. Thank them for their time, offer your services, and terminate the interview.

As soon as the subordinate departs, critically evaluate your personal performance. What did you do right and what would you do differently if you had it to do over again? Were you successful in getting the other person to discuss performance? Was the other person satisfied with the way you appraised his performance? Should his job description be updated to cover new responsibilities? Were new goals established that will benefit both the employee and the organization? Did he depart with a positive attitude?

Make a copy of the appraisal for the employee, yourself, and the personnel department. Your supervisor may also require a copy. Many would argue that the meeting should be private and the resultant appraisal is a concern only for the supervisor and the employee. However, with the lawsuits and problems that arise today, it is best for all concerned to file a copy in the personnel jacket.

Employees can be given their copies in a few days. At that time the supervisor can check to see how they are progressing toward the agreed-upon improvements.

The Performance Improvement Process

This crucial step can take place at the end of the appraisal interview or another time can be established to develop a plan for improvement. When the interview was positive and upbeat, it may signal an opportunity to prepare a solid plan. If all did not end as you hoped, perhaps another time would be better.

Performance Improvement

The first step is to develop performance improvement goals for the next appraisal period. The rules established earlier fit well here. No one should be exempt from the improvement process because performance always can be improved. There is much at stake for all participants, beginning with the need for organizational survival and ending with the potential for reward.

The supervisor and subordinate should work on goals they feel are important. Again, mutual input and agreement is important. Priorities should be established for each goal in terms of payoff and benefit to both parties.

The supervisor must then ascertain what kind of support is needed for the subordinate to reach these goals. Perhaps additional training is a requirement. Coaching may be a necessary ingredient in certain areas.

Both the goals and the required actions of both parties should be listed on the form. If the supervisor agrees training is required, it should be stated on the form and provided by the supervisor. Supervisors have just as much at stake as subordinates. Any required check-back times, progress reports, and completion dates should be established. The form should then be signed and dated by both parties.

As time progresses, the supervisor must continually review progress in a positive, supportive way that provides encouragement. Improvement is recognized as it occurs and the supervisor continues to question if there is anything else required to make the plan work.

Improvement Plans

When an improvement plan is required, take the time to develop one. The supervisor will know whether this is required prior to the appraisal and can have it ready along with mental notes on a possible course of action. It is important to think them through even though you won't construct them until the employee is with you. It is the employee's plan and not the supervisor's. A sample improvement plan is shown in Figure 6.4.

A few simple rules should govern the use of improvement plans.

1. The plan should cover one problem.

2. The most significant problem should be tackled first.

3. It should be the employee's plan as much as possible.

4. The supervisor must declare what he will do and must ensure that training and support are provided.

5. Check-back on the agreed-upon dates is mandatory.

Performance Problems

There will also be cases that require counseling about poor performance. A determination may be required whether the person should be retained on the payroll. This action should not be taken lightly. The person should be given the support required for improvement to a satisfactory level.

The initial step in working with performance problems is to define the exact problem specifically. Once this is accomplished, the problem's seriousness can be determined. These determinations set the stage for an action plan to correct the situation.

Name_____ Department _____

Supervisor _____ Date_____

Job Title _____

1. Problem/deficiency:

2. Plan of action:

3. Training or other support required:

4. Supervisor action required:

5. Check-back dates:

_____ _____ _____ _____

6. Action taken as a result of the checkbacks:

7. Preventive actions:

Sign-off date and results: Date _____

Employee signature _____

Supervisor signature _____

Figure 6.4 Sample Improvement Plan

The second step asks if it is a cannot or a will not problem? Could the employee do it if he really wanted? If the answer is that he cannot, then it must be decided if there is a skill or knowledge deficiency that training and/or coaching could overcome. Often it is wise to review past performance to see if the person could ever complete this work correctly in the past.

As performance improves and the requirements for additional improvements get tougher, the job may go beyond the capabilities of some workers. Perhaps the person can produce marginally acceptable performance, but never progresses beyond that. The supervisor must make the decision as to whether the person can actually perform to new, higher standards. At this time reassignment to a more appropriate job could be a solution.

Perhaps the person just doesn't want to do it. In this case the reason must be determined. Perhaps there is no reward for improved performance. Maybe the system will punish improved performance by causing some people to work themselves out of a job by higher performance. Who wants to do that?

Nonperformance can also be rewarding. I know of an organization that provides overtime for people to get their work accomplished without seriously questioning how they spent their normal workday. More than a few people waste their work time so overtime is required. Then they don't work too hard because no one is there to supervise them.

Conditions actually may prevent subordinates from achieving higher performance. Machine tooling or dies may be worn, systems may be antiquated, procedures or policies sometimes interfere with performance, and red tape can get in the way. All of these possibilities should be reviewed for applicability. Those that apply must be removed or reduced before further performance improvement can be expected.

Disciplinary Actions

When performance problems are caused by willful actions or complete disregard for the welfare of the organization, action must be taken to correct the situation. Most organizations have designated actions that are taken for specific infringements. For those that don't, that subject is beyond the scope of this book.

Some disciplinary guidelines are appropriate for discussion here because they support performance management and the quest for improvement.

1. *Be responsible*–Supervisors have the responsibility and the legitimate right to confront poor performance.

2. *Be honest*–Explain the circumstances as you view them, without emotion, exaggeration, or reservation.

3. *Be constructive*–Remember, the idea is to improve performance and not to vent frustrations, put an employee down, show your authority, or any other such reason.

4. *Be consistent*–Treat similar situations the same for everybody. This does not mean some people won't need more of your time than others; it means that you cannot discriminate in disciplinary matters.

5. *Never accept excuses*–Always revert to goals, performance criteria, and agreed-upon similar standards. The person must live up to these standards or face discharge.

6. *Never threaten*–People soon realize your threats are idle with little force, or they quit caring and wait for you to carry out your actions. Follow through with any warnings that are given.

7. *Base all confrontations on performance*–Be specific about the performance problems. When behavior is a problem, identify the exact behavior to which you are referring. Leave references to drug addiction, alcoholic problems, and personal problems to trained counselors. Don't hesitate to refer employees with these potential problems to the proper people for help.

8. *Strive for acknowledgment*–The individual must acknowledge the problem or little will come out of the meeting.

9. *Work toward an agreeable solution*–As always, it is best if an employee-generated solution can be reached.

10. *Gain commitment*–Once the plan has been agreed on, ensure that both parties sign it. The improvement plan format readily adapts to this situation.

11. *The next step*–Ensure that the employee knows what the next step will be in terms of both the positive or the negative. Then proceed with that step as required based on the individual's performance.

Make sure minor infractions are handled as they occur. This often prevents more serious problems later. Make sure all individuals understand the rules, policies, and procedures as they apply to them. Employees cannot be held accountable for what they do not know.

Record all disciplinary meetings and the resultant actions. The employee and you should sign such paperwork and record it with personnel. For most individuals, this action will be sufficient.

A few individuals never seem to get the message and termination may be required. Once the decision is made that the person will not or cannot perform, or will not conform to standards, termination should be immediate.

The only alternative is for the supervisor to decide to tolerate poor performance forever. Not many are willing to do that.

Summary

1. Performance improvement is the payoff part of the performance management system. It provides a basis for appraisal, the appraisal process, an improvement process, and support efforts.

2. Performance goals are established by the employer and supervisor. The supervisor has the responsibility to ensure the goals meet performance improvement needs.

3. Performance appraisal measures to what extent performance met the established goals. There is some disagreement concerning performance appraisals, but they play an important role in performance management.

4. Improvement plans are used to guide required performance improvement efforts.

5. At times, disciplinary action may be required because of poor performance. Guidelines were provided to ensure disciplinary actions remain constructive.

Bibliography

Alexander Hamilton Institute. *How to Develop a Job Description Program,* New York: Modern Business Reports, 1980.

Baird, L. S., Beatty, R. S., and Schneier, C. E. *The Performance Appraisal Sourcebook,* Amherst, MA: Human Resource Development Press, 1982.

Bemis, S. E., Belenky, A. H., and Soder, D. A. *Job Analysis—An Effective Management Tool,* Washington, D.C.: The Bureau of National Affairs, 1983.

Dailey, C. A. and Madsen, A. M. *How to Evaluate People in Business,* New York: McGraw-Hill, 1980.

Famularo, J. J. (editor-in-chief) *Handbook of Human Resources Administration,* New York: McGraw-Hill, 1986.

Fear, R. A. *The Evaluation Interview,* New York: McGraw-Hill, 1984.

Ghorpade, J. V. *Job Analysis—A Handbook for the Human Resource Director,* Englewood Cliffs, NJ: Prentice-Hall, 1988.

Grant, P. C. *Multiple Use Job Descriptions,* New York: Quorum Books, 1989.

Johnson, R. J. *The Appraisal Interview Guide,* New York: AMACOM, 1979.

King, P. *Performance Planning and Appraisal,* New York: McGraw-Hill, 1984.

Kirkpatrick, D. L. *How to Improve Performance Through Appraisal and Coaching,* New York: AMACOM, 1982.

Landy, F. J. and Farr, J. L. *The Measurement of Work Performance,* New York: Academic Press, 1983.

Maddux, R. B. *Quality Interviewing,* Los Altos, CA: Crisp Publications, 1986.

Mager, R. F. and Pipe, P. *Analyzing Performance Problems or You Really Oughta Wanna,'* Belmont, CA: Fearon Pitman Publishers, 1970.

Maier, N. R. F. *The Appraisal Interview: Three Basic Approaches,* La Jolla, CA: University Associates, 1976.

Mohrmand, A. M. Jr. and Resnick-West, S. M. *Designing Performance Appraisal Systems,* San Francisco: Jossey-Bass Publishers, 1989.

Morf, M. *Optimizing Work Performance—A Look Beyond the Bottom Line,* New York: Quorum Books, 1986.

Morrisey, G. L. *Performance Appraisal for Business and Industry,* Reading, MA: Addison-Wesley, 1983.

Plachy, R. J. with Plachy, S. J. *Performance Management—Getting Results from Your Performance Planning and Appraisal Systems,* New York: AMACOM, 1988.

Rae, L. *The Skills of Interviewing,* New York: Nichols Publishing, 1988.

Wolff, R. H. *The Complete Portfolio of Prewritten Job Descriptions,* Brentwood, NY: Asher-Gallant Press, 1988.

CHAPTER 7

Planning for Quality

Organizational success depends on the ability of its managers to see the future in terms of how it could develop and then make provisions to prepare their team to take competitive advantage of that future as it will exist. This future vision becomes the basis for a planning evolution that produces the structure which guides the organization on its trip into the future. In this context, planning is an organizational attitude that concerns performance, quality, customer focus, and the goal in terms of tomorrow's requirements.

Planning could be defined as the formal process of establishing a mission with objectives and goals, along with the process to attain them. It is a reflection of the best current processes combined with an estimation of the timing requirements, actions, and strategies necessary to develop solutions to problems of today and tomorrow. Planning is a dynamic, ever-changing structure that supports our efforts to harness the opportunities, both present and visioned.

Planning is the foundation that guides every other managerial action. The following factors are a part of planning.

1. *Vision*–The ability to view the future in realistic terms.

2. *Strategic thinking*–The technique of deciding what must be done, how to do it, and how to prepare the organization to accomplish it.

3. *Problem solving*–The planning evolution requires solving problems for future operations.

4. *Decision-making*–These decisions define states as they are desired in the future.

5. *Goal orientation*–Targets are planned that best position the organization to meet future challenges and opportunities.

6. *Commitment to change*–Continuous improvement cannot happen without continuous change.

7. *Commitment to measured performance*–The act of planning produces the standards in terms of goals and objectives against which performance is measured.

8. *Awareness of the possibility of failure*–"What can go wrong will" and plans must be made accordingly.

Planning places several demands on leaders. It requires the ability to quickly envision end results in terms of goals that are mutually acceptable by all parties. It requires objectivity and realism, without which it is an effort in futility. Repetition is required because the assumptions, premises, and performance requirements must be reviewed time and again to ensure they meet current and future requirements as they are known.

Planners must commit to the endless details involved in developing and carrying out the planning efforts. They also must be dedicated to the *goal* as it is developed for each organization. Successful planning efforts receive their energy from the boundless enthusiasm generated by visionary leadership, without which the planning process remains little more than a paperwork drill.

Planning is a simple process in concept, but difficult to carry out. It is a series of small steps to get from where you are to where you want to be at the time you want to be there. These steps are developed through a two-way evolution. Planners first look forward into the future from where they are to ascertain the steps that need to be taken to reach the goal. The second look requires them to step into the future, stand on the target, and look back to see what steps were taken to get there. The combination of these two observations provides a fairly solid plan for taking the journey.

Plans are self-fulfilling prophecies. Good plans become the foundation for success while poor plans generate failure. Therefore, it is important that the only plans that are produced are plans that will be accomplished. To prevent failure or unnecessary setbacks, alternatives should be developed for crucial steps, and procedures for changing plans should be produced along with the plans. This provides flexibility and prevents the problems that stymie rigid systems.

Problems

Consider the difficulties when an organization has no vision, plans, or goals, when concrete plans don't exist. Correct choices become difficult if not impossible to make because they are guesses with a high probability for failure at best. This leads to a hesitancy to make decisions or choices. It also encourages a policy of satisfying immediate needs and wants rather than working toward long-term requirements. Budgets aren't followed since they retain little meaning without a strategic plan. Profitability is easily lost as the focus switches from policies which guide long-term growth to political expediency. Without the guidance that accompanies planned evolutions, seemingly endless meetings are held to debate the most basic issues which generally end without constructive conclusions. No one wants to be blamed for the mess that is created, so considerable time is spent blaming the problems on other groups in the organization. "It isn't our fault manufacturing can't build 'em; we just produce the designs."

Consider an example easily recognized by all. Without strategic operational plans, the United States went from being a great creditor nation to the greatest debtor nation on Earth in one decade. We developed huge budget and trade deficits and spent money faster than it could be generated. With 75 million illiterate or nearly illiterate Americans incapable of completing most technical jobs, many of our political leaders are pushing to fast-track, assembly-type jobs out of the country. Since there is no plan to allocate resources to strategic development, money is thrown at every situation that comes along with little concern for how that money will be generated. The result is that service on the national debt has become the biggest line item of the federal budget. What other organization could survive with this sort of leadership?

It is important to examine what kinds of problems impact on the obtainable results through planning exercises.

Planners and doers–Many have commented that organizations have planners and doers. Most doers involved in planning situations are not truly committed to the planning effort. Too often they see planning as an end product that uses a lot of time while serving no positive purpose. It is not terribly exciting work. Doers are busy folks. They don't have a lot of time to invest in processes that add little or nothing to the productive efforts of their work group, and they are working about as hard as possible, all things remaining the same.

Conversely, planners always seem to find time for planning. They enjoy the meetings, talking about the things that might happen if . . . . For planners, planning is the end product. They expect others to put forth the effort to carry out their plans. They always seem to know the benefits that will follow if the doers do things their way. These diverse actions impact heavily on an organization's ability to develop workable quality plans.

Plans without purpose–Many organizations invest a major portion of their management teams efforts in detailed planning cycles that have no payoff. Executives use the plan as a coordinating effort of sorts, but receive all their decision-making information from other sources. Managers view the plan as a useless hassle, but have no way to get out from under it. When all the planning meetings are attended, there is little time left for the day's work. A cause could be made for such planning details if they were the guiding structure for such organizations, but they seldom are.

Plans of this nature are purely demotivational. They serve no useful purpose, needlessly absorb huge amounts of resources, and interfere with the day's work. It need not be this way. The assets expended on planning should be equivalent to the value received from the planning exercise. This suggests that developed plans must be followed to pay off.

Poor planning–Poor planning is another part of this problem. Too much is left to chance and chance will not support TQM. This process takes an ongoing commitment leaving nothing to chance. Without workable plans to guide an organization, every event has the potential to become a disruptive emergency that can burn the organization. Enter the firefighter. The following sign says it all:

> Bad planning on your
> part does not
> necessarily constitute
> an emergency
> on my part.

Planning doesn't support TQM–Planning evolutions based strictly on profit or the *goal* without addressing all the quality needs will not produce the quality products and services necessary for survival. TQM planning requires that the plan address the three separate entities that make up this system: customer focus, employee commitment, and the proper use of the quality tools necessary to obtain quality in that environment. These three factors must happen in unison as the standard way of doing business or a quality program will not happen. This requires solid planning and committed leadership.

Plans are viewed as guidance for managers only–Considerable time is spent developing organizational plans. Executives then neglect to follow the plans even though managers are expected to meet each detail. Problems arise when the manager needs some asset or counts on some action that won't be forthcoming because plans were changed at headquarters without amending the plans and notifying lower management.

Plans require change–People aren't committed to change until they see a reason for changing, which takes time and must be planned. A solid vision accompanied by the benefits that will result generally produces reason for change. This, however, cannot be a static evolution. The vision must be continually updated, refined, and expanded to keep participants interested and create the desire in more people to become involved.

Planning Concepts

The commitment to planning (like the commitment to quality) must begin at the top. Without commitment there will be little long-term success in the organization. Everyone can point to examples where divisions in organizations were led by performance-minded visionary leaders who planned for and achieved high quality and production without much guidance from the organization. This happens occasionally, but generally does not survive if that leader departs.

A local site manager became disenchanted with the constant hassle created by poor planning in other areas of the organization. He departed for another position. The attention to strategic planning, quality, and quality training ended the day he departed. Quality and production suffered, customers became disenchanted, and employee morale plummeted. Soon the sharpest people were interviewing for positions with other companies and many departed, often for less money but more satisfaction. Unfortunately, this is not an uncommon situation.

Time

Solid planning evolutions take precious time that is always in short supply and heavy demand. The planning time must come from somewhere. However, that time almost always is available within the current workday. It is disguised as work effort, but virtually every person has some discretionary time currently filled with activity that produces little. Perhaps there are current planning efforts that are less than productive and can be curtailed in favor of quality planning.

Every manager we know of or have read about who is involved in a successful TQM program admits that getting the quality ball rolling requires considerable additional time. Much of this time, however, will come from previously unproductive use of time. This alone may not do it. Management may be required to invest additional time to get the program started.

How will you find this time? Well, you know where you can find the time in your day because you know what is being done that doesn't have to be or shouldn't be done. Your people and other managers are another question. Over the years we found the best way to find this time is to ask them, "What are you doing now that can be put aside so that you have about three hours a week for quality planning, training, and TQM?" If the program is worthwhile the people will find the time initially. The trick is to keep the time productive enough so that they want to continue to find time for it. Don't be discouraged when a few do not become part of the team; they are probably fighting other parts of the organization as well and you just don't know it.

The investment in planning time at the beginning can pay handsome dividends over the long run. The plans must be dynamic instruments, understood by the entire team, fully utilized, updated, and continually improved as an ongoing evolution. This is the only way that a lasting quality program will be achieved. Chapter 14 will assist employees with this time situation.

Publicizing the Quality Program

Everybody in every part of the operation must be tuned to find and correct each discrepancy that evolves in their area of responsibility. It is difficult to keep people in production areas keyed in to constant quality improvement if their checks are incorrect, their benefits are poorly handled, and work areas are dirty. True quality savings occur only when every person in every area is tuned in on quality procedures for a quality work environment and is working to make them pay off for the organization. The development and follow-through of plans have the ability to keep everybody focused on the organization's quality programs.

Coordinating Efforts

Each organization must have the capability and desire to produce quality. Capability comes from having the equipment and machinery available to produce quality goods and services, and the trained people to be able to optimize the utilization of these assets. The desire comes from making quality the priority, or as Ford Motor Company states, "Quality is job ONE."® Every action the organization takes must be a witness to the quality mandate. Nothing less will do. This requires asset coordination throughout the organization.

Planning Requirements

Planning for quality must cover several separate actions. The plan must ensure the current level of quality is maintained while quality improvement is planned and implemented. The plan also provides ways to decrease substantially the time for bringing new products and services to market with quality built in when they arrive.

Two areas must be taken into account during the planning process: strengths that provide competitive advantage and weaknesses that result in a competitive disadvantage. Some issues to consider include the following:

- Personnel
- Performance achievement (production and quality)
- Marketing
- Sales
- Customer relations/services
- Vendor relations
- Facilities
- Products or services
- Financial status
- Research and development

Factors outside the organization also must be considered. Current and future conditions are assessed. The discussion of future conditions provides an understanding of changes that have a probability of occurring and how those changes will impact on the organization. Some changes to consider include the following:

- Customer preference
- Social change
- Literacy level of the potential work force
- Availability of trainable workers
- Environmental concerns
- Governmental dictates
- Technology
- Competitors
- The economy

These internal and external factors provide the basis for planning strategies to provide organizational direction. Some factors (such as growth, retrenchment, and diversification) provide guidance on the types of job and position skills which will be required in the current and future organization. Planning and change management are further discussed in Chapter 11.

The quality plan provides basic management control for the TQM process. It does the following:

1. Encourages systematic, forward thinking.
2. Provides a quality outline and coordinates quality efforts.

3. Ties together business plans, budgets, marketing plans, and training plans to promote organizational quality.

4. Transfers customer needs and expectations into plans for finished quality products that meet these needs and expectations.

5. Creates performance awareness as measured by production and quality. This is accomplished by planning and inserting quality into every part of the operation so that quality is planned and built in rather than inspected into each section.

6. Provides a basis to measure results against target values that control performance.

7. Exerts continuous awareness and influence for the TQM process and quality planning throughout the organization.

8. Supports the quality manual and serves as a basis for its upkeep.

9. Prepares an organization to take advantage of emerging opportunities through quality products.

10. Provides a guide for suppliers and subcontractors.

11. Designs a process to meet quality goals under operating conditions.

There are several distinct parts to the performance improvement process which must be considered in planning: the vision of excellence, the quality plan itself, quality control, and continuous improvement. The vision provides a look into the future in terms of the benefits that will result for everybody in the quest for quality. The quality plan is a road map designed to take us from the current level of quality to some superior quality level. Quality control serves to maintain the status quo or current level of quality while we search for methods to improve quality. Process improvement produces the action steps and quality measures taken to move the organization to the new level of performance that has been planned.

Leadership commitment is the major determinant of success through quality planning. This commitment must be observable through example, communications, management philosophies, policies and procedures, and the quality visions of the leaders. Other factors that impact on success include the commitment of resources, a solid, ongoing training program, and rewards for success. Each of these must be communicated to every member of the organization.

In all probability, there will be some measure of quality without a quality plan. However, it is doubtful if this quality will be the best the organization can produce. In fact, it may not coincide with the customer's needs and expectations.

Understanding Planning

Planning, like TQM, is an ongoing process that provides direction to efforts. It is not an event or task that has a beginning or an end. Rather, it is a dynamic structure that gets us from where we are to where we want to be.

Planning has been described as a formal written guide around which one must deviate. Planning provides a set of interrelated actions devised to accomplish agreed upon objectives and then focuses efforts toward these objectives. The reality of life in any organization is that these objectives are ever-changing. As quality improves, processes and procedures are reevaluated, higher objectives are established, and operations are improved. Planning assumes that change is desired. This is the heart of TQM.

The planning process involves asking questions and making choices to reach stated objectives. Some of these might include: who has the ultimate responsibility for this action? Do we have enough information to reach a workable solution? Is the information accurate? How much time is available. Do we have the assets required? Who will make the final decision?

These and other appropriate questions provide the basis for systematic steps to implement quality procedures. Planning efforts will not eliminate all risk, but it can reduce the surprises.

The following are six important basics for all planning situations.

1. *Simplicity*–The quality plan should be kept as simple as possible.

2. *Flexibility*–The plan must be easily adjusted so that it can accommodate change to meet emerging needs and take advantage of new opportunities. It also must accept the changes required to fix plans that go awry as they have a habit of doing.

3. *Credibility*–The plan must be believable by the entire team. This requires that it be the collective work of all participants and that all participants adequately represent the people on their teams. The plans must be seen as valid, worthwhile, rewarding, and in their best interest.

4. *Operational*–The plan must meet the needs of the operating people that must make it work. This requires that the majority of all quality planning is a functional activity of line personnel and not a task relegated to staff planners.

5. *Achievability*–All plans must be viewed as achievable by the people who are affected by the plan. For this reason, plans should be basic at the beginning, providing for small successes. These successes provide a basis for larger undertakings with greater successes. The elephant must be eaten one bite at a time. Elaborate plans with unbelievable goals will result in failure.

6. *Visionary*–The plan is the vehicle for bringing the visions of the organization's leaders to reality through team planning. The plans solidify vision, give them form, and provide the means for accomplishment.

Planning is a structured process that provides a road map to reach some goal, in this case improved quality through TQM. It delineates who will do what to get where, as the organization marches off on the quality journey. The following nine principles are extremely important if the planning is going to pay off in increased performance.

1. *Goal determination*–Definitive goals must be established for every achievement that is desired. Data must be secured and analyzed until the exact goal is understood. Once this goal is determined, all activities are designed toward reaching this goal.

2. *Action steps*–Once goals are determined, action steps are constructed in narrowly defined increments and in great detail. Care must be taken to ensure these steps are in the correct order of performance. Gaining commitment to change is much easier through small increments than large changes because people view the change as doable. People are willing to be led through small, achievable processes. The small successes provide confidence for the bigger steps that will come later. Small increments also are more controllable so there is less chance for setback. Almost all quality improvement comes one step at a time, or as J. M. Juran says, "project by project." This consistent progress is the nature of successful TQM processes.

3. *Plan with events*–Many plan with processes or activities. The plan itself is the process. Activities contain no measurable actions and thus promote little accountability. Events carry a measurement factor that can be dated and checked because they focus on results and not just efforts. On the other hand, activity (which by itself is useless) focuses on efforts. Too much time is spent on activity rather than accomplishment. Activities include marketing reports, data analysis, and feasibility studies. These activities can be changed to events according to the following examples:

"Submission of the marketing report by . . . ."

"Review of the data analysis on . . . ."

"Completion of the feasibility studies with review by . . . ."

4. *Develop specific objectives*–Objectives must be trackable and measurable. Performance measures must be established for each objective. This provides the means to compare progress toward the objective with that objective and determine a factor or percentage of completion. Tracked

and measured objectives provide accountability and promote execution because there is now a success/failure standard that encourages action.

5. *Identify responsibilities*–Plans must identify the person or team leader responsible for each objective. This provides accountability and without this accountability there will be little success. The responsibility lies with one person. Placing groups in charge is equivalent to saying no one is responsible. If everyone is in charge, no one is in charge. Plans also identify events and the people responsible for bringing these events to life.

6. *Plan for effectiveness*–Planning gets time on your side, which promotes effectiveness. Effectiveness is doing the right things, in contrast to efficiency which is doing things right. Completing tasks correctly is of little use if they are not the correct tasks to complete.

7. *Plan for success*–Success is directly proportional to the effort, wisdom, and common sense generated during the planning exercise. In effect, plans are self-fulfilling prophesies. Well-prepared plans that are carried out generate excellent results. No matter how well poor plans are executed, they will deliver poor results.

8. *Planning and forecasting are different*–Forecasts predict the probability of something happening while plans make things happen. Plans are designed to affect positively the performance of people in specific ways. Quality progress will happen only through well-led people in the organization.

9. *What if*–Plans should include the possibility of failure. There should always be contingency plans that answer the "what if" questions.

Another area to consider before beginning a quality plan is the organizational environment. An environment hostile to the quality process will make TQM a difficult or impossible endeavor. A list of questions has been designed to ascertain if the environment will host TQM. If it won't, there are two possibilities: work to change the environment, or don't waste your time planning for what will surely end in failure. The questions for planning follow.

1. Is our organization's senior leadership committed to TQM?
2. Is our management team committed to TQM?
3. Where is our present quality program?
4. How do our current customers and people perceive our quality program?
5. Where do we want our program to be?
6. How can we get from where we are to where we want to be?

7. Is our organization, if properly led, willing to put forth the effort required to reach for quality?

8. Are assets available to launch a quality program?

9. If assets are not available, are there ways to overcome these deficiencies?

10. Do we have or are we willing to acquire the training capabilities necessary for a solid quality program?

11. Will the organization's business plan, marketing plan, budget, and training plan support TQM?

12. Is our organization anti-TQM? Do we believe any of the following:

"Quality is not all that important to our customers. They buy for cost and generally can't tell the difference in levels of quality."

"We are the experts in our field and know more about what our customers need than they do."

"TQM is just one more program that will go the way of the buggy whip."

"The major problems with quality is generally unconcerned workers."

"Quality costs money which doesn't help our bottom line at year's end."

"TQM is a process related strictly to manufacturing and service production departments. The rest of the organization doesn't need and can't use it."

"You cannot produce on-time, cost-competitive products when you are so concerned with quality."

"TQM might work in some places, but our situation is unique."

"Success in our organization comes from strategic leaps rather than continuous improvements."

"If it ain't broke, don't fit it."

There are four areas that input into the quality plan and impact on the TQM process. Two of these are internal inputs from within the organization and two of them are external to the organization. All inputs must be planned.

The first internal input is the *human element.* This includes the senior leadership of the organization, every staff and operating department, all special teams or groups, the quality council, and the TQM manager (where one has been appointed). It is important that all groups are represented and have access to input into the quality plan. The exclusion of any group for whatever reason will have negative impact that will develop problems as time passes.

Other internal plans comprise the organization's second internal input. The quality plan must consider the other planning documents of the organization and, in turn, become a part of these other plans as time passes. The budget, business plan, marketing plan, long-range strategic plan, and training plan must all be considered in development of the quality plan. The reasons are fairly obvious in every area.

The first external input comes from the supply side. We must *receive quality goods and services* to provide the same. Every organization can help its suppliers improve. In fact, when any organization fails to help its suppliers improve it does itself and its suppliers a disservice. Therefore, it is recommended that suppliers become a part of the planning team where appropriate.

The second external input is from *the customer.* This input is crucial since TQM is a customer-focused process. The customer also can serve as a valuable member of one's quality planning efforts. The following questions will help focus efforts on customer needs.

1. Who are our customers?

2. Who is our competition for these customers?

3. Why did these customers choose us to supply their needs?

4. How well are we taking care of our customers?

5. How do our customers perceive our quality, price, and customer service?

6. What improvements would our customers like to see us make?

7. How can we improve our offerings to our customers?

8. What other customers should we be marketing?

9. What are these customers' needs?

10. Can we meet all of their needs or only part of them?

11. Does this open new fields that we should enter?

The needs of all customers and potential customers should be considered. Some of the most important needs are safety, prompt delivery, no interruption of service, fast repair and installation services, all training should be provided, well-documented and easy-to-read instructions, correct billing, and prompt, courteous replies to all phone calls and requests for assistance or information. These seem standard, but are often overlooked in the heat of battle.

There are other steps to take that show our customers we want their business. We should look for services that show them how important they really are. Often there are services that can be built in that cost little or nothing but make a big difference to the customer and the way they perceive us. We know of one organization that shares appropriate training with customers. The organization already has paid for the program and allows customers to fill the empty seats. That action has cemented those relationships. Every organization will find these kind of services once they begin searching for them.

Goals of a Quality Plan

The major goal of a quality plan is to produce products—goods and services—that satisfy customer needs and expectations. This sounds simple enough until one considers that both the customer needs and expectations are continuously changing. Much of the change is due to the desire for higher quality products that do more things at less cost—in other words, the desire for real bargains. This is understandable. After all, the major American pastime is not baseball or even football, it is shopping. The thing people are shopping for is a real bargain. What is this real bargain? Only the customer knows for sure.

Identification of Need

The first part of the quality plan must be identification of need for customers both internal and external to the organization. This will outline the overall quality plan.

The first step requires identification of the people who make the buying decision and those who can influence the buying decision. Almost anyone in the customer's organization can influence the buying decision. Engineering will question quality and fitness for use; purchasing will examine cost, availability, and customer service; manufacturing will study ease of use and quality. The receptionist can have input based on contacts with the people from your organization, the people on the shipping docks can input on the way products are shipped and received, and so forth. The idea is that each part of every organization can have an input on the buying decision, so every area of the organization must be considered in the quality plan.

The second identification step determines the key decision-making factors. Do the factors include quality, form fit and function, cost, features, availability, quality customer service, follow-up service, warranty, or ease of doing business with the organization? Regardless of what the customer sees as the key factors, the organization must place quality at the top of their supplier's list of key features. It is paramount for long-term success. This quality must be in both goods and services. Studies show the main reason for the loss of customers is the lack of concern for customers' needs.

Customers' views will change over time. Economic conditions, changing tastes, and emerging needs all play a part in the buying decision. The human factors also influence all transactions. Personalities, experience, knowledge, and customer relations impact heavily.

All employees in the organization must tune themselves to the changing requirements of their customers. Customer feedback often comes in unexpected ways. Employees become goodwill ambassadors for their teams and organization. Every attempt must be made to understand exactly what the customer needs and wants. This can be difficult. The language of the customer and the supplier may be quite different. Interpreted and actual needs may be different, and the customer may not know what is actually needed.

I can attest to this principle. Some time ago I went into a tire store to purchase tires for my truck. I knew what I wanted the tires to do, but I didn't know which tires I needed. The person at the counter asked how he could help me. I told him my truck needed tires. He asked what kind of tires I wanted, and I told him I wasn't sure. Before I could explain how I used the truck, he cut in, "Mister, if you don't know what you want there isn't any way I can know either. We aren't mind readers here." I thanked him for his observation and since the supervisor wasn't available, departed for another store that could help me.

Less than two blocks away I found a K-Mart tire store in which the manager listened to my needs, made a recommendation, and supplied me with new tires. He made me feel like I made a wise decision by shopping there. The tires were top of the line and exactly met my needs. There was not much time involved buying four tires there and there was a lot less frustration. I do all of our tire shopping there to this day.

Product Quality Deployment

Product quality deployment is the creation and delivery of a quality product that meets or exceeds customer needs and expectations. It matters not whether it is an internal or external customer or the product is goods or services. The step produces effectiveness and creates considerable goodwill.

In the past there have been problems in this area. There are those individuals who believe they can successfully tell the customer what they want rather than produce what the customer wants. Often organizations have decided to produce a product of their choice and then sell the customer on that product through slick packaging and aggressive marketing techniques. Sometimes it works; often it doesn't. Coca-Cola provides a good example. The company developed the new Coke and tried to sell their customers on the idea that it was exactly what they wanted. When sales plummeted they listened to their customers and gave them a choice in the matter. This resulted in bringing back the original Coke with the new name Coke Classic.

Another problem has been designing products to sell based on price rather than value. Price alone seldom generates return business. Witness the Yugo car. After the price is forgotten, the value of whether it is good or bad still remains. That part of the transaction is not forgotten and conceivably brought about the bankruptcy of Yugo America, Inc.

Creation of Values

The next step is to develop products with the characteristics that customers desire. Ford took this step with the Taurus and Sable automobiles. They asked the customers what they wanted and then provided that product to them. These cars are quality products with the desired features. Their success says that Ford "did a good job."

This process involves creating target values for each desired characteristic. This is the ideal value even though it may be difficult or impossible to reach at start-up. Where applicable, intermediate goals also should be set. They should be accompanied by targets such as numbers of products, dates for performance, and other quantifying numbers so accomplishment can be measured against goal to determine success.

For some services, intermediate goals would not be appropriate. Heart surgeons would not be expected to have intermediate performance goals. The same is true for safety engineers, firefighters, brake repair specialists, and so forth.

Creation of target values should be a participative function with the people responsible for reaching these values having a hand in setting them. A strange phenomenon happens. The people responsible for the production effort generally set higher targets and intermediate goals than the management team would establish. They generally meet or exceed the goals they set because they are their own goals.

Is there something we don't understand about this? The answer is "yes." Nobody in the organization knows more about the workings of a team than the individuals in that team. They know how to be more productive. The question then becomes, "Why aren't they?" There are two reasons. First nobody asks them how to do it better, quicker, with more quality. Perhaps no one bothers to listen to them when they try to tell management how to improve the process. The second part of the situation is that generally there isn't anything in it for them if they do improve the process. Remember, you receive the action you reward.

The goals of each different area must be balanced so that resources are available to bring the entire quality program along at an acceptable rate. This can be difficult. Each team tends to believe its efforts are the most important. Without continuous focus it sometimes becomes quite easy to lose sight of the customers and their expectations.

These values must include improvement of process capability. This does not mean purchasing all new equipment or initiating entirely new processes. Too often this is the wrong answer. Chances are that many of the problems stem from improper training. People do not know how to optimize the use of their current equipment or they do not fully understand the capabilities of their current process.

Examples of this philosophy are easy to find. A local machine shop and tool and die operation uses many older machines. In fact, it buys some old equipment and rebuilds it to its own specifications. This is supplemented with new computer-controlled equipment in critical areas. It has an excellent in-house training program and an apprenticeship program. Both programs are demanding. However, it knows how to do the job by fully utilizing its equipment. It produces excellent quality and is cost competitive.

On the other hand, a service organization establishes a different example. It has cash flow problems, paycheck problems, billing problems, customer relations problems, and the obvious personnel problems that plague a system in this shape. It has hired and fired financial officers, bought new computer systems, and discussed the problem to death. To date it has not planned for quality processing in this area, provided system training on the systems it has, or cross-training for its people. It has the patent excuses about computers this or that—"You can't hire good people any more," and so on. It believes in quality programs in its production areas. It also provides outside training on quality and management subjects for every part of the organization except one. You're right. No one from the finance department ever attends these sessions. They are too busy fighting the fires, and besides, "Quality management doesn't really apply to finance in a direct way."

Target values should not be considered the *good enough* point. From initial planning on, it must be understood that "when we get to this level we must already have plans in the wings to hold this while we work to new levels." Quality improvement always must be considered as the nature of the business with solid plans for improvement.

Summary

1. Organizations seem to have planners and doers, and they seldom want to combine their roles. Too many people see planning as an end result rather than a process to provide guidance for the organization.

2. Planning is an organized effort that is coordinated between all operations of the organization. Without coordination, there is generally considerable unnecessary duplication.

3. The quality plan provides basic management control for the TQM process.

4. Planning is an ongoing process that provides direction to effort. It is a dynamic structure that gets us from where we are to where we want to be.

5. Plans should be simple, flexible, credible, operational, achievable, and visionary. The major goal of the plan should be the production of quality goods and services desired by the customer.

6. To provide the goods and services desired, customer need must be correctly identified. This requires the producers to know their customers and who has the buying decision power.

7. Product quality deployment is the creation and delivery of quality goods and services that meet or exceed customer expectations. The followup is the development of products with characteristics desired by the customer.

Bibliography

The keys to successful quality planning are much the same as for any other technical planning activity. The need for planning and the planning process must be understood and applied to the TQM process. The following books will help with the planning of a quality program.

Branch, M. C. *Comprehensive Planning—General Theories and Principles,* Pacific Palisades, CA: Palisades Publishers, 1983.

Crosby, P. B. *Quality Is Free,* New York: McGraw-Hill, 1979.

———. *Quality Without Tears,* New York: McGraw-Hill, 1984.

Ellis, D. J. and Pekal, P. P., Jr. *Planning for Nonplanners,* New York: American Management Association, 1980.

Gitlow, H. S. and Wiesner, D. A. "Vendor Relations: An Important Piece of the Puzzle," *Quality Progress,* pp. 19–23, January 1988.

Groocock, J. M. *The Chain of Quality,* New York: John Wiley and Sons, 1986.

Hagan, J. T. *A Management Role for Quality Control,* New York: American Management Association, 1968.

Harrington, H. J. *The Improvement Process,* New York: McGraw-Hill, 1987.

Hayes, G. E. *The New Challenge*, Wheaton, IL: Hitchcock Publishing Company, 1985.

Ingle, S. *In Search of Perfection*, Englewood Cliffs, NJ: Prentice-Hall, 1985.

Juran, J. M. and Gryna, F. M., Jr. *Quality Planning and Analysis*, New York: McGraw-Hill, 1980.

Kacker, R. N. "Quality Planning for Service Industries," *Quality Progress*, pp. 39–42, August 1988.

Liberatore, J. A. "Supplier Team Adds Values for Customer," *Quality Progress*, p. 43, February 1990.

Melcher, B. H. and Kergner, H. *Strategic Planning: Development and Implementation*, Blue Ridge Summit, PA: Tab Book Inc., 1988.

Morrisey, G. L., Below, P. Jr., and Acomb, B. L. *The Executive Guide to Operational Planning*, San Francisco: Jossey-Bass Publishers, 1988.

Parson, M. J. and Culligan, M. J. *Back to Basics Planning*, New York: Facts On File Publications, 1985.

Randolph, R. M. *Planagement*, New York: AMACOM, 1975.

Sloma, R. S. *No-Nonsense Planning*, New York: The Free Press, 1984.

Stursberg, P. A. *One-Day Business Planning*, Radnor, PA: Chilton Book Company, 1988.

CHAPTER 8

Implementation—The Critical Step

There is no one correct way to implement TQM, just as there is no one right way to run your organization. Sure, there are accepted practices that have been proven to work and incorrect ways of doing things that can get you into big trouble. Between these two extremes lies the gray area that also must be used. Such will be the case of any TQM program.

Reasons abound why there are so many variables in the TQM process. First, TQM fits all organizations from giant industries to small education systems. The needs vary greatly with the type and size of the organization. The framework and ultimate goals will remain the same, but the training format, the quality manual, and so forth may be different.

The second, major reason TQM processes may vary is because TQM's main ingredient is employee involvement. People are different. The needs of people on an assembly line and in a school system are different. The work they do, their educational backgrounds, their customers, and so forth are different.

A third reason each TQM installation effort varies is because of the organization's current status. Some organizations have a long history of quality performance with a significant training program. Others are just now embarking on the quality journey, perhaps because they are in their infancy and may not have a training program or training department.

Regardless of where the organization is in its struggle for quality, the basic concepts are identical. The base for the program is employee involvement; the focus is on the customer, both internal and external; and certain quality tools are required to implement and maintain the TQM process. The first two requirements can be considered virtually the same for any organization. The quality tools, however, are different. For example, SPC is not nearly as important in an education system or restaurant chain as it is in a high-tech manufacturing environment. This does not mean a working knowledge of SPC will not benefit these organizations, it simply means that other quality tools probably will be more important.

TQM is a long-term transformation process evolutionary in character. This mandates change throughout the organization. Different planning requirements, new systems and procedures, different leadership and management styles, new work habits, and new employee human relations skills will all be part of the change required. The necessary changes will vary in degree depending on the aforementioned differences.

The TQM process requires patience. It is a long-term process that takes time. It also requires continuous change. These changes are best implemented in small steps. Organizational leadership must show evidence of change before change will be accepted by other members of the organization. It isn't realistic to expect everybody else in the organization to change to a TQM process while the leadership continues in their same path. TQM requires leadership change from the top down and, requires substantial additional effort by the organization's leadership. Luckily, much of the time for the effort can be found when the wheel-spinning activities are curtailed.

TQM builds on the strengths of the organization and creates plans to overcome weaknesses or quality-deficient areas. This requires organization assessment prior to the actual quality planning stage. Normally, the people involved in this assessment become the quality council or quality steering committee as the TQM process progresses. These people include the leaders and managers of the various departments and divisions within the organization. *The planners and the doers must be the same people in TQM.*

Potential Obstacles

As in most things, awareness of the potential obstacles that may hinder the TQM process will help prevent many of them from happening. Forewarned is forearmed. Many of the obstacles will be present with or without TQM. Luckily, TQM provides a framework to discover and overcome problems and obstacles that exist in every organization.

Every organization will not face all of these obstacles, but they will face many of them. They all are important enough to list.

1. Top management is not committed to and does not get actively involved in the installation and operation of the TQM process. If the top management group is not willing to commit itself to the leadership and energy required for a successful program, it is best not

to begin. Of all the premises of a TQM program, this is the one item with which every quality guru appears to be in agreement.

2. TQM is not a quick fix. It is a long-term process that requires continuous leadership and extended patience. It can take a significant amount of time for the organization's leadership and management style to become totally tuned to the quality processes. The organization's quality attitude follows this leadership example.

3. The TQM program will be viewed cautiously by the work force. After all, most of the work force have seen other management plans and quality programs come and go after a brief flurry of action. Many have witnessed programs, such as quality circles, expire because more attention was placed on form than substance. The work force must see continued interest in TQM from the top down in order to maintain its commitment.

4. Labor unions may provide considerable resistance to TQM efforts. They want assurance that this is not another program to improve the bottom line at the expense of the work force. They do not want to work themselves out of jobs. Most union representatives can quickly point out examples where employees make the difference in a program and someone else receives the rewards. There are now many examples where union leaders are quality leaders. The Chrysler Corporation serves as one example of a union that has high-level input into corporate management.

5. There will be some people problems that may be accompanied by a temptation to change groups of people to solve quality problems. This temptation must be resisted because it usually is ineffective and it sends a negative signal to the work force. Some individuals may need to be replaced for cause, and this is generally accepted, but work groups almost always can be brought into the quality team environment through leadership.

6. Some will try to equate higher quality with a singular benefit such as increased profit. When this benefit does not come about rapidly, there is a loss of interest. Increases in profit are to be expected, but they generally won't be immediate. TQM is a total package and must be sold with all its benefits. Potential benefits include improvements in pride, performance, customer service, customer relations, job security, and profits with accompanying decreases in reworks, scrap, customer complaints, and employee turnover.

7. Often there is a tendency to appoint a TQM manager to oversee the process without providing that manager with the support,

cooperation, and authority to gain success. The TQM manager must be a proven leader and an integral part of the management team.

8. Often TQM is made overly complicated, especially at the beginning. In many cases, initial effort centers around SPC training without the leadership and human relations training required to change the organization's way of doing business. Any training program receives a better reception if it begins with the basics and attempts to train to topics as they are needed and can be utilized. People then see purpose through need which is a healthy motivator to learn.

9. The quality program may be held back by equipment or machinery that is not capable of performing to the expected level. This may not show up until the TQM program is underway. At this point, the decision becomes, "Do we acquire the equipment necessary to gain the required quality or do we . . . ?" Remember the words of Henry Ford, "If you need a piece of equipment but don't buy it, you pay for it even though you don't have it."

10. The work procedures and/or quality procedures are such that they do not support TQM. This problem will become quickly evident as the program takes shape.

11. There is an organizational problem that often restricts TQM. Leaders within the system see the organization strictly in terms of chain of command. TQM requires that all employees also see themselves as customers, suppliers, and team members.

12. The TQM program will meet resistance. Often there is a tendency to meet this resistance with force rather than patient leadership. Force generates sabotage which is manifested in a multitude of ways only limited by imagination. The leader, however, who realizes there is an informal organization with loyalties that exist outside of the formal organizational needs, and works with these groups on their level, will find resistance more easily overcome. People will accept change when they are a part of planning the change, while they will resist someone trying to change them. A great contributor to successful implementation of the TQM program is sound human relations skills.

13. The last obstacle, and the major one in many organizations, is the presence or lack of a reward and recognition system. Too often, the reward system does not fit the TQM program. High productivity might be rewarded when increased quality is desired. Managers may receive personal rewards for their team's efforts without rewarding proper recognition for the team. Team awards and rewards are most supportive of the TQM program. However, outstanding individual

contributions also must be noted. The awards system is like the TQM process in that it must be tailored to the organization. A well-thought-out reward program will provide solid support for the TQM process.

Program Implementation

Like the TQM program itself, there is no one correct way to introduce TQM to the organization. Certainly, there must be an orderly transition into the new way of doing business. This transition builds on the current strengths of the organization and tackles the areas that impact the greatest amount on performance first. The following introductory sequence works well and serves the needs of virtually any organization.

Commitment Letter

This letter is the organization's introduction to TQM. It should be signed out by the organization's senior leadership. This letter outlines the reasons for the TQM process, discusses the basics of how the program works, covers the importance of teamwork for success, and provides the benefits of TQM for the organization's membership. TQM is defined in terms of a long-term, goal-oriented process. The letter ties TQM to the customer and the corporate motto, in the following case, "Quality Through Professional Excellence." Most importantly, it commits that senior person to this program.

Mr. Gary Carter, president of Summit Technologies, Inc., headquartered in Springfield, Virginia, permitted use of the message from his commitment letter.

Dear STI EMPLOYEES:

Summit Technologies is growing up. We are moving toward the point where we will graduate to big business. To ensure we are competitive in this arena, we must operate smarter. That is why I have elected to initiate a total quality management program.

Total quality management (TQM) is a process that encourages each individual at STI to manage the quality of the products and services to which he or she contributes. TQM also allows people to have more control over their work environment. We currently have the people within our team who can develop this process in order to ensure that our company is productive and provides for quality, cost-competitive products.

Total quality management (TQM) is the new way STI will conduct business. This is not a miracle quick-fix program with a near term completion date. It is a permanent goal-oriented program that will guide our

STI team in all endeavors. Through our total quality management program, our organization will meet the challenges of the future as well as the demands of the present. We will move forward and grow as a dynamic, quality team.

For this program to succeed, each person must realize that his or her efforts are equal in value to the efforts of every other team member. Every member of every department or work site must think quality, produce quality, and provide outstanding service with a smile. There is no other way for success. We must completely immerse ourselves in the total quality management program.

This then is our task:

> Be a competitive team
> Produce outstanding customer service
> Deliver on-time, quality products

Our corporate motto summarizes our goals and our way of doing business. "QUALITY THROUGH PROFESSIONAL EXCELLENCE." Together, as Team STI, we will excel and grow through total quality management.

On behalf of our team, I pledge myself to this effort.

Gary J. Carter,
President

Introductory Speech

This speech usually is presented by the same person who signed out the commitment letter. An appropriate place for presentation is the first meeting of the quality steering council or committee. This speech follows the commitment letter and orally commits the organization's leadership to TQM.

This speech covers and reiterates the same subjects as the letter. Over the course of time, TQM presentations must be made over and over again, followed by action that says we are committed to a quality product through quality excellence in every area of the organization.

This introduction to TQM will discuss the importance of total quality management and quality planning, basic program requirements, the potential benefits for everyone, and program expectations. It discusses the importance of the big three of TQM: employee involvement, customer focus, and the use of quality tools through training and practice. It covers the framework for quality including the quality council or committee and a TQM manager, if there is one. It projects the use of current assets in the quest for quality and discusses training needs in addition to the current training program. The speech should end with the speaker's commitment to the program over the long term.

Although there are many fine examples, we did not use an actual speech. We chose to use a broad approach that can be universally applied. It provides an outline with useful ideas for all organizations.

The first paragraph should reflect where the organization is. The sample is for a situation where there aren't major problems and TQM is being implemented to improve performance, or increase customer focus, but there is no crisis situation.

Where there is a problem, that problem should be called out in the first paragraph. A potential for that opener is provided first because it is fitting for so many of today's organizations.

Sample First Paragraph

We lost money the last six months. When I leave this meeting I am headed for the bank to secure loans to continue operations. When asked at the bank, I will be forced to tell them we have lost market share and our competitors are giving us serious competition. If we can't turn this situation around during the next three months we must cease operation at this plant and close down. This will be a terrible blow to all of us because it means the end of our jobs and the cessation of an operation to which we have all devoted our working lives. Our community also will suffer because we have been a good employer. Turning this operation around, however, will save our jobs and pay dividends in many other ways. Most of all, we will prove that we can still face adversity and come through as winners. I firmly believe we can pull this off and become more competitive than we ever were before. The way we can do this is through the installation of a total quality management process. We already have much of the required structure in place. Do you want to hear more?

Some leaders will want their message to be much more forceful and this can be accomplished by changing the last sentence in the paragraph. A sample follows that is a veritable quote from an introductory speech by a recently selected president of an organization that had such problems. The speech made a significant impact on most attendees, enough so that one manager could quote most of it.

Damn it folks, I am not a loser and I came here committed to turn this operation around. I intend to do that. Those of you who wish to support me, I need all the support you can provide. We have our work cut out. Those of you who don't support our efforts can consider yourselves shortlived at _____. Your efforts and actions will tell me which of you are team players and which of you should be watching the classified ads for more suitable employment."

From there he continued with the outline of his plan. The turnaround is well under way and the company will show a profit for the year rather than the projected loss. It hasn't been easy for them, but the people there seem to be enjoying the challenge. Now for the other version in its entirety.

Why TQM

America and its organizations are at a crossroads in the global marketplace. We are regaining our competitiveness because of performance improvements, most of which are quality-related. But, it is only the beginning and every organization, ours included, must join the fight for quality.

I have decided we must institute a total quality management program to remain competitive and build our market share. Without TQM, our very survival as we now know our organization, may be questionable. With it, we can improve our performance in all areas and each of us can enjoy the many benefits that this improved performance will certainly bring.

Total quality management is a performance management process that focuses on quality through solid planning efforts. It provides the quality link between our strategic planning efforts, business plan, market plan, training plan, and budget. Sure, none of us like to plan, and we may resist change. But good enough is not good enough to remain competitive. This quality plan is a must if we are to enjoy the success we all desire.

To make quality planning more acceptable, we must make sure it is a KISS (Keep It Simple, Sam) plan. We will also ensure that it is a dynamic plan that successfully guides us to continuous process, production, and quality improvement.

The TQM program mandates that we understand and use participative leadership practices whenever these principles are applicable. We must work to become closely united teams working together to make *our organization* the quality leader in our customer's eyes.

Yes, our customer is the one who decides if we are a quality organization. We must, therefore, acquire the knowledge of what our customers truly need and desire, and then we must provide those products and services in a competitive manner. This requires us to become a team with our customer and our suppliers. Together, this team, which must include our customers, our suppliers, and every member of our team, can become the market leaders we all desire to be. This will require close working relationships that might be somewhat foreign to us now.

I am totally committed to TQM. This will become our new way of doing business. Research has proven to me that American organizations which are competitive in the global market remain competitive through total quality management. My expectations are that we will unite as a strong quality conscious team, leading our people into the 1990s and beyond.

We intend to begin this program with our own assets. Each leader down through supervisors and group leaders has been asked to fill out one of our quality assets forms. I intend to share these forms with each of you at this meeting. I can tell you our potential in-house assets are far greater than those for which I had hoped.

As we determine the need for additional training or outside consultants to support this effort, these assets will be acquired. Until then, we will begin with what we have. I intend to begin our training program with two separate sessions: An Overview of the TQM Process and Participative Leadership.

Each person at this meeting, our leadership team, will be members of our quality council. I have also chosen Ms. Albright as the TQM manager. She will serve as the focal point for the process during implementation. Our job will be to plan for quality, train for quality, teach quality processes, and preach quality at every opportunity until quality becomes our very way of life. Thereafter, we will continue in this same vein until we are truly the best of the best.

Thank you all for your support in this endeavor. It is appreciated.

Regardless of which type of speech is made, leaders must take their rightful place as the head of this quality process. These same people must be prepared to make this speech throughout the organization so every employee knows what the plan is and who is leading it. Nothing less will do.

The Quality Council

Many possibilities exist for the makeup of the quality council. The membership of this vital group will be determined by the type of organization. Our favorite scenario for business is one where the department managers are members of the quality council with the site or plant manager serving in a dual capacity as the TQM manager. This arrangement follows the standard chain of command and is simple. However, it may not always be practical. Certainly the department managers should be a part of the quality council if it is to be effective. Other members should include union representatives where applicable. Customer and supplier representatives also are appropriate for many sessions, especially when planning is taking place that affects either of these groups.

Finance, administrative services, contracts, human resources management, maintenance, and other support departments should be members. If these departments are not producing quality products with high-quality support, it is unlikely that the other employees will want to be high performers, either.

An education system might have the school superintendent as the TQM manager and chair with membership of the principals. Representatives from the counselors, teachers, secretarial staff, other support staff, maintenance, bus drivers, and students might make up the quality council.

The Quality Control Mission

Regardless of the organization and its makeup, the mission is the same. That mission is to install TQM throughout the organization. The 10-step process follows:

1. Determine where the organization is now in each vital area.
2. Determine where the organization wants to go.
3. Determine the need which is the difference.
4. Design improvement processes in each area of need.
5. Develop workable strategies.
6. Develop quality guidelines.
7. Determine progress measurements.
8. Assist and support implementation.
9. Produce a training program to support and enhance the quality program.
10. Produce quality action plans to meet the determined needs. Ensure they require the involvement of the employees in every area of the process.

The TQM Training Program

There is no standard training program because each organization is different with unique requirements. Most organizations will have adequate resources to begin the program using their present in-house assets. The challenge is to marshal those assets now on board in order to produce a productive quality training program. These four volumes will provide virtually all of the background information required to get your program up and running.

The available assets will be determined from the quality assets form, resumé review, and the knowledge of the personnel within the organization. Some people may have skills they were hesitant to list, so it is best to use multiple sources.

The first training scheduled should be training for the prospective trainers. If train-the-trainer resources are available in the organization, they should be called on to prepare this program. If not, organizations in conjunction with local universities, provide this type training. A part of this training should be development of ways to tie quality and quality improvement for the home organization and its particular needs into every training session. Trainers must be aware of the quality action plans that have been developed so the training can assist in accomplishment of the projects.

Training for management and those in leadership positions should begin with an overview of successful TQM and the process for program implementation. This should be followed closely by leadership training. W. Edwards Deming in his book *Out of the Crisis* emphasizes on the need for leadership and training from the beginning. The message is the same in works of other quality authors. Among the topics covered should be leadership styles, participative leadership, visioning, selling yourself and your ideas, and effective communications. Other important sessions should include initiating change, building teams, correct rewards and recognition efforts, various human relation topics, and leadership strategies for TQM implementation. Quality customer service also should be a subject taught in the early stages.

The technical aspects of TQM should follow in regular training sessions. Organizational need ultimately determines the training subject order. Leaders must become familiar with the technical aspects of the work produced in their area. This is extremely important to successfully lead people. You must be knowledgeable of the work they do from their perspective.

Employees should begin training at the same time. They should begin with training on the successful TQM program and quality customer service. This provides the background reasons why the training they will receive on the technical aspects of their jobs is so important. Process control training is a subject that must be taught early on because quality hinges on it. In most organizations employee training often will include a much higher percentage of on-the-job training. Work skills are best developed on the shop floor and not in the classroom.

Cross-training is extremely productive. It produces well-rounded employees who can fill in for others during personnel absences. It also provides for a pool of trained people to cover rush orders and other such requirements. Perhaps the biggest benefit comes from people learning how their product affects other employees and the challenges other employees face in their jobs. Many great ideas for performance improvements come out of cross-training sessions. It also encourages employees to respect the efforts of their fellow workers.

Training requirements that cannot be met with current assets must be procured from other sources. Particular needs should be noted. Often these can be filled when hiring new employees. Investment for some personnel in one of the quality colleges or institutes will fill many of the training holes. Quality seminars are becoming available in more locations. Additionally, colleges and universities are beginning to add quality subjects to their curriculums. Outside trainers and consultants are available to fill virtually every quality requirement. It is important to choose the source of outside training carefully. It should be tailored to the needs of the organization and use the organization's material where possible. This makes outside training a part of the organization's training and quality team, and it makes the training more acceptable to employees.

Training should be spread out over time. Most sessions should be one to four hours in length. Taking small steps at close intervals keeps enthusiasm high and allows the material to be assimilated into the work processes more easily. The material will become habit only if it is used on the job soon after the training sessions. Unused training is a waste of resources and can be a demotivator since the people invested their time in training that had no payoff.

Paced training also keeps minimal negative impact on current production. In organizations where there are end of the month production crunches to get orders out, it often is best to schedule training for the beginning of production periods. During these times employees are kicking back after the end of the period rush and there will be no noticeable impact on performance. Hopefully, the training will help spread production efforts out over the production period. It is difficult to achieve quality when there are production crunches; the two tend to be mutually exclusive.

Quality Council Meetings

Quality council meetings must be planned so that a productive output results from each meeting. Unproductive meetings waste time, demotivate the doers, and impact negatively on quality. Quality meetings must be progressive in nature and demand action by all participants. There is a great deal of work to do. The product from every meeting should be a quality plan, action plan, or some other product that guides the team toward its quality goals. These meetings must create a sense of urgency and develop a commitment to TQM. Anything less must be considered unsatisfactory.

The initial quality council meeting will set the tone for the TQM program and future quality council meetings. Therefore, it is important to start productively. A possible format for that meeting follows.

1. *Introductions–senior manager.* The CEO, president, or division manager should deliver the TQM speech.

2. *The opening speech–senior manager.* The meeting then may be turned over to the TQM manager, if one has been selected.

3. *Select a recorder.* A volunteer should be encouraged.

4. *The TQM need, responsibilities, and benefits–TQM manager.*

5. *Customer requirements both internal and external–marketing manager.*

6. *Results of quality assets survey–TQM manager.*

7. *Requirement for action plans–TQM manager.* Some of the action plans should include:

   • Quality policy draft

   • Define quality in terms of the organization

   • Quality plan draft

   • Quality awareness plan

   • Training plan draft

   • Outline of a quality manual

   • Implementation plan draft

   • Awards and recognition plan draft

   Note: There probably won't be time to develop any of these plans at the first meeting and that's good. They can be assigned for action so that each manager can tackle one of these prior to the next meeting. They should be assigned to members by name so the person accepts responsibility. Council members who have knowledge or interest in specific areas should be encouraged to volunteer for those areas. These people can then go to their respective departments and obtain assistance from their employees on the action plan. Employee involvement is a crucial ingredient of the TQM program. Work on these initial plans will promote teamwork.

8. *Pass out handout–TQM manager.* This handout will be developed prior to the meeting. We recommend that it contain three subject areas: draft duties of the TQM manager, draft quality council responsibilities, and a list of questions that should be answered, preferably at the second meeting. Details of this handout are in the next section.

9. *Determine when the next meeting will be held.*

10. *Adjourn.*

The Meeting Handout

TQM manager duties and responsibilities

- Chair the quality council.
- Attain membership in the American Society for Quality Control (ASQC).
- Prepare quality council meeting schedule and agendas.
- Coordinate the quality training program with HRM.
- Organize quality presentations.
- Coordinate all quality action plans developed by the quality council.
- Coordinate quality teams assembled to overcome specific quality problems. Team leadership will be assigned to those people responsible for the problem area.
- Other such duties as assigned by *appropriate authority.*

Quality council tasks

- Successfully complete action plans (listed on the agenda).
- Assist the TQM and HRM managers with quality training.
- Continual assessment and improvement of the quality process.
- Continually promote TQM awareness.
- Develop and assist with implementation of strategies to improve the quality program.
- Develop input for other organizational plans.
- Develop quality measurement standards.

Questions that should be answered

1. What business are we in? The organization's business and marketing plans contain this information and every staff department and line operation should know it.

2. Where are we now? What do we do well? Where do we need improvement?

3. How do we measure where we are now? There are many measurements. Prime determinants of measurement requirements are the type of organization, the purpose of the department, and the goods produced. Some area of measurement might include:

   - Profit
   - Customer satisfaction

- Product rejects
- Cost of rejects
- Percent of reliability
- Sales increases
- Number of new customers
- Mean time between failure
- Rate of repair
- Cost of repair
- Employee turnover
- Number of adverse labor actions

Education might measure

- Number of dropouts
- Performance on standardized tests
- Discipline problems

4. Where do we want to be? Clearly defined goals are a must. These goals must be easily understood by each person involved in the TQM process. Guidance for these goals comes from the president down, with input from every employee involved in the particular operation. Goals must be realistic, achievable, and measurable. Vague goals soon become no goals. Goals must be quantitative. Our goal for 199___ is to:

- Improve sales 20 percent through improved customer satisfaction.
- Reduce rejects from 15 percent to 5 percent by _____.
- Reduce scrap from 20 percent to 10 percent by August 199___.

5. How do we get where we want to be? What are we doing now? What must we do different? What must management do? What must employees do? What assets and resources are needed for the job? What support must our staffs provide? What must we do in design, development, marketing, systems, and testing?

6. What training is required for management, employees, and joint management/employees?

7. How do we begin the quality improvement process? What changes are necessary to build quality in rather than inspect junk out?

Training that will be a part of future quality council meetings

1. *Analysis techniques*–Simple statistical methods, graphing techniques, and charting operations that will provide large quality and production improvements at modest cost.

2. *Design reviews*–These will help quality-conscious leaders plan for review of every process step from design to marketing and sales.

3. *Computer analysis*–This training will cover various computer programs available covering techniques such as computer simulation methods, finite element analysis, and so on.

4. *Performance reviews*–Techniques to address both aspects of performance, which are quality and production. Both components must be addressed.

5. *Problem-solving techniques*–This training will cover general problem-solving techniques that can be applied to any situation.

The Quality Policy

The quality policy will be the next official proclamation. This policy must be the cooperative effort of the executive staff, the quality council, and the employees in order to gain support from all members of the organization. The policy will state the quality policy in simple terms so that each person within the organization can understand it. The quality policy of Quality America, Inc. follows:

Policy

Quality education is the foundation for our management and quality programs. We are committed to excellence and dedicated to customer satisfaction. It is our policy to:

- Consistently provide training, seminars, courses, and consulting services that meet the quality and performance expectations of our customers.

- Actively research every topic in our inventory to promote ever-improving quality and state-of-the-art information.

Philip B. Crosby in his book *Quality Without Tears* lists many corporate policy statements that he has displayed at his Quality College. These serve as excellent examples of quality policies.

Summary

1. Implementation is the critical step in the TQM process. There is no one correct way to implement the process, but there are accepted guides that will help with installation.

2. There are many obstacles to implementing TQM. Some managers may not get on board at the beginning of TQM. Others will see it as a quick fix, which is an idea that must be overcome. Other groups also may resist initial implementation.

3. Program implementation usually begins with a commitment letter from the organization's chief executive. The letter introduces members of the organization to TQM.

4. An introductory speech is important to TQM. This speech also is made by the chief executive. In large organizations, the executives of individual operations probably will follow this with their own speech.

5. The quality council is an important part of TQM, especially at the beginning of the process. In time, the duties of this group may migrate to the department leaders who handle the organization's other group affairs.

Bibliography

Branch, M. C. *Comprehensive Planning—General Theories and Principles,* Pacific Palisades, CA: Palisades Publishers, 1983.

Crosby, P. B. *Quality Is Free,* New York: McGraw-Hill, 1979.

———. *Quality Without Tears,* New York: McGraw-Hill, 1984.

Deming, W. E. *Out of the Crisis,* Cambridge, MA: Massachusetts Institute of Technology Center for Advanced Learning, 1986.

DiPrimo, A. *Quality Assurance in Service Organization,* Radnor, PA: Chilton Book Company, 1987.

Ellis, D. J. and Pekal, P. P., Jr. *Planning for Nonplanners,* New York: American Management Association, 1980.

Garvin, D. A. *Managing Quality,* New York: The Free Press, 1988.

Gitlow, H. S. and Wiesner, D. A. "Vendor Relations: An Important Piece of the Puzzle," *Quality Progress,* pp. 19–23, January 1988.

Hagan, J. T. *A Management Role for Quality Control,* New York: American Management Association, 1968.

Harrington, H. J. *The Improvement Process,* New York: McGraw-Hill, 1987.

Hayes, G. E. *The New Challenge,* Wheaton, IL: Hitchcock Publishing Company, 1985.

Ingle, S. *In Search of Perfection,* Englewood Cliffs, NJ: Prentice-Hall, 1985.

Juran, J. M. and Gryna, F. M., Jr. *Quality Planning and Analysis,* New York: McGraw-Hill, 1980.

Juran, J. M. *Juran on Planning for Quality,* New York: The Free Press, 1988.

Kacker, R. N. "Quality Planning for Service Industries," *Quality Progress,* pp. 39–42, August 1988.

Liberatore, J. A. "Supplier Team Adds Values for Customer," *Quality Progress,* p. 43, February 1990.

Melcher, B. H. and Kergner, H. *Strategic Planning: Development and Implementation,* Blue Ridge Summit, PA: Tab Book, 1988.

Morrisey, G. L., Below, P. Jr., and Acomb, B. L. *The Executive Guide to Operational Planning,* San Francisco: Jossey-Bass Publishers, 1988.

Parson, M. J. and Culligan, M. J. *Back to Basics Planning,* New York: Facts On File Publications, 1985.

Randolph, R. M. *Planagement,* New York: AMACOM, 1975.

Sloma, R. S. *No-Nonsense Planning,* New York: The Free Press, 1984.

Stursberg, P. A. *One-Day Business Planning,* Radnor, PA: Chilton Book Company, 1988.

Townsend, P. L. *Commit to Quality,* New York: John Wiley and Sons, 1986.

Walton, M. *The Deming Management Method,* New York: Putnam Publishing Group, 1986.

CHAPTER 9

The Quality Manual

The quality manual provides the structure within which we can repeat our successes. It is a dynamic guide to quality, rather than a static once-and-done publication. The outline provided is intended as a starting guide to provide ideas for putting together a quality manual. Much of the required information is readily available within the organization. Many parts of this chapter are presented in outline format to facilitate the construction of a manual and the attendant plans that support it.

We recommend a minimum of five separate sections. They can have many titles, but the following divisions will get the manual started.

- Philosophy
- Internal quality
- Supplier certification
- Customer service and customer relations
- Awards

Philosophy Section

The philosophy section should lead off the book and begin with the quality motto. Two examples of a quality motto follow.

"Quality is job ONE"®

–Registered Trademark of Ford
Motor Company

"Quality through Professional Excellence"

–Summit Technologies, Inc.

The philosophy section generally contains some common topics. Usually it begins with a philosophy statement, "It is the philosophy of *our company* to:

1. Provide on-time deliveries of defect-free products.

2. Place quality customer service as our most important job.

3. Promote true teamwork of the internal and extended team which includes our suppliers, our customers, and ourselves.

This will be achieved through:

1. Demonstrated commitment by all employees.

2. Quality goals that seek to improve products and processes continually.

3. Continued education for all team members:

   a. Quality customer service training for every employee.

   b. Management personnel training includes leadership, team building, quality, planning, process improvement analysis techniques, and problem-solving techniques.

   c. First-line supervisors' training includes the same subjects as the management team. Much of the training can be as a part of the management team training. They also will receive training on statistical techniques, statistical data display, and the proper methods and procedures for quality manufacturing.

   d. Production personnel training includes methods and techniques for quality manufacturing, recording process information, and basic data interpretation. Ongoing training will be provided on problem diagnosis and correction steps possible for operator/production personnel.

Our company will develop a quality working environment conducive to quality performance.

Policy

The policy already discussed should be entered here. Many organizations choose to expand their policy statement with paragraphs on intent and responsibilities. The Quality America, Inc. corporate quality policy statement is included here as an example.

CORPORATE QUALITY POLICY

Policy

Quality education is the foundation for our leadership and quality management programs. We are committed to excellence and dedicated to customer service. It is our policy to:

- Consistently provide training, seminars, courses and consulting services which meet the quality expectations of our customers.

- Actively research every topic in our inventory to promote ever-improving quality and state-of-the-art information.

Intent

Quality education and consulting practices will be our major thrust. It is our sole reason for existence as an organization. Therefore, we will:

- Strive to understand the exact needs and goals of our customers and accept only those challenges we can perform in a professional manner.

- Develop quality educational programs to meet the existing and emerging needs as defined by our customers.

- Stay current in every aspect of our business to provide the services demanded by our professional customers.

Responsibilities

Each member of the Quality America, Inc. team is responsible for:

- Communicating our quality policy to each associate.

- Providing quality services at all times by tailoring those services to exact customer needs.

- Continuing self-education programs on all aspects of quality.

- Ensuring that each associate and consultant remembers the following at all times:

  (1) Our ideas are not the only correct way of meeting the stated objectives.

  (2) Our way of viewing any problem is not the only relevant viewpoint.

  (3) Our presentation methods are not the only acceptable method for a given subject.

(4) Our solutions are not the only workable solutions to a situation.

- We will ensure flexibility in all professional environments to encompass the ideas of each participant to arrive at the best possible solution for each given situation.

- We understand that in every session, there will be participants who have substantial knowledge about any given subject. It is our duty to facilitate idea exchanges that bring this material out for the benefit of all participants.

- We will monitor and continually improve the level of customer satisfaction.

Key Principles

Several key principles are important to understanding and implementing TQM and should be included in the quality manual. Four of these are outlined.

1. *Defining quality*–Quality is personal to the organization. The statement could be "Quality is defined as . . . ." Some examples are:

   a. "Conformance to requirements."–Philip Crosby

   b. "Efficient production of the quality the market expects."–Dr. W. Edwards Deming

   c. "Fitness for use."–Dr. Joseph M. Juran

   d. Regardless of how it is said, the thought conveyed should be one that says we will produce quality, cost-competitive products *the customer needs and wants.*

2. *Performance standard*–Philip Crosby says it all with zero defects

3. *Description of the quality system*–The system should include:

   a. The quality plan.

   b. Quality control and quality assurance to meet the quality plan.

   c. Quality improvement to provide continuous process improvement.

4. *Quality measurement*–There should be a simple statement that says something like, "Our quality measurements will be detectable improvements in customer satisfaction and cost savings through quality process improvements."

The section may also include copies of the letter of commitment and the president's opening speech. These are good reference pieces that should be referred to occasionally in order to measure how the organization is progressing against the commitments that have been made.

Quality goals are outlined in the philosophy section. This is a nuts and bolts outline of program goals. The need for goals should be developed in a few paragraphs. Some of the verbiage can include competition in the global market, the customer demand for quality goods and services, the need for continuous improvement, and the fact that survival itself may depend on quality performance. The goals should be listed as they are currently known. These could include the following:

1. Produce cost-competitive, defect-free products our customer needs and wants.

2. Introduce a TQM program throughout our organization.

3. Preach and teach the TQM message until it is the very nature of our organization.

4. Assist every individual in our organization in becoming the best they can be.

5. Build a quality work environment where people enjoy coming to work.

6. Establish a true team relationship with our customers and suppliers.

7. Continually improve our production and quality processes so we eliminate waste, reduce costs, and improve quality.

Internal Quality Section

The internal quality section outlines the way the TQM process will be organized for implementation and operation. At times, initial implementation will have a temporary structure to get the program implemented at which time operational responsibilities will be shifted to the normal chain of command. Another setup is a TQM organization functioning within the chain of command. Many smaller organizations follow the chain of command from inception. This provides an excellent working arrangement because the leadership of the organization is directly responsible for all aspects of the performance improvement process.

Quality Control/Quality Assurance

The internal quality control/quality assurance system is one part of the internal quality section. It addresses the way these two separate factors work within the quality process. One must remember these factors address the status quo, maintaining quality at some level. TQM concerns improvement above this level.

TQM concepts have been covered before but they should be listed again. TQM is a quality improvement process that moves the organization forward from the current controlled level to ever-improving quality levels. These include the following:

1. Prevention vice detection through final inspection.

2. Continual process improvement.

3. Supplier relationship and responsibilities.

4. Customer relationships and responsibilities.

5. Problem solving requirements.

6. Corrective action procedures.

The Quality Plan

The quality plan is developed in a format designed to coincide with other plans used within the organization. A common format makes it easier for people to relate to the way they must put the plan into use. Individual responsibilities are outlined where they are crucial to the program's success. A process is developed to update the plan on both a scheduled and as-needed basis. This, too, should be something common to the way other plans are updated. The last consideration deals with the way the organization will utilize this plan to implement and continue the TQM process.

The quality plan is a dynamics guide to continuous production and quality improvement. It can and should be updated whenever goals are reached. A sample quality plan is provided in outline format for easier use.

1. List quality-related goals.

    a. List each goal.

    b. List measurement standards for each goal.

    c. List check-back dates.

    d. List completion dates.

2. Develop action plans for each goal (responsible managers with input from their teams). Action plans with formats are provided in Volume III.

    a. Objective.

    b. Justification/benefits.

    c. List key tasks.

    d. Assign responsibility.

    e. List the schedule.

    f. Potential roadblocks.

    g. Team members.

    h. Training required.

    i. Projected costs.

    j. Potential return on investment.

3. Develop specific procedures. This is a bottom up process that uses the knowledge and talents of each individual in the concerned process or section. It also is the step where teams are developed that provide the real success that occurs with TQM.

    a. Foremen, supervisors, and group leaders work on written quality goals to meet action plans. This group should be a part of the original action plan development for maximum success.

    b. These quality goals include measurement and schedules.

    c. The manager collects these goals. They are critiqued against action plans, condensed or added to when required, and become a part of the development quality and action plans.

4. A review schedule is developed by the quality council and TQM manager. Care must be taken to ensure that the schedule is not so cumbersome it precludes completion of the job responsibilities that go with production. A red tape overkill must be carefully avoided. TQM should reduce red tape and not increase it.

5. Each department must have a TQM plan so that every person in the organization is addressed in the plan at least once. These departmental plans become subsystems of the main organizational quality plan.

6. Each department plan should address the following as a minimum:

    a. Goals.

    b. Action plans.

    c. Procedures.

    d. Internal audits.

    e. Training.

    f. Process control.

    g. Process improvement.

    h. Needs and requirements of continual quality improvement.

    i. Benefits of TQM.

    j. Statistical data display.

    k. Internal relationships and teamwork.

    l. Responsibilities to:

        (1) Customers.

        (2) Suppliers.

        (3) The organization.

        (4) Ourselves (includes self-training).

    m. Schedules.

    n. Follow-up.

TQM Manager

A TQM manager is not always appointed. In some cases it is the plant or site managers who have the TQM manager responsibilities as either an assigned part of their normal duties or a collateral duty. This is especially true when the organization is small and lacks the additional resources that can be taken away from production for a considerable part of the time. This section should include:

1. Duties and responsibilities.
2. Reporting procedures.
3. Authority.
4. Reporting requirements.
5. Quality plan requirements.

Quality Council

The quality council may be a full-time body designated to implement TQM. In smaller organizations it may be a part-time assignment with membership which follows the established chain of command. When possible, this is an ideal situation because these departmental and operations managers are the people responsible for performance and customer quality service within their work area. This section contains the following:

1. Makeup of the quality council.
2. Duties and responsibilities.
3. Authority.
4. Meeting requirements.

5. Reporting requirements.

6. Quality plan requirements.

Process Control

The process control section outlines the desired process which becomes the standard against which the actual performance or process will be measured. A subsection is allotted for each department. A copy of the process control section for each department is maintained in the work space for ready reference by the people in that department. The master is filed in the quality manual. The breakdown of process control follows.

1. Flowcharts are prepared for each operation or process. The flowcharts show each step in relation to others and what comes in and goes out of that step as a product. Complicated processes and operations are further broken down to subprocesses.

2. Process comparison and verification steps are clearly noted. These steps should be detailed. In many cases there will be operator self-checks. At other times the process automatically checks itself and reads out the information. In some cases, inspectors make checks in specific points of the process or operation.

3. Statistical processes are noted wherever special information is gathered to develop the various charts and graphs that are used to control the process.

4. Statistical data displays also are noted on the flowchart. These pictorials display statistical information in a simple format.

5. Deviation policy. It is important to note the deviation policy, which might be "there will be no deviations." Whatever the policy is it should be recorded.

6. The feedback process is detailed. The people involved must know how feedback information is handled and who receives it. It also is a good idea to list what actions are required by these people with the information.

7. The process control input to the quality plan is outlined so process control is continuously being updated and improved in order to improve quality continuously, the base purpose of TQM.

Receiving Process

Every organization receives incoming goods, services, raw materials, and so forth. This section outlines the process to handle receivables correctly. The subsections that must be developed follow.

1. Control of received materials.

2. Control of received services.

3. Supplier-furnished quality information.

4. Lot sampling.

5. Deviation policy (if any is acceptable).

6. Feedback process.

7. Inputs to quality plan.

Product Verification

The product leaving any operation or organization should be verified as being a quality product. The verification process ensures this will happen from product conception to customer utilization. The subsections that need to be developed follow.

1. Design and engineering responsibilities for TQM.

2. Vendor and supplier control and quality verification.

3. Validation and testing.

4. Outgoing sampling.

5. Quality verification information.

6. Customer setup plan.

7. Compliance visits procedure with suppliers and customers.

8. Quality survey feedback form to customer.

9. Deviation policy.

10. Inputs to quality plan.

Internal Audits

Internal audits and assessments on an ongoing basis support the quest for quality. Quality management can be effective only if the responsible people have a handle on what is happening in the operation. Administered correctly, audits determine what is going right and areas that can be improved. In this sense they are a positive tool in the TQM process. Quality audits are covered in Volume III, Chapter 2 and Volume IV, Chapter 7. The subsections that must be developed for this section follow.

1. Policy.

2. Procedures.

3. Frequency.

4. Checklists.

5. Input to quality control plan.

Quality Plan Evaluation

This section outlines how the quality plan will be evaluated to determine whether it is successful and signifies the period within which the evaluation process takes place. An evaluation is important to ensure the plan remains a dynamic one that supports the TQM process.

Supplier Certification

Supplier certification is vital to the program. An organization cannot produce quality goods and services if it is receiving low-quality materials, goods, and services as the input to its operation. This is true in any organization although I would hesitate to call the input in the education system low quality. Perhaps *undertrained* would be a better phrase in that case.

There are many benefits of a sound supplier certification program that is conscientiously carried out as routine. The receiving organization can expect improved quality of received goods and services, reduced prices, increased satisfaction with received goods, and improved working relationships with the suppliers and vendors. Combined, these factors develop long-term commitments with shared research, development, and training which increase quality and reduce costs and variation. This leads to increased business and profits because the organization is recognized for quality goods and services.

The supplier benefits because of the increased business and long-term commitments that improve its competitive position. It also benefits from improved working relationships and shared research, development, and training. The suppliers can expect increased profits because of the recognition for quality.

Customers share the benefit through improved quality products and services with the attendant increase in satisfaction. They also benefit from reduced prices, long-term commitments, shared knowledge, and improved relationships.

Requirements

The requirements of a supplier certification program vary with the type of supplier or vendor and the products or services supplied. Serious consideration must be given to a certification program of some kind for all suppliers whether they be products, components, or services ranging from engineering to janitorial services. Quality is important in every area. Areas appropriate to each vendor or supplier can be selected from the supplier certification list provided to aid development of the subsections of this program.

1. Zero defects vice acceptable quality level.

2. Records and documentation.

3. Quality verification.

4. Process control.

5. Process improvement.

6. SPC.

7. Supplier rating procedures.

8. Supplier ratings. Guidelines for certification ratings (lowest to highest) are as follows:

   a. Approved supplier status.

   b. Qualified supplier status.

   c. Certified supplier status.

   d. Preferred supplier status.

Note: Each supplier's objective should be certification as a preferred supplier. The certification steps for each level must be determined by the receiving organization or customer. Actual certification steps are beyond the scope of this program because they vary from one organization to another.

A process for decertification also should be developed. This process should be available for presentation to potential suppliers and vendors during the discussion of possible business. When presented in a nonthreatening matter-of-fact way it serves to highlight your commitment to quality and the quality commitment expected from the vendors supplying your organization. The outline for developing this section follows:

1. Conditions for decertification.

2. Warning of possible decertification.

3. Decertification.

4. Procedures for recertification.

Customer Service/Customer Relations

This section is crucial to TQM because the emphasis is on quality customer service. Quality-oriented organizations continually sample their success in these critical areas. The potential feedback can originate and should be required from every part of the organization.

- Marketing
- Manufacturing
- Engineering
- Shipping
- Finance
- Contracts

From this feedback the organization can determine:

- Customer quality requirements
- Customer desires
- Customer needs
- Customer strategic plans

Every employee should receive both initial and regular follow-up customer quality service training. Every training session should highlight the need for attention to detail, continuous process improvement, and all the benefits that accompany them.

Product quality deployment must be a part of every quality organization. Each of us must continually strive to develop and produce quality products. Every effort is made to ensure peak quality service through *service supreme*. We must produce product features the customer needs and will use.

The Awards and Recognition Program

No section is more important for success in a TQM process. As Dr. LeBoeuf says, "You don't get what you want, need, or desire. You get what you reward." The awards program is limited only by the imagination. It does not have to be an elaborate program to be successful. People need to be loved, accepted, and recognized. It is a measurement of their worth as individuals. People do not do what an organization or other people want them to do, *they do tasks that will reward and recognize them*. Therefore, rewards and recognition must be the foundation for a successful awards program.

As stated, the awards program does not have to be an elaborate, expensive program. Many companies are restrained by finances, but that isn't a problem. Often simple is better. The suggested objectives of the award program follow.

1. To express the organization's appreciation for superior performance.

2. To stimulate continued superior performance through a recognition program.

3. To improve morale in the quality environment through recognition.

4. To encourage all members of the organization to participate by thoroughly communicating the performance and successes that were acknowledged in the rewards program.

5. To stimulate a united, "we are a team," environment between management and the work force that will willingly tackle the quality and production problems.

Six different types of awards usually are a part of the TQM process.

1. Group public recognition.

2. Individual public recognition.

3. Private recognition.

4. Certificates, letters, trophies, and other nonmonetary awards.

5. Monetary rewards.

6. Financial compensation packages.

Group public recognition is the most effective recognition for team-building. It creates a sense of belonging and improves organizational loyalty. The ways of recognizing group performance are limited only by imagination. Some recognition methods include the following:

1. Group recognition at employee meetings.

2. Videos about the group's contribution that can be shared with other groups. These provide great incentives for both contributors and would-be contributors. It also can support marketing efforts.

3. Articles about the group's contribution accompanied by photographs printed in company newspapers, trade journals, and local media. This action is a great morale builder and excellent publicity for the organization.

4. Group mementoes such as pins, pens, calculators, tie tacks, ball caps, and jackets.

5. Recognition lunches and picnics with top management. Additional media coverage can be generated with these affairs.

6. Team plaques for specific contributions to display in work spaces or some common area.

7. Special company-sponsored training programs above the normal organizational training program.

8. Sponsorship to technical conferences or symposiums.

9. Visits to customers to see how the contributions help customers.

Individual public recognition also is important where one individual made a contribution above and beyond that which is expected. There is no limit to individual recognition. Some ideas follow.

1. Promotion with an official ceremony in front of peers. Many companies, military organizations, and other groups find the ceremony the most effective individual reward.

2. Other employee recognition at organization meetings.

3. Videos, news releases, and write-ups in organizational newspapers, trade journals, and the local news media.

4. Improved office spaces.

5. Organization-sponsored vacations or meetings where family also can attend.

6. Training programs that benefit both the individual and the organization.

7. Annual conferences, especially those where additional recognition is given.

8. Plaques, jewelry, clothing, etc., that recognize the contribution.

9. Customer visits and/or supplier visits.

10. A major award board located in a common area so everyone can see the contributor's "Hall of Fame."

Private recognition also can be an important reward under the right circumstances and they can be used to support both team and individual public recognition. Some ways of doing this follow.

1. A personal letter sent to the contributors' homes thanking them for their efforts. This letter can be used for individuals or groups.

2. Thank yous by members of the management team.

3. Thank you cards sent to the contributors' homes, enclosing a restaurant gift certificate for two.

4. Personal notes on reports, suggestions, and letters thanking people for their input.

5. Acknowledgment in performance appraisals. Special appraisals that note specific accomplishments are especially appreciated.

Nonmonetary awards prove supportive of both team and individual efforts. Ideas for nonmonetary awards abound at businesses that sell these items. Some possibilities include:

1. Specialty catalogs and shops have ideas for cups, clothing, jewelry, and similar items.

2. Trophy and plaque shops have all kinds of appropriate samples.

3. Printing shops have a variety of samples for certificates, standard awards letters, and similar terms.

Monetary awards can be a strong part of the rewards program. Categories can be developed for suggestions, team contributions, training programs, and patents. Some specific contributions to be considered include:

1. Scientific or engineering contributions, especially those above and beyond the normal duties of their job.

2. Patents.

3. New concepts and ideas for process and performance improvements.

4. Training programs that support in-house training needs.

5. Marketing successes by nonmarketing personnel.

6. Professional or commercial achievements.

7. Prevention awards in such areas as the safety program.

8. Managerial and leadership excellence, especially that which builds successful, high achieving teams.

9. Ideas that generate economic savings.

Potential types of monetary awards that should be considered include:

1. *Savings bonds*–Bonds support the United States, and they carry a face value at maturity that is twice the purchase price.

2. *Cash*–Cash is especially liked by employees for many reasons.

3. *Bonuses*–Bonuses are excellent tools as long as the requirements are well-known and the size of the bonus is equivalent to the contribution. This also is true for cash awards and bonds.

4. *Company stock*–Provides employee ownership and pride. Some businesses require employees to purchase stock as a requirement for initial hiring. The belief is that people commit to performance in organizations where they own a piece of the action.

Financial compensation packages that reward employees for *exceptional efforts* can be supportive of TQM. Rewards that connect performance and pay are most beneficial for all concerned. These are listed, but additional study through the HRM manager is recommended before implementation because when used incorrectly rewards can be a negative factor which detracts from TQM.

1. Commissions.

2. Employee stock plans.

3. Piecework pay.

4. Gain sharing or profit sharing. The Scanlon plan is an excellent example and is readily available for study.

5. Bonuses for both team and individual.

TQM Sample Award Program

1. Quarterly award

   a. Savings bonds—winner (team or individual)

   b. Certificates for section runners-up

2. Criteria

   a. Originality

   b. Human resource utilization

   c. Asset utilization

   d. QA results—impact

   e. Customer satisfaction/service improvement

   f. Production impact

   g. Potential value to customer:

      (1) Savings

      (2) Quality

      (3) Time

      (4) Product/System Improvement

   h. Potential value to organization

      (1) Customer satisfaction

      (2) Quality

      (3) Increased business

      (4) Cost reductions

3. Review panel

   a. TQM manager

   b. Quality council

   c. Department heads

4. Eligibility—all teams or employees other than panel

5. Awards

   a. Quarterly awards—end of March, June, September, December.

   b. Annual

6. Cut-off dates—fifteenth of the award month for quarter awards and first day of last fiscal month for annual awards

7. Format—recommended

   a. Current situation—outline procedures, problems, etc.

   b. Effects of current situation

   c. Potential solutions

      (1) Possible negative impact of each drawback

      (2) Value of each

   d. Recommendation with any additional reasons

   e. Benefits for

      (1) Customer

      (2) Supplier

      (3) Our organization

8. Certificate–Keep it simple

   a. Certificate for participation in the TQM suggestion program

      (1) Name of participant

      (2) Description of suggestion

   b. Signed by committee chairperson and/or the organization president, and dated.

9. Letter from organization president—congratulations and thanks for the support.

Summary

1. This chapter provides an outline for the construction of a quality manual. A minimum of five separate sections are recommended: philosophy, internal quality, supplier certification, customer service/customer relations, and awards.

2. The philosophy section would include the organizational motto, its philosophy concerning quality, and the policy it will follow in the pursuit of TQM.

3. Internal quality concerns quality control, quality assurance and the TQM plan. It outlines the various people and groups who will support TQM and the processes that take place.

4. The benefits of supplier certification are discussed. This process benefits everyone involved. The requirements list details the various aspects of a certification process.

5. Customer service and customer relations are important to the TQM process since it is customer-focused. Feedback is important from each department.

6. The awards and recognition program is extremely important for the success of TQM. A comprehensive program is outlined in this section.

Bibliography

Branch, M. C. *Comprehensive Planning—General Theories and Principles,* Pacific Palisades, CA: Palisades Publishers, 1983.

Crosby, P. B. *Quality Is Free,* New York: McGraw-Hill, 1979.

————. *Quality Without Tears,* New York: McGraw-Hill, 1984.

Deming, W. E. *Out of the Crisis,* Cambridge, MA: Massachusetts Institute of Technology Center for Advanced Learning, 1986.

DiPrimo, A. *Quality Assurance in Service Organizations,* Radnor, PA: Chilton Book Company, 1987.

Ellis, D. J. and Pekal, P. P., Jr. *Planning for Nonplanners,* New York: American Management Association, 1980.

Garvin, D. A. *Managing Quality,* New York: The Free Press, 1988.

Gitlow, H. S. and Wiesner, D. A. "Vendor Relations: An Important Piece of the Puzzle," *Quality Progress,* pp. 19–23, January 1988.

Hagan, J. T. *A Management Role for Quality Control,* New York: American Management Association, 1968.

Harrington, H. J. *The Improvement Process,* New York: McGraw-Hill, 1987.

Hayes, G. E. *The New Challenge,* Wheaton, IL: Hitchcock Publishing Company, 1985.

Ingle, S. *In Search of Perfection,* Englewood Cliffs, NJ: Prentice-Hall, 1985.

Juran, J. M. and Gryna, F. M., Jr. *Quality Planning and Analysis,* New York: McGraw-Hill, 1980.

Juran, J. M. *Juran on Planning for Quality,* New York: The Free Press, 1988.

Kacker, R. N. "Quality Planning for Service Industries," *Quality Progress,* pp. 39–42, August 1988.

Liberatore, J. A. "Supplier Team Adds Values for Customer," *Quality Progress,* p. 43, February 1990.

Melcher, B. H. and Kergner, H. *Strategic Planning: Development and Implementation,* Blue Ridge Summit, PA: Tab Book Inc., 1988.

Morrisey, G. L., Below, P. Jr., and Acomb, B. L. *The Executive Guide to Operational Planning,* San Francisco: Jossey-Bass Publishers, 1988.

Parson, M. J. and Culligan, M. J. *Back to Basics Planning,* New York: Facts On File Publications, 1985.

Randolph, R. M. *Planagement,* New York: AMACOM, 1975.

Sloma, R. S. *No-Nonsense Planning,* New York: The Free Press, 1984.

Stursberg, P. A. *One-Day Business Planning,* Radnor, PA: Chilton Book Company, 1988.

Townsend, P. L. *Commit to Quality,* New York: John Wiley and Sons, 1986.

Walton, M. *The Deming Management Method,* New York: Putnam Publishing Group, 1986.

CHAPTER 10

Quality Teams

This chapter concerns the development and employment of quality teams in the TQM process. Remember, some work groups may not develop into teams that can solve performance problems. It takes well-trained, committed people who are dedicated to continuous improvement while functioning as quality teams.

The differentiation between work groups and teams is important. Groups can be any assembly of two or more members while teams are work groups with common goals and resources working together in an effective manner. Teams provide a division of labor that comes together with specific skills which, when used together, multiply the potential for results. Relatively minor inputs from one member may develop into a significant contribution when the idea is worked over by a team. This multiplication of effort is called *synergism*.

Successful teams exhibit five common traits not found in other work groups.

1. *Common purpose*–Team goals are developed and take precedence over individual goals.

2. *Joint effort*–Everyone pulls together toward common goals.

3. *Straight talk*–Communication is in terms of, "Here's the way it is without hidden agendas, bickering, or behind-the-scene power struggles."

4. *Commitment to each other*–People respect each other for their performance and what they contribute. It has little to do with liking each other, although that is a bonus.

5. *Respect for the team leader*–The team leader is respected for knowledge, skills, and leadership ability that is provided the group. It has little to do with liking the person, although that helps. The leader builds this respect from mutual trust, openness, and the desire to support subordinates.

Quality teams laboring together against a common process enemy share common experiences that provide a greater appreciation for the struggle for continued performance improvement. They realize that the subject can be complex and difficult to grasp. For a team bent on success, this tends to make the victories sweeter.

Perhaps these highly beneficial entities would be better named performance teams because they do work on both factors in the performance equation, quality, and production. However, we will stick with quality teams because that is the name they have already acquired in practice.

Quality circles are not discussed as a major part of this training. This is not a put-down. Quality circles are an effective entity in the situations with which they deal. Quality teams are presented because they include managers with access across operational lines. This important difference, management membership and interdepartmental access, makes a significant difference in the types of projects that can be successfully tackled and the assets that can be brought to bear on the problems.

Management participation is extremely important. Most quality problems are either management-*caused* by placing production priority over quality; out-of-date process methods and equipment; low investment for capitol equipment and little emphasis on performance; or management-*allowed* through acceptance of poor quality; poor or no training on process or quality; inattention to the quality process; ignorance of quality processes themselves; and/or dereliction of duty. Therefore, management must be an integral part of the solution process or there will be no solution.

Many managers and administrators are not educated on quality and the TQM process. Ignorance of quality and quality teams is not a problem if it is admitted up front so that all parties concerned can work toward training and solutions. There must be a concentrated effort to overcome these shortcomings with everyone involved realizing that quality is a lifetime evolution and not a quick fix.

Workers apart from their work groups will tell you that they believe in quality and would like to be able to put more effort toward production of higher-quality products. The problem they face occurs when management places emphasis on throughput or quantity rather than performance that includes quality and production. It is a simple matter to induce measurement standards and controls in most work environments so workers in all organizations can measure both productivity and quality. Currently production is the dominant concern in too many organizations, and workers perceive whatever is emphasized as important.

Leadership Requirements

Several leadership-based requirements exist within successful quality teams. These are outlined as follows.

1. *Visionary leadership*–The leader provides a quality vision. Team members must know the mutual benefits of a quality operation. This includes where the team plans to go; the commitment level of team members, team leaders, and the organization; and the potential for reward when they reach that target.

2. *Participative or delegative leadership styles*–Leaders must exhibit the willingness to share equal idea input with an agreement to let everyone accept a level of responsibility for team output. Where possible, individuals or subgroups are delegated portions of the effort.

3. *Drive*–The leader must exhibit personal drive and be willing to pull others to use their fullest potential. Most individuals operate far below their potential unless this type of leadership is evident.

4. *Positive supportive environment*–The working environment must be one of mutual trust and support built with open communications up and down the chain. Leadership builds the supportive atmosphere through agreement, understanding, and cooperation. Every effort is made to reduce or eliminate conflict. Training supports every aspect of TQM, and there is a shared time consciousness that endeavors to get today's work out today.

5. *Interdependence*–Performance requires team members to work together for an end product. No one has all the required skills to finish the product.

6. *Energy*–The leader must exhibit energy and a willingness to work well beyond minimum expectations.

7. *Commitment*–The leader and every other team member must be committed to performance improvement which is evidenced through quality, productivity, customer service, and training to meet needed requirements.

8. *Creativity*–Performance improvements demand creativity. Continual change is required which demands that every member stay tuned into innovations and ideas that will improve process and performance. The leader serves as a facilitator to bring out the creative ideas of each participant.

9. *Excellence*–Leaders produce excellence and demands it of their teams. Nothing less is acceptable. Team members cannot be allowed to simply get by or survive. They must produce excellence.

10. *The teams must contain people with a stake in the final outcome*–The leader and each individual must have some part in the process and see a benefit, or they seldom put forth the additional energy necessary for performance improvement.

11. *Responsibility*–The leader never forgets who is ultimately responsible for the team's success.

12. *Communication is natural*–Honest, considerate, and positive communication creates a climate of trust that searches for answers and finds them.

13. *Focus*–The leader retains focus on the task at hand and applies the team's total energy to the solution.

14. *Change-oriented*–The leader understands and thrives on the fact that growth and the future depend on change.

15. *Action attitude*–Leaders insist on putting ideas to work to solve assigned tasking. They maintain a "roll up our sleeves and get at it" attitude.

16. *Rapid response*–Immediacy is a byword. Identification and action on problems and opportunities is *now*-oriented.

An Overview of Quality Teams

Quality circles provide the basis for quality teams. They operate as a small group of workers from a common work center who meet voluntarily on a regular basis to analyze problems of that work center and recommend solutions *to management*.

Quality circles have proven several things. No one knows more about the work being performed than the work force performing that work. Employees want to produce quality and share a desire to solve the quality and performance problems as they see them. Workers know the value they receive from producing quality goods and services—their jobs depend on it. Given the opportunity and support, quality circles can solve the problems that occur on the shop floor.

Quality circles tend to have shortfalls, although they are not evident in every situation. They are structured and that goes against the traditional concepts of many American workers. They tend to create a we–they attitude between quality circle members and workers who are not members of quality circles. Nonmembers may view members as arms of management. Quality circle members and managers may be at odds because managers are faced with solutions they had no part in generating. Some labor organizations are not interested in their members being involved in quality circles. In the United States, there generally is a low volunteer rate for quality circles.

Studies indicate the highest quantity of problems are solvable at the work level while the highest dollar value problems are solvable at the management levels. This serves as further evidence as to the value of management participation. Quality teams have replaced quality circles in many American organizations which now accept the concepts of the work force assisting with performance improvement. This team idea builds on the concepts of "my company," and "we are all in this together," and attempts to involve 100 percent of the people. It utilizes managers and workers who have a stake in the outcome. This turns the *we/they* into *us* for at least the duration of the team. Management personnel empowered to make decisions are required in the problem solving/solution process.

Team makeup often crosses departmental lines to reach all players. This allows for faster action at a more involved level. The concept of quality teams has the potential for 100 percent involvement if input is solicited from every department which has something at stake in the outcome.

Teams generally are nonvolunteer so they reach people who would often decline to volunteer for quality circles. Because managers are a part of the team, the need for quality presentations to management concerning the problem–solution process is eliminated. Employees want to have job input, but do not seem to be challenged by their current efforts. Studies indicate the overwhelming majority believe they could be significantly more effective on their jobs than they are at the present time.

Quality teams can be a solution to performance problems, but some questions must be asked. If they cannot be answered affirmatively, quality teams may not be the answer and performance could suffer because of team involvement.

1. Do the executives and managers readily support the quality team concept?

2. Are these executives and managers supportive of participative and delegative leadership in team situations?

3. Will the organization support the training requirements for successful quality teams?

4. Will the organization benefit from quality teams and their efforts?

5. Does the organization's efforts require quality teams because of inter-dependence of tasking?

6. Will the efforts of the quality team be accepted as a general rule?

7. Does organizational leadership have the energy needed to power high-performance quality teams?

There are many positive aspects of quality teams. Additional resources become available to solve common problems. People or groups from many parts of an organization can come together on a project that benefits the organization as a whole. Participants become more willing to undergo training and grow together. Individuals have a vehicle to use their particular talents to improve the organization while leaders have the opportunity to grow in both technical and leadership areas.

Each participant has the opportunity to become a team member jointly responsible for an effort with deadlines, contribute to solving problems, share in the rewards, and celebrate the *success*. The organization benefits from better utilization of people and assets, newfound talent, and better processes for quality, production, and customer service improvements.

There also is potential for negative results. Leadership and management problems may be highlighted. Building successful teams takes time and resources; the organization may be short of both commodities. Team efforts and recommendations may not be compatible with the organization's structure. Team members occasionally have hidden agendas which detract from potential team performance. The organization may find it cannot support the team at the level the team wishes and does not desire or is not able to sufficiently reward the team.

Several concepts are necessary for building quality teams. Teams must be kept to a workable size, preferably four to eight individuals. Those who are affected by the team's efforts should be represented on the team. Team members must be carefully briefed and receive continuous updates on quality operations, services, and products. Training, including proper orientation, must be planned ahead and carried out over the course of the team's existence.

Project agendas are developed early and supplemented by agendas for each meeting. Reports are completed for each segment of the project followed by an after-action report when the effort is completed. Determination is made at the outset concerning how long the team will exist even if this date has to be revised later. Communications tailored to the team efforts are a challenge. Team challenges, progress, achievements, and final success should be communicated widely. This motivates the team and may persuade others to join in team efforts.

Rewards must match results. There is little incentive to continue the extra effort required to improve performance if there is no reward and, even worse, if there is a potential to work yourself out of a job.

Team leaders generally are the senior manager or a designate. There are other means, that are covered later. Leaders must be flexible and remember that every teaming exercise will be a learning experience and a strong test of their leadership ability. Team morale is an all-important factor fueled by the leader's vision, enthusiasm, positive mental attitude, integrity, and service to the team.

Barriers to Teamwork

There are several barriers that prevent united efforts. They restrict the team's effectiveness. Discussing them should help prevent their impact on most teams.

1. *Grabbing credit*–A common problem occurs when the leader or factions of a group take credit for the group's success. Coach Bear Bryant provided guidance to prevent this situation. His theory was, "When there are failures, *I* was responsible; where the effort is just satisfactory, we did that; and when the effort was superior, I'm so proud of their accomplishments." The leader never has to take credit for a project. People will assume his leadership was responsible, whether good or bad.

2. *Playing favorites*–This can occur without the leader being aware of it. Selective input is one cause of this barrier. The input of some participants is listened to while that of others is not. Some people may have more usable ideas, but the team should listen to everyone.

3. *Poor followup action*–The black hole theory is one where ideas funnel into a black hole (the boss' office) and are never heard from again. The all-talk problem occurs where plans are always being talked over with no follow-through action. The mushroom syndrome—kept in the dark and fed manure—is a common one found in many organizations.

4. *Procrastination*–Another performance preventer is the procrastinator's work savers—putting off starting until . . . . This is closely related to indecisiveness, "Maybe yes, maybe no." The leadership rule is, "Do something, even if it's wrong."

5. *Dealing in personalities rather than performance*–Some leaders make the mistake of dealing in personalities rather than contributions. This is not to say abrasive people must be accepted as they are. It means that even people with less-than-lovable dispositions can provide significant performance improvement suggestions and efforts.

6. *Killer phrases*–Negative comments or judgments kill participation, which is the key ingredient of teamwork. Several of these killer phrases follow.

- "We've never done it that way before."
- "We're not ready for that."
- "That's just too radical."
- "We'll never sell that idea."
- "We do all right without it."
- "We could never meet that schedule."
- "Who would buy that concept?"
- "We never did it that way before."
- "We must be realistic."
- "It costs too much."
- "That's not my job."
- "Get serious."
- "We don't have time for that."
- "That's not our ball game."
- "We don't have the experience."
- Any statement that ends in "but."

7. *Leadership failures*–Leadership failures erect barriers that prohibit TQM. Many of these are rooted in personalities, which can be changed. The aloof, arrogant individual who is insensitive to others' needs has little chance of gaining team cooperation. Another fault is the person who follows personal objectives that are at cross-purposes with the team or the organization.

8. *Conflict and performance problems*–Many managers are hesitant to handle conflict and performance problems. Too often these problems are overlooked as if they didn't exist. This is a certain way to enlarge the problem and occurs when situations are allowed to continue without attention.

Some managers have difficulty as they endeavor to develop teams. There are some common reasons for this. They do not provide a vision with goals, plans, and strategies. They may try to manage people, instead of leading them. Their ineffectiveness leads to strained working relationships both within their team and with other leaders within the organization, including their boss. Any of these traits in a leader can devastate team-building efforts.

The team leader must be trained to understand and accept the role of both leader and facilitator. Both roles are important. Team leaders learn a sequence for quality team problem solving–decision-making. They should be trained on team building, leadership techniques, and the proper ways to handle meetings. All of these factors find considerable importance in team evolutions.

Developing the Quality Team Foundation

There are many difficulties to overcome before teams can become effective in the quality battle. Turf protection is one area that adversely impacts on team efforts. It breeds infighting, which prohibits solid solutions, prevents interdepartmental cooperation, and promotes compromises that are not the correct answer to the situation. Another problem in this area is the tendency to fix blame rather than problems. Blame is not important, improving performance is and must be the common goal of all participants.

Teams must be carefully selected so they share common goals and objectives or they will not function. The leader encourages them to establish common goals, priorities, and work load distributions for the projects on which they work. Group interaction is most important to the team structure.

Members must be oriented to the team and understand that each individual is important to success. This requires them to understand why they were chosen, so they realize they can make an important contribution. The team must have interests that coincide with the team membership. Prospective members who are not interested in the projects that will be tackled and see no benefit in contributing to these efforts will not become contributors. Without contributions, there will not be true membership.

Mutual trust is another important ingredient that builds teams. Trust promotes openness and frankness, which encourages two-way communications. Truthfulness is mandatory because without it, members will withhold information that is required in the execution of team duties. Trust is not a static function. Rather, it is a dynamic function varying according to the displayed leadership and the team's makeup. All members must work to understand each other's needs. This requires a sharing and caring attitude. Team effort can be prevented by one individual—the proverbial apple spoiling the barrel. This cannot be allowed.

Certain questions to members must be answered with a "yes" for mutual trust. Will this group maintain confidentiality? Is each group member committed to the task, or will the leader make sure those not committed are removed and replaced? Are all members now technically competent and are they willing to improve themselves to meet emerging needs. Will I be accepted by this group as an important and equal team member? If so, can I meet their expectations? Am I willing to immerse myself in self-development programs where required?

Goals must be established and clarified. Areas where there is latitude are defined and priorities are established as task assignment understanding is reached. When the group establishes the goals, the group must define the exact goals and subgoals with parameters, establish priorities, and define each person or subgroup's individual contributions needed including their personal goals.

Meeting schedules are then agreed on as required. A means must be developed to clarify issues. Brainstorming is one way this can be accomplished. All issues must be discussed without finger-pointing and each must be resolved. The exact requirements of groups and each subgroup is established including deadlines, asset limitations, and final product parameters. The leader should then list the potential results of success in terms of "real benefit to you" for each participant. Some of these could be experience, awards, training, improved potential for promotion, and the opportunity to showcase one's talents.

Direction is important in team development. Every meeting agenda covers success to date, roadblocks that come up, and concrete ways to overcome roadblocks. Additional assignments and potential schedule or asset requirement changes are discussed along with any additional help that subgroups may need, and who can provide this help.

Ownership must be established for all assignments. Tasks and assignments that are not owned by specific groups probably will not receive much attention. It is "somebody else's job" even though the somebody has not been established. A good way to establish ownership is to ask questions. "How can you help with this problem?" or "Who has the knowledge or skill to do this?"

The leader must continually ask the following personal questions:

1. As a team do we properly understand the direction we must move in?

2. Are we heading in that direction?

3. Will our time schedule of events get us there in time?

4. What are the potential roadblocks we may not have previously seen or understood?

5. Are additional assets required?

6. If so, can we obtain these assets?

7. Are we functioning as a team or are we simply a group working together?

8. Are we improving as a team?

The leader continually promotes superior performance through leadership excellence. Strong leadership provides vision and training which result in success. Each member feels team membership, the team needs each member, and need fulfillment occurs. Team members feel the need for excellence and understand the value for superior performance which encourages their need to contribute.

Encouragement and the need to contribute by each member promotes synergy, the force where $1 + 1 = 3$. The creation of synergy may not be a concrete function that can be seen. Rather, it is a force that can be felt, but the results can be seen. Leadership and the leader's attitude has a great deal to do with the synergy level and the resultant performance improvement.

Individuals get caught up in the action when they experience success. Personal contributions may then be at a level far above what their previous ability seemed to be and often they are more creative. They feel a need for higher personal performance because of the high performance of their teammates. Success breeds success. Each small success fuels the desire for bigger successes. At this point, synergism is reached in most cases. Strong leadership must be maintained. Every aspect of the team's effort must be tracked, coordinated, communicated, and completed.

A cycle becomes evident in team development. It begins with problem recognition and closely follows the problem-solving outline. Data are collected and analyzed. The data are shared and the confirmation of the problem is checked. The causes are determined and an attempt is made to uncover any hidden problems. Data are summarized into three categories: items the team can work on; items the team cannot handle, but some other group can; and items that are probably not changeable, at least at the present time.

From this, solutions are developed and are placed on action plans with implementation suggestions outlined. Action plans turn into team plans with leader and team commitment. Team members must react to their individual schedules. Strong communications must continue so each subgroup's activities happen on time in order to mesh with the efforts of other associated groups. Simultaneous operations are coordinated. Roadblocks are communicated so every team member can work to remove them, and newly discovered issues are resolved.

The leader must require accurate progress reports and ensure every subgroup remains informed of overall team progress. The leader continually reviews results searching out signs of resistance and problem areas while tracking team progress against goals and schedules. Enthusiasm and positive mental attitude are generated through positive reports of accomplishment. These are reinforced with the success stories that occur through the team.

Team Development

Team selection is crucial. The composite skills, talents, and experience of this team determines the results its members are capable of achieving. The overall ability of the team, when the group becomes one, will be greater than the sum of its parts. This team's potential can be further enhanced by the subject matter experts within the organization, but who remain outside the team's borders. The responsibilities assumed by the team and individual team members depends on their talents, the tools with which they have to work, and most of all, the leadership in the team and the organization. Their relationships within the team provide the answers to who does what, when, and how. Team and team commitment are dependent on organizational support and the leadership abilities of those people in leadership positions. As in all endeavors that require a great deal of effort, the level of success achieved is almost always directly related to the leadership committed to the effort.

Teams must have access to the correct tools required for each assignment. Volume III provides a thorough overview of mechanics required for TQM and performance improvements and Volume IV covers the training needs. In addition to training and the mechanics, communications is an all-important tool. The environment with its operating rules, principles, and procedures is listed as a type of tool. Tools can be beneficial if there has been an effort to remove the deadwood so it can support the TQM process. The individual talents of team members coupled with the organizational assets provide the means to tackle the existing performance problems. In almost all cases, the individuals within the organization are able to handle almost every problem they encounter. For success, they must be provided the opportunity and be rewarded for their successes.

The team must have the ability to outline each project in terms of what the project is and who owns what part(s) of the project. Some parts of the project may not be initially expressed or understood. Task leaders may not know exactly what is needed when projects are undertaken, but that may be clarified as they proceed. Often this is the case in the efforts of quality teams. This requires the team leader to stay on top of each project to assist members when new information becomes available.

There is often resistance when teams are formed. Many people have never been a member of a successful team, and there is fear of the unknown. Perhaps they have experienced a poor or unsuccessful team building effort in the past. Perhaps a friend told them a horror story about an unsuccessful effort. Other people are afraid their performance will be questioned in front of the group. Many see little personal benefit in team efforts. Time and organizational policy restrictions must be handled above the team level. The traditions of too few people and too much work, poor past performance by management, and lip service (in past efforts), are problems that build resistance.

This resistance can be overcome. It must be confronted with honest answers. If not confronted, resistance will surface later, often showing up as a lack of commitment. Leaders should discuss common resistance factors for the team at initial meetings and explain how each of these problems will be prevented from occurring. They must stress that personal criticism and confrontation of members is not conducive to team development and will not be tolerated. The leader must also establish that any member has the right and responsibility to question any action they believe is destructive to the team.

The team-building agenda should be established and circulated prior to the first meeting. It can then be modified at the meeting. The agenda answers many of the following questions that impact on the team and its performance.

1. What business are we in?

2. What are our goals for:

   a. This session?

   b. Our team?

   c. The organization?

   d. Each individual?

3. What are the strategic plans as they apply to this team?

   a. One year

   b. Three years

   c. Five years

4. What is expected of this team?

5. Who will make the decisions for this team?

6. Who will be chosen and how will they work with other organizational groups?

7. What are the problems we will tackle?

8. What are our relative strengths and weaknesses?

9. How will we receive feedback on our recommendations?

10. Make sure there is time for an extended session.

The First Session

The first meeting session of the team is extremely important. It sets the tone for future meetings and establishes the leader's credibility. The operation of this meeting is outlined because of its importance.

1. The team leader is in charge even if a consultant is part of the exercise.

2. Cover housekeeping details such as breaks, lunch, etc.

3. Review and allow for changes to the agenda.

4. Discuss characteristics of an effective team.

   a. Discuss common goals.

   b. Discuss commitment to goals.

   c. Discuss commitment to each other.

   d. Team members identify strengths and assets and are willing to use them.

   e. Willing listeners.

   f. Work for successful communications.

   g. There is a climate of trust.

   h. Differences of opinion are encouraged and they are freely discussed.

   i. Conflict is surfaced and resolved.

   j. The team routinely critiques its performance on:

      (1) Its agenda

      (2) Its goals

      (3) Its team

   k. Flexibility is a byword.

   l. Energy is directed toward problem solution rather than internal conflict or competitiveness.

   m. Mistakes are treated as learning exercises.

   n. Membership equality is a byword.

5. Discuss conditions for a successful team.

   a. Leader must lead and provide vision.

   b. Each member must acknowledge the leader's position.

   c. Leader and each member must be committed to the team effort.

   d. Each member must accept responsibility for the team's success.

   e. Each member must continually critique her own performance and that of the team.

   f. Each member must meet their obligations and commitments.

   g. Each member must understand successful teams are built over the long term through:

      (1) Action planning

      (2) Implementation

(3) Evaluation

(4) *Hard work*

6. Cover the agenda–Ensure notes are taken. There could be a different note taker/recorder each time.

7. Decide who will draft the report of the first meeting.

   Note: (1) This will be a requirement of every meeting.

   (2) The report preparer and recorder are in power positions.

8. The leader must answer these questions after the first and every succeeding session.

   a. What unexpected problems came up at this session?

   b. Were these problems solved effectively?

   c. How was conflict handled?

   d. Was feedback provided to those involved in conflict?

   e. Was there a spirit of trust?

   f. How was the session valuable?

   g. How could it have been improved?

   h. Was satisfactory progress made on the problem?

Getting Past the First Session

Difficulties arise when meeting schedules are established. Travel schedules, conflicting demands, and sick or vacation schedules get in the way. Such is life. They must be worked around just like any other situation. Subsequent meeting dates should be established at each session. Only bonafide emergencies will then be reason for schedule changes. A good rule to follow says training and quality meetings will not be changed or cancelled without permission. Too often meetings are changed for relatively insignificant reasons until everything gets in the way of them and the process grinds to a halt.

A few people may attempt to monopolize meetings. Volume III, Chapter 1 provides the means to handle this and other situations that occur when teams meet. The leader exerts positional authority to give everyone a chance for input. If the leader is a problem, it should be discussed with him outside of the meeting by a team member or members.

Initial meetings may lack structure, but an agenda will alleviate most problems. Providing just the right amount of structure to ensure the agenda is met without impacting on the level of discussion can be a problem. Any difficulty in this area should be discussed in the meeting. Time should be allotted for each topic on a "not-to-exceed-this-amount-of-time basis." When it goes past this time limit, there is a good chance that more preparation is required. Should there be group consensus, a topic discussion could run longer than planned, generally based on real progress being made.

When bickering erupts, it is the leader's responsibility to take charge and stop it. Often there are underlying reasons in addition to disagreeable people for this type of problem. It is better for the leader to explore this problem early on in an effort to ascertain the underlying problem. This bickering must be overcome rather than pushed aside or the group will not become a team. If it can't be overcome, it is probably better to replace one or more of the bickering parties.

There are other session problems. At times, leaders make deals with individuals outside of meetings. This can defeat any team building attempt. Other group members wonder why one or some members receive preferential treatment. They also will be concerned that the group is meeting for the sake of meetings and not for real problem solution. It is better to conduct team business as a team. There may be times when a leader and a team member have business outside of the team effort, but care must be taken so that it does not appear to be anti-team maneuvering.

The leader may run into a period where her leadership is questioned. This is not bad. Often it is the sign of a high-performance group looking for any indication of team weakness. There are several things the leader can do. The first is in the way of prevention. Constant application of the tactics discussed under visionary leadership help prevent serious problems in this area. The leader must be aware of the strengths and weaknesses of team members. By deferring to team members when discussion topics are in their strength areas, a sense of teamwork is encouraged. The team is more productive, and members certainly feel better about the leader.

The challenge may be distasteful, but it can be a positive factor. Only when the team feels strong will they be open enough to challenge the leader. Strong leaders move through this opportunity and carry the rest of the team with them toward the goals.

Team Requirements

Leaders must take the initiative in all matters that pertain to performance as seen by their teams. Being bosses is not enough. They must encourage and train members, oversee their efforts, and offer encouragement.

Communication is critical. Communication builders include openness, empathy, and equality of participation. The leader and the team must be problem-oriented instead of personality-oriented. Leaders carefully describe their personal thoughts and those presented by others, "I see it this way and wonder how you see it," or "Jack, you feel that . . . and that is an understandable position." Listening is an important skill for all members. The leader must enforce listening so everyone can participate.

Communications barriers must be carefully avoided. Manipulation through communications with hidden motives is a problem. Judging actions is another problem. Statements such as, "You are wrong." hamper the efforts to get everyone committed. This happens when a person suggests to another what the problem is. They don't dispute it and the person then judges performance or problems based on off-hand judgments. Projection of an air of superiority causes immediate problems: "My thoughts are better than yours." Certainty is another misguided effort: "I know what's happening, so don't confuse me with facts." Attempts to control alienate others: "I'll tell you how to do that." Indifference can cause just as many problems: "It just doesn't matter to me what you people do."

Problem definition is important. Look at the problem as it is given and analyze each problem for broader implications.

- What is the problem?
- What created it?
- Who owns it?
- What are they doing about it?
- What else has been done?

Discuss the problem creatively. Look at it from all angles. It is important to change parameters so the problem can be diagnosed from many angles. Some techniques include narrowing possibilities, broadening possibilities, and adding or subtracting from the original situation.

The problem solution steps are outlined in Volume III. A brief recap is listed here so the chapter can stand alone.

- Gather facts.
- Redefine the problem.
- Generate ideas for solution.
- Evaluate the ideas.
- Combine ideas for solutions.
- Generate a *best* solution.
- Generate an implementation plan.

The next step is the creation of an action plan. Action plans are encouraged to handle situations that need correcting. Action plans have proven to be an effective tool when they are carefully developed and conscientiously followed.

Achieving Results

Members from every department or group that has ownership or knowledge of the overall process become a part of the team's knowledge bank. In this context, a quality team can have members from most departments. There can be and often are full-time members who have ownership supplemented by part-time members who have special knowledge about some specific area. Each must be empowered to work on specific problems. Special teams may be disbanded when a specific problem is corrected. This does not mean their quality efforts are complete. All teams should work on other problems, and may unite together on other situations.

Usually, team leadership is known when the quality team is empowered. The senior person responsible for the problem's correction has real ownership. She is supported by a designated subordinate who is appointed as a team leader. The person is probably a leader who has experience in the problem area. Quality teams often uncover problems that can be decided on the spot. The decision-maker is part of the team. Teams are balanced with optimists, cynics, and pessimists. Such balance tends to force deep thinking and long-term workable solutions.

Quality teams are part of a process rather than a program. The term program suggests a plan with a beginning and end. TQM is not like that. Rather, it is a process which is an open ended evolution bent on evolutionary quality reform.

Quality teams receive high-level support often lacking in quality circles because management is a part of the team. Leaders receive the initial training with quality teams. This is training that also supports other aspects of their job. By definition, quality teams involve everyone. It is understood that commitment will vary, but the goal is 100 percent involvement to benefit everyone. Quality teams tackle three important areas of quality problems: worker initiated/controlled, management initiated/controlled, or system initiated. In labor situations where labor leaders block workers from joining managers, managers may join the workers.

Overcoming Team Problems

Getting started and maintaining order can be challenging. Preparation of an advanced agenda with time schedules by topics is important. It should be circulated among team members for additions and deletions ahead of time. Publish a final agenda one day before meeting. Allow time for discussion of team rules and guidelines, then follow the agenda.

The boss may be the problem. He may be a domineering, know-it-all, who also lacks leadership ability, or he may be a procrastinator who is indecisive.

Regardless, the boss often is unaware of the problem or misunderstands the severity of his problem. There is a tendency to be hesitant about confronting the boss. Members may fear reprisal because of the shoot-the-messenger approach to any criticism, no matter how well intended. One might like and respect the boss and not want to ruin a relationship. Or, it may be believed that it won't do any good and one is just asking for trouble.

Diplomacy always is required and action is demanded for success of the team. Discuss it with the boss one-on-one with no other observers. Approach the discussion with the sincere desire to help the boss and the team. Listen. It has amazing power. Give advice only if asked and keep advice impersonal. Never disclose the meeting or its outcome to anyone. To do so is a breach of ethics and when you are found out, your actions will be remembered.

Problematic members may be disruptive forces who offer negative comments about the project and participants. Some individuals block progress without reason. These people attack the thoughts of others by attacking the person. They vote against ideas everyone else agrees with and refuse to follow through on commitments. They may miss meetings without reason and be a disruptive force when they attend. No matter how these people are viewed, they are problems that must be overcome.

Some questions must be asked. What does this person add to the team or the organization? How does this contrast with what he detracts from the organization? Should we get rid of him? If so, how?

Confrontation is the only way to handle the problem. This would first entail a confrontation between the leader and the problem person. Do it in private when possible. "Praise in public—reprimand in private." Privacy may save the leader considerable embarrassment.

Confrontation also is a possibility between other team members and the problem person. This keeps the problem from appearing as the boss' personal bias. Confrontation must be positive and controlled. It begins with a description of the problem behavior. Identify the negative impact and present the consequences of this action. Ask for cooperation. Often this settles the issue.

The leader also may limit the troublemaker's participation to listening during the meetings with any input coming after the meeting. The leader can assign additional responsibility. The person may have valid comments and she can be assigned an additional project which often encourages people to "put up or shut up."

The meeting "clam" may be a member with the most potential for contribution yet he is hesitant to add anything. Call on the person in his area of expertise. Assign a report or special assignment. Ensure that person knows before the meeting if there will be areas where he will be asked to contribute.

Some people tend to lead the team away from the agenda. Politely remind them of agenda subject and time constraints. Seek to solve one item at a time.

Ask how the new turn of discussion ties in with the subject. If relevant, it may be best to go with the flow. If not relevant, but worthy of discussion, request permission to put it on a future agenda.

The leader is responsible for meeting control and success. Team efforts are a test of one's leadership ability. Quality demands commitment by all team members. The contributions of the team are limited only by its vision and the leader is responsible for the team's future vision.

Who Leads?

Most often, quality team leadership follows organizational lines. The positives are that the section manager and team leader are the same person. This person has the most to gain or lose with the team. This provides emphasis on success. This manager also would be a member of his boss's quality team which should improve information flow, accountability, and support for team efforts.

There can be drawbacks when the manager's leadership style has been directive instead of participative or delegative. Quality teams demand more.

Managers may select assistants to lead in their absence. Managers may already have a full schedule with insufficient time to lead a team properly. In this case, there is no best method to select assistants, and it is an extremely important process. Several possibilities are presented; however, trial and error may prevail. Team leaders are the quarterbacks of quality teams. Organizations must demand the positions be filled with the best leaders, those who are committed to quality.

This person may be selected by management based on proven leadership ability. The positive aspect is that the person is chosen for leadership ability and would have management support. Management could ensure the person had the proper amount of time. Management support of the leader's program legitimizes the program. It would free up the manager's time. The leader may be more acceptable to the work force. The leader would have an opportunity to showcase her abilities.

There are drawbacks. The work force may consider the person a management mouthpiece, which would mandate he walk a tightrope between management and the work force. Without adequate support from management, this leader would automatically be in a losing position.

There is a third method promoted by some organizations. This is a co-leader situation with a manager and a work force representative. We don't recommend this because if everybody is in charge nobody is in charge. However, the idea is presented because some swear by it. The positive benefit is that management and work force are represented in leadership positions. It can accommodate travel schedules and provides the possibility for considerably greater energy from the leadership position.

One drawback is that shared leadership positions are inherently difficult. If the manager dominates the team, it could mean loss of the work force input, and if the work force representative dominates, it could mean loss of management support.

A fourth method is election of the leader. The positive advantage is that there automatically is support from a majority. The elected leader would be intimately known by the team. As far as the work force is concerned, an undesirable would not be elected.

There are drawbacks here, also. Democratic elections often elect people for wrong reasons. Elections become popularity contests, or the person is selected because of leadership ability on the bowling team.

Employing Teams

There are many ways to employ quality teams successfully. The first way is along the lines of organizational chain of command. Teams are comprised of that operation's managers, supervisors, and work teams. These teams then receive training as a team. This is an effective way to begin quality teams. Members become familiar with other members of their work team in a different manner. The leadership can exhibit their commitment to quality through training, carrying it over to the job.

When teams train together, the leader then knows what level of knowledge team members possess. Assistance can be provided during training which often helps the leader discover areas of strength and weakness. High-performance military teams practice as a unit because of the camaraderie and trusting relationships that develop.

This is a valuable way to implement quality as the normal order of business. People soon search for anything that can negatively impact on performance in their area. It should be no surprise when members begin searching through reference works for the answers to problems they encounter.

Members of work centers may become members of quality teams apart from their work group. Subject matter experts may be called upon to solve a problem that occurs in another part of the operation. This is valuable use of quality teams. Members can bring the experience they have gained in their areas to problems in other work centers. Combined with the experience and knowledge of others, all grow and become even more valuable when they return to their own work groups.

Often team members are requested to assist with the training of other work groups in some special area. Quality teams from one area or operation may be used to audit some other part of the operation. Both training and audit experience broadens the knowledge of individual team members.

Some organizations are now using the trained quality teams who have been successful to train groups from other organizations. The 1990 Baldrige award winners were unanimous in their praise for previous winners and other high-quality organizations for the training they provided and other assistance they received from them.

Quality team participation should be viewed as an assignment and not strictly voluntary. Everyone must become involved in the performance improvement process. Projects should be assigned to teams when the idea for the project was not forwarded by a team as its own project. Every problem must be tackled by somebody and assignment places responsibility on someone, thus producing accountability.

It must be understood that teams cannot simply look at problems and solve them. Team meetings will be involved, information must be gathered, and only then can the problem-solving process begin. Volume III is entirely dedicated to this process.

A tracking system must be put in place so that projects can be tracked effectively. Without tracking, progress may be nonexistent and projects can get lost through the cracks.

Actively tracking projects leads to the final comment. The tracking system will show where teams are stymied. At this point help must be forthcoming or the team will generally stagger around until it surrenders. Organizational leadership, members of the quality council, and subject matter experts can assist the team.

Assistance is a key word here. The project should not be taken away from the team unless all else fails. Helping the team through its current dilemma can be the best of all possible training. The idea here is to help the team help the organization.

Quality Team Rewards

Rewards are discussed in several chapters, but because of their importance additional comments are necessary. Quality team recognition is extremely important if success is to continue. It reinforces team activities, a crucial concept. It precludes separating some individuals for rewards at the expense of others.

Prompt rewards are important for success. Rewards not promptly awarded lose effectiveness. People forget the reason for the reward. Teams lose interest when promised rewards are not forthcoming. Rewards to successful teams can be great motivators to other teams, so it is important to cash in on this benefit early.

High-level personnel should present awards to increase the importance of the awards. The higher the executive, the more effective the reward. We all thrive on attention from the top. The higher the level of the person presenting the award, the bigger the reward appears.

The personal touch is most important. Warm, hearty handshakes are appreciated by all team workers. Each person should be queried about her achievements. Pictures of the presentation are especially appreciated and are good for publicity. News releases to internal organs and to the news media make people feel good and are the best publicity an organization can receive. Bulletin boards serve well for achievement notices and not just routine announcements. Members of the quality council should be given wide recognition for their successful efforts. Create achievement notices for the bulletin boards. It is catching!

A quality celebration to end the year is a rewarding concept. The potentially most important reward is the change in corporate culture. The work force becomes more organizational and quality conscious. Management becomes more aware of the potential for contribution by the work force and the value of a participating work force, especially as it applies to quality. Performance, as measured by improved quality and increased production, is ensured.

The following teamwork exercise can be used to assist team leaders in their initial efforts with their teams. It gets individual members thinking about teams they can relate to and the achievements they had.

Quality Teams—Where Should We Be Headed?

The value of quality teams cannot be overstated. As organizations continue to improve, they place greater emphasis on their quality teams and the value they hold for the organization.

Most organizational problems could be resolved at the level of front-line supervisors. Most aren't, not because of capability, but because of built-in structural roadblocks which preclude them from doing so without permission from above. Doesn't this tell us that this first supervisory level should be the leader of the quality team where the problem exists? Doesn't it also show a need for removing the rules and regulations that hinder performance improvement before we begin team efforts?

Through this program we learned how to progress with our people through the situational leadership styles to the point where delegation becomes a standard method of doing business. We studied empowerment so that the teams were provided the power and authority to handle more and more projects and decisions at lower and lower levels. Continuous training prepares people for greater achievements.

This alludes to an often unseen benefit of quality teams. The continuous exposure to new ideas and concepts—working through situations that weren't even considered previously and training each other on the various topics that come up—increase the knowledge and skill levels of all active participants. It also focuses attention on the importance of the internal customers within an organization. Exposure across department lines brings a new awareness to the organization and, as teams work together, a new commitment to cooperation.

Based on all these factors, I don't believe it is possible to even perceive how far properly trained and empowered teams can go. The two greatest limiting factors will be:

1. The self-confidence level of management which will either hinder team performance or support teams to prosper through delegation.

2. The limits placed on the rewards and recognition system that pays the involved teams for the performance improvements they create.

Hold it Newt—We're Not Finished Yet

Any discussion of teams cannot be considered complete without answering a final question, "Are teams always the way to go?" The answer to that must be, "No." When an individual has the capability to handle the situation, teams make no sense at all. In fact, the members would be in each other's way. Attempts to use teams in situations where an individual can handle it equally well or better amounts to team overkill and can easily result in long-term problems and ineffectiveness in areas better-suited to team utilization.

Few individuals are willing to give up their total identity to the team. Each person has unique needs and wants, some of which are not supported by team concepts. There must always be a place for both team work and individual efforts within an organization. These efforts must be supported by management and positive results must be accompanied by both individual and team recognition and rewards.

Teamwork Exercise

1. Briefly describe a team of which you were a part.

2. Our accomplishments included:

3. The team was effective when we:

4. The group was ineffective when we:

5. List some of the benefits when a group operates as a team.

6. Everyone is a leader. List some actions you can take as a leader to foster teamwork.

Summary

1. Quality teams are an important part of the TQM process. They get individuals working together to overcome the performance problems they encounter in their work centers.
2. Successful quality teams require sound leadership. They must also have common goals, interdependence, and commitment to quality.
3. Quality teams are an American outgrowth of quality circles, which also was an American concept. Quality teams are generally nonvolunteer and attempt to get everyone involved. Quality teams must be formed for every department and operation in the organization or the organization will experience limited success in the TQM process.
4. Three separate barriers restrict the implementation and operation of quality teams. Generally, these are the same factors that impact on any leadership situation.
5. Quality teams do not just happen, they are carefully developed. Team training, orientation, and mutual trust are vital to team development.
6. Team meetings are an important part of quality team operations. The basics for quality team operations meetings are covered with hints to make these meetings effective.

7. There are many ways that quality teams can be employed. They follow normal chain of command lines and function within their work centers. They can be made up of subject matter experts from many work centers who will work on problems throughout the organization. There is no limit to the way they can be successfully employed to support TQM.

8. Quality team rewards for quality team successes are a critical factor which encourages ongoing participation in the TQM process.

Bibliography

Bennis, W. and Nanus, B. *Leaders, the Strategies for Taking Charge*, New York: Harper and Row, 1985.

Blake, R. R., Mouton, J. S. and Allan, R. L. *Spectacular Teamwork*, New York: John Wiley and Sons, 1987.

Buckholz, S. and Roth, T. *Creating the High Performance Team*, New York: John Wiley and Sons, 1987.

Burns, J. M. *Leadership*, New York: Harper and Row, 1978.

Crosby, P. B. *Quality Is Free*, New York: McGraw-Hill, 1979.

———. *Quality Without Tears*, New York: McGraw-Hill, 1984.

Deming, W. E. *Out of the Crisis*, Cambridge, MA: Massachusetts Institute of Technology Center for Advanced Learning, 1986.

DiPrimo, A. *Quality Assurance in Service Organizations*, Radnor, PA: Chilton Book Company, 1987.

Garfield, C. A. *Peak Performers*, New York: William Morrow and Company, 1986.

Geneen, H. *Managing*, New York: Doubleday, 1985.

Heany, D. F. *Cutthrough Teammates*, Homewood, IL: Dow Jones-Irwin, 1989.

Juran, J. M. and Gryna, F. M., Jr. *Quality Planning and Analysis*, New York: McGraw-Hill, 1980.

Juran, J. M. *Juran on Planning for Quality*, New York: The Free Press, 1988.

Katzan, H., Jr. *Quality Circle Management*, Blue Ridge Summit, PA: Tab Books, 1989.

Quick, T. L. *Quick Solutions*, New York: John Wiley and Sons, 1987.

Schatz, K. and Schatz, L. *Managing by Influence*, Englewood Cliffs, NJ: Prentice-Hall, 1986.

Townsend, P. L. *Commit to Quality*, New York: John Wiley and Sons, 1986.

Team Building, Blueprints for Productivity and Satisfaction, Alexandria, VA: NTL Institute for Applied Behavioral Science, 1988.

CHAPTER 11

Managing Change

Change can be threatening and may scare people when it isn't understood. Some people look the other way and pretend it isn't happening. Worriers sit and watch it happening, wringing their hands while they pray something will intervene and slow things down. Others smile and calmly announce, "Might as well learn to live with it. There isn't anything we can do about it." Some individuals try to control change by wrapping themselves around it, dragging their feet trying to halt that which they don't understand. Still others try to understand change, endeavoring to forecast what the change means in terms of opportunities, visioning themselves into position so that it can be harnessed for organizational benefit.

The latter area is where everyone must be as we strive to improve performance through the TQM process. The power to constructively use change to support the transition to an organization of excellence comes from two factors: *knowledge,* which allows us to use change for continuous performance improvement, and *desire,* which provides the initiative to lead our organizations to operate differently. This chapter provides the basis of understanding for both of these factors. The good news is that your people are waiting for the process to begin because they either see other organizations changing around them or they see circumstances developing that mandate change or a different style of living they are not ready to accept.

There are a great many causes of change that impact on all of us. Offshore competition is changing the way we compete in the global markets. Our textile industry is hard-pressed by foreign competition. The semiconductor business and steel industry are in the same fix. Thirty-five percent of the American automobile market was lost to foreign competition in the last

10 years while manufacturing lost 25 percent of its markets during this same period. Many individuals have lost high-paying jobs in these sectors and others are threatened. Change is definitely affecting us all, negatively in these instances.

At the same time, the United States is creating jobs at a rapid pace. Manufacturing facilities that are being closed by the giants in manufacturing are being reopened by others and are surprisingly successful. The Geneva Steel Plant in Utah was closed by USX and sold off because it was no longer competitive for all the reasons commonly offered. Two years later Geneva is thriving, its 2,600 employees are producing steel for the United States, Japan, Belgium, and Argentina. Their clean air and water standards surpass federal agency requirements, and they are installing new equipment to produce higher performance. They share their wealth with employees through profit sharing which can only improve worker commitment to Geneva.

Management practices in some organizations prevent this kind of breakout into the future. Unwilling to experiment, they stick with familiar ways of operating, familiar products, and familiar markets. Nor do they expect changes in their people. Conformity to "our way of doing business" is demanded. They continue to fight outsiders who expect their operations to move into the future in terms of EPA requirements, personnel policies, and so forth. TQM has little hope of survival in such operations because it is a process designed to improve our performance into the future, not learn how to live with the past. This requires change.

The current profit situation stops some organizations from installing quality even though TQM is a proven performance improver that quickly pays for any initial outlays. The investment in current facilities or ways of doing business precludes many from seriously considering any kind of change. Others have a psychological commitment to existing organizations, processes, and/or products which chains them to the past when they should harness themselves to the future.

Union resistance to such change must be managed. Union power and survival can depend on changes that are made. Many distrust the hidden motivation for the installation of TQM, and in too many cases, unions can point to an organizational track record that would demonstrate reason for concern.

Many fear change of any kind because it has the potential to disrupt their lives. Some individuals consider TQM as a process that will improve performance to the point where they work themselves out of a job without any reward for doing it. Organizations see quality improvements strictly in terms of the cost of implementation. They remain ignorant of the benefits in terms of performance improvement and customer service that can be achieved.

The need for performance improvement is the driving force behind change, but often this need is ignored until circumstances are overpowering. The last major oil crisis prompted Americans to want small economy cars. American companies stayed with large cars of questionable quality, maintaining profit per vehicle. Americans switched to Japanese manufacturers for smaller, fuel-efficient, quality vehicles. Now 35 percent of the vehicles sold in the United States are of foreign manufacture, which robs our nation of a considerable amount of tax revenue necessary to support schools and services.

A great many errors result from neglecting change. Things seldom remain the same; they get better or worse, move up or down, and go slower or faster. Business examples abound. The belief that yesterday's solutions are right for tomorrow's problems sinks many organizations. Detroit's failure to pioneer smaller vehicles of higher quality led to a huge market loss. Eastern Airlines' refusal to buy jets when they first came out led to a market loss from which it had difficulty recovering. Pennsylvania Railroad experienced the same sort of problem. Instead of seeing itself in the broader concept of a huge transportation network, exploiting those opportunities, it remained a railroad and disappeared. In the short term, each stand appeared correct, but the true nature of the problems these companies faced (because they didn't adapt to the times) soon became apparent.

The potential opportunities for new products and processes remains hidden for many. Examples abound where people met constant refusal of their ideas by major organizations until someone finally helped them develop and market the ideas. At that time those products became instant successes. J. C. Penney's five and dime concept was presented to the store owner, where Penney first worked. He pleaded with this owner, but could not prevail. He started his own business based on his theory of selling inexpensive products with a high turnover rate and the rest is history. The owner who had turned Penney down discussed it later and said he believed it cost him millions of dollars for every time he had turned down Penney. Another often-quoted example concerns Chester Carlson, who finally found acceptance for a new idea with Haloid after DuPont, IBM, Kodak, and others had all turned Carlson down. Carlson persevered with his idea, and Haloid become Xerox. Faster copiers were indeed a worthwhile invention. Changes in priorities, attitudes, preferences, wants, and desires continually create new markets for new products.

Misunderstanding the nature of change is one of management's biggest problems with the most opportunity for disaster. Bringing ideas to market ahead of their time can mean outright rejection of that idea. Witness the sleek, aerodynamic Kaiser vehicles in the early 1950s. Although they led the change in this direction, they did not find acceptance themselves. Another example is when someone quits before the need is fully developed. International Harvester withdrew its pickup and four-wheel-drive lines just as the market went wild for these vehicles.

We must assume that little in life or business will remain unchanged for long. There must be a refusal to simply ride out changes as we learn to harness change as a partner to improve our organizations. Currently, the greatest competitive advantage most organizations can gain is in performance improvement. The benefits of productivity improvements have been long understood and now the benefits of quality and customer service also are becoming extremely evident. These will come about only through change.

The Changes Managers Face

Change marches on swiftly. Technology is rapidly changing life as we know it. There are all kinds of spin-offs from the space programs. Lightweight materials, food products, medicines, and a new understanding of the planet are just a few changes. Fiber optics are improving human lives in many ways. Lasers are used for both eye operations and smart bombs, thus saving and destroying.

Computers are changing the face of all organizations. They help sort, calculate, and store vast amounts of information which might otherwise be lost. They also can generate so much information there is no way to digest it all. In real estate, computers quickly provide information on all aspects of the property being considered, and they are rapidly expanding into nationwide networks providing services that weren't even considered a few years ago. Manufacturing examples abound. Computer-aided design/machining (CAD/CAM) changes the way all kinds of products are brought to market. Robotics assisted by laser sensors, ultrasonic probes, automatic welding, and automatic testing procedures change the face of manufacturing operations.

Changes are taking place with government rules and regulations. Those in government would have you believe they are removing red tape, making it easier for businesses to compete. Those outside of government see a never-ending stream of paperwork that limits, controls, and confuses.

Policies, procedures, rules, laws, and standards rapidly change the management environment. Regulations concerning the handicapped are changing building design and construction techniques. The need for additional restroom facilities for women finally has been recognized, and this need is being incorporated into design. The change in smoking rules also impacts on design and requires designated smoking areas. Sexual, racial, and ethnic bias regulations impact heavily on the way people are hired, discharged, and promoted.

Training requirements change rapidly. One third of the American adult population, or 75 million Americans, are either functionally illiterate or only able to read and write at the most minimum levels. Some organizations are *dumbing down* their operations so less-educated workers can handle the jobs. Others are now working through this problem with new order training programs to elevate workers to the point where they can meet modern quality, production, and manufacturing requirements. Human relations also are receiving more favor as workers are trained for better adjustment in the work environment.

Technology is aiding training programs as computer-driven training, interactive videos, advanced simulators, and improved training practices are employed to help Americans learn new skills and knowledge. Simultaneously, our education system is suffering for a lack of all of these and is turning out more illiterates each year; the number of high school dropouts is staggering.

Consumer demands are changing rapidly. People want a variety of quality products at the right cost. They demand convenience and choice in the services they use. They also demand quality customer service, which is changing the way organizations respond to customer need. They have learned the power of the dollar as they buy from the businesses that produce the quality, style, choice, and convenience they want at the price they can afford and with the service they demand.

American organizations now compete in a global market with new competitors appearing almost daily. These same American corporations shop around the world for materials, products, technology, business partners, and labor. Communications technology makes unbelievable amounts of information instantly available. Technology gives all organizations the potential to continually become more competitive and those who don't use it likely will pass out of existence.

Working conditions are changing as more attention is paid to the working environment. Noise, dirt, and pollutants are systematically reduced. Managers are learning to lead, rather than boss. Workers participate in manager–worker integrated performance teams, which rapidly improve production and quality where they are applied. Workers are gaining freedom to change operations and processes at their level, which produces immediate improvements. Organizations realize the importance of rewards and are integrating these into their quality plans.

Management is progressing to flatter organizations that more readily adapt to the TQM process. Managers are learning and using different leadership styles. Even more important, they are becoming more in tune with their work centers as they lead implementation of quality systems. This reflects a new importance paid to human relations within the work environment. It does not signify a total giveaway of management authority or responsibility. Union negotiations have progressed to give-and-take bargaining sessions based on organization needs and worker wants. Both must be considered for long-term survival in this new global economy.

Great emphasis is being placed on work force participation in all areas of many organizations. A measurement of how far this is going is the number of union members on corporate advisory boards, a trend introduced at Chrysler. Management is becoming increasingly aware that people doing the work are best qualified to improve it. Decision-making powers are being pushed down to the lowest possible level. Management now has examples of how worker participation improves job satisfaction and commitment to the organization. They can see the work force as it is, a tremendous resource pool of ideas and energy waiting to be unleashed. Participative programs, such as quality circles, performance teams, and quality teams, are active groups gaining greater acceptance. Specific examples include IBM's PRIDE (People Responsibly Involved Developing Excellence) and Goodyear's EI (Employee Involvement) programs, which are producing results in many areas.

Workers' beliefs about job security are changing as new contracts contain worker protection clauses. Leisure time gains importance with each passing year and some would have us believe the work ethic is changing. American workers, however, are still the most productive in the world and getting better. Sure they want their quality of life to be better than it used to be. Why not? Isn't that the American way? We can continue to have this improving standard of living if we develop ways to improve performance continually. Isn't that the major challenge we face?

Change Facts

Change is a *balance* between the stable environment required for normal productivity in the past and the ability to readily adapt to global demands for high-quality products and services that are desired in the marketplace. New technologies and information processing systems change the way operations and processes are handled throughout all kinds of organizations. The changes are the results of pressures from the market, work force, management, government, and various special interest groups. For some the changes are painful, for others welcome, but in the long run everyone will benefit by the tremendous emphasis on quality products, services, and quality of life. Hopefully, this demand for quality will pressure educational systems to follow the march to quality.

Change is providing significant improvements on a great many fronts. It also may make things worse if great care is not taken to ensure progress. Murphy's Law still seems to impact on our efforts.

Response to change is an attitude. How you see change will determine how you face it. Those who consider technology a godsend and work to harness it for good search out the changes that will improve their organizations. Others view most technology as the potential for environmental disaster. Many people would like to go backward in time to a simpler life. They have a problem of major proportions because time will not be turned back.

Visionary leaders' existence depends upon change. They paint the picture of a positive future with its benefits for all, which can only occur through change. This provides the needed energy for change.

Other leaders focus on controls and outcomes rather than employee concerns, believing that most employees will fight change anyway. The resulting problems include short-term change gains followed by long-term resentment. Cooperation disappears and the work force allows problems to happen because it sees no benefit in preventing them.

A third type of leader focuses too much attention and energy on work force concerns about change and not enough on the creation of vision which would eliminate much of the worry generated because of change. Problems include the loss of momentum for change, poor employee leadership, and projects that tend to flounder. As outlined in Volume I, leadership success demands a combination of leadership styles tailored to environmental needs at the time.

Solid change demands careful planning with inputs from all levels of the organization. Carefully timed action steps support change implementation. This requires answers to the who, what, when, where, and why.

1. Is our organization's leadership prepared to lead the change effort?

2. Do we have our organization primed for planned changes?

3. Is our organizational structure ready to support change?

4. Do our team members have the right mix of skills to make the changes happen?

5. Can we be reasonably sure the implementation process will be successful?

6. Are the required organizational people properly committed to the planned change?

7. Are our resources sufficient to meet the requirements of change?

8. What other questions should be asked?

Reaction to Change

Resistance to change can be anticipated. The form such resistance takes depends upon leadership actions and the people who are involved. Many workers fear personal loss of security in the form of job loss or potential salary and benefit reductions. Often this is accompanied by loss of status, especially when layers of management are flattened or there is a reorganization. Many workers fear job title, responsibility, and authority reduction. Pride and satisfaction can suffer if they end up with a job that doesn't use their knowledge or skills. They may lose freedom if procedures, policies, or a new boss rescind authority to make management decisions. Working conditions could change if they are moved to a small office or an undesirable job site. Loss of friends can accompany these changes if a physical relocation to another area is involved.

Requirements could increase with the change leading to resistance. The change might be accompanied by a need for more education, training, or knowledge. More energy and effort could be required to meet emerging requirements. This may not be readily accepted, especially if it is perceived as a wasted effort or a speed-up process designed to extract something for nothing from the workers. More paperwork could accompany change and this is not greeted with a great deal of enthusiasm. Many current improvements are accompanied by an increased use of MIS equipment. Learning to operate this equipment can be traumatic for many. Increased span of control with increased responsibility almost always accompanies flattened management structures. This change is more readily accepted if it is planned for ahead of time and the involved people can see some reward for their extra efforts. Likewise, TQM takes additional effort and commitment to change and all involved must be prepared for these challenges.

Change may cause more harm than good if the work force is not confident in the early stages. Often this is prevalent when there was no input from the rank and file or lower management, or this group perceives top management doesn't know what is happening on the shop floor. There also will be resistance if there is no perceived need, "Things are okay the way they are," or no benefit, "What's in it for me?"

Management attitude can destroy change initiatives. Attitudes that must be avoided like the plague include:

1. "We are the bosses, you are the workers."

2. "Take it, or leave it."

3. "The decision is made—here's the plan."

4. "We make policy, you carry it out."

5. "We're paid to think, you're paid to work."

6. "From our position, we can see the whole picture."

7. "Our positions demand we make all the decisions."

Change surely will meet resistance if the work force does not respect management and previous management decisions. Poorly developed or misunderstood policies cause nearly as many problems. The actions and attitudes of certain individuals and departments can cause great loss of respect for the entire organization, especially if they operate a department key to worker morale such as the HRM department.

Negative attitude can eliminate any possibility for change. This could happen when the work force does not see this change or any change as positive. The lack of input is equally damaging. "If I'm not important enough to be part of the decision, they don't need me for anything else either." Poor communications feeds negative attitudes. The "no one tells me anything" problem causes people to use the grapevine for information. Few positive comments ever travel the grapevine. Gossip doesn't work that way.

Force begets force, the stiffest form of resistance. Some find a need to challenge those in authority for whatever reason: "I won't do it and you can't make me." Others are just obstinate by nature.

Timing is crucial. People tend to resist if they already have significant problems such as completing a major change or current reorganization endeavors. Those facing layoffs and salary or benefit reductions will not be terribly excited about changes that further increase these risks.

It is the leader's duty to separate real reason for resistance from stated objections. This can be difficult. The best way to make this determination is to ask those resisting why they are resisting. When the objections are known, eliminate those objections with known facts. Many would-be leaders fear this one-on-one interaction because it requires a knowledge of people, product, and customer.

Barriers to change can make it almost impossible to institute any new process. Some of the main barriers that affect change include the following:

1. Lack of organizational leadership.

2. Employees are not aware of the goals or are not committed to them.

3. They are satisfied with the status quo.

4. Vested interests in keeping things as they are.

5. Inadequate training for change.

6. Hostile attitude toward the proposed change or those who propose the change.

7. No reward for changing.

8. Threat to security.

9. Lack of organizational support.

10. Poor communications.

Acceptance of change comes more easily when there is the potential for personal gain. Job security may be higher because they are using more of their skills. There could be potential gains in salary and benefits. Status could increase with a new title, position, or authority and responsibility. Pride and satisfaction increase when workers are assigned a job that uses more of their skills and knowledge. There may be more freedom through reductions in procedures and policies, or a new boss may give them more decision-making authority. They could acquire better working conditions through a new office or relocation to a better area with the accompanying new friends and professional contacts that occur with relocation. Leaders must be aware of each of these potential benefits, how they would affect which of their people, and be prepared to point out benefits as they apply. In this process, the leader becomes a salesperson of the highest order.

Some look forward to change that requires more education, training, and knowledge, or an increased span of control and more responsibility. Any increase with the promise of reward will meet much less resistance. Early work force and lower management input and work force perception that top management understands what is happening on the shop floor strongly supports change alleviating resistance which might otherwise occur. Employees also commit when they perceive a need or see a benefit that can be best presented in terms of, "The real benefit to you is . . . ." This should be a part of management's ongoing awareness program which brings awareness of organizational survival, performance improvement, and customer service needs to the shop floor.

Management attitudes that strongly support change and build respect include:

1. "We are all in this together."

2. "This may not be the only or the best solution. How do you see it?"

3. "We see a need for change. We need your input."

4. "Policy is effective only when it meets the needs of those who work with it."

5. "We all hold important positions in this organization. It takes all of us to make things work."

6. "From our position, we may not see the whole picture."

7. "Our positions show we need your input on most decisions."

8. "Our survival depends on the contributions of all of us."

Respect also is improved when management track records and previous management decisions are positive. Positive, supportive policies promote positive attitude, and the work force sees this change and change in general as being in its best interest. Early input tells the worker, "I'm important enough to be part of the decision, I had better make it work." Solid communication allows people to know what's happening from the beginning, especially when official communications beats the grapevine version. The use of sales and persuasion strongly supports the implementation of change.

Workers are more likely to assist those in authority when such assistance is encouraged and appreciated, followed by credit for work force efforts and success. Participative and delegative leadership styles strongly support change because the players are empowered to make changes in the processes of which they are a part.

Good timing supports change. Seek to implement change when things are upbeat. Keep change simple and understandable. Change things when the work force can see it improves competitive positions. When things are tough and demand change, ensure people understand the need and know their personal needs are most important considerations in the decisions which must be made. It is the leader's duty to lead, inspire, and establish a positive example. The way credit is addressed is most important. Someone wrote about the important words in the English language as follows:

Five most important words: "I am proud of you."
Four most important words: "What is your opinion?"
Three most important words: "If you please."
Two most important words: "Thank you."
One most important word: "We" or "Please."

Change generally meets with mixed reaction. Some people are for change, others against change, and still others are neutral concerning change. Some individuals don't seem to care one way or the other. Not everyone resists or welcomes change. Acceptance or rejection can depend on whether the person is an optimist or pessimist, how change is approached, and the expected outcome. Other factors that impact are concerns about the organization and personal feelings about the leadership/management team. Participation is a *most important factor*. People want to be important within the organization. They wish to contribute and they want their ideas considered. Workers like their ideas used, and where they can't be used, an explanation why they are not. When they reach this level of participation, they are strong supporters of change. When they are not a part of the change, there is little chance they will support it and, in all probability, will resist it in some way.

Leading Change

Change will only occur when discontent with the current situation is greater than the fear of change. Change is forced because leaders are dissatisfied with the way things are and decide to change them. Dissatisfaction alone is not enough; each leader must develop the inner drive and initiative to move without orders to do so. To wait for direction is to lose. Leaders must know the boundaries of their responsibility and authority, work to those limits as required, and be willing to expand those limits when necessary. Most leaders would rather rein in their subordinates because they went too far too fast in their enthusiasm to improvement efforts than to have to continually spur them into action.

Evolution of change begins when pressure on top managers makes them discontented with present conditions. Most major corporations relate that the driving force that pushed their decision to install TQM as a process was the will to survive and grow. This push to action is followed by an audit process to determine where the firm is in terms of its competitors, followed by development of plans to change.

Plans to change are designed to overcome the problems they face. Solutions are developed and tried, refined and retried, and placed in operation. Results are analyzed and changes occur as a result. This can be the beginning of an ongoing performance improvement process, or it can be a one-shot deal because "we fixed the problem and should let well enough alone."

Leaders discover there are four times when change can be most readily made: when they are new on the job; when they receive new training; when they have new technology; or when they are impacted by outside pressures such as the market, stockholders, higher management, the government, and the work force itself.

Employees expect change whenever their organization comes under new leadership. In most cases they are not disappointed as can be witnessed at GE when Jack Welch took over. New coaches and managers in sports come under the same phenomenon. Because change is expected, employees seem to accept it more readily as the "new way we will operate."

Likewise, employees expect changes when their bosses receive new training or new technology. They can see it coming and are more receptive to it. They also understand when outside pressure is driving change, their leadership will either change the way they operate or their leadership will change. They know change is coming one way or another and await its arrival.

Leaders may face three separate conditions as they work to implement change. First, there is implementation of change demanded by task requirements with no need to refer to higher authority. Ideas may come from quality groups, performance teams, individuals, and oneself; the decision to change rests with the leader.

The second condition involves the implementation of changes after receiving the go ahead from higher authority and the leader agrees with these changes. The first step is to ensure understanding of the requirements. Necessary team members are prepared for the change and the reason for the change is explained. The leader must be prepared to address benefits, problem areas, resource requirements, exceptional needs, and training requirements. Enthusiasm is an important ingredient of success for the leader facing this condition.

The third condition arises when leaders do not agree with changes demanded from an outside source, including those received from higher management. Choices must be made. They can immediately quit and begin searching for a new position. They may insist higher authority is wrong and demand they change their directives to conform to the realism of the work environment. They could carry out the change, but make sure subordinates know "those idiots in the ivory tower demanded this action."

Any of these choices must be carefully considered because of the obvious implications. Another possible action occurs when leaders provide their thoughts about the advantages and disadvantages of the change and hope for a correct solution. If still overruled, leaders should implement the change as if they agreed on it and support the actions to carry forward. This may be impossible if the proposed action is inconsistent with the leader's values. At that time, she may need to opt for other employment.

All leaders are faced with situations where they cannot agree with a decision, but also have duties that accompany their leadership position and the requirement, in turn, to support the leaders appointed over them. I kept a sign on my wall for many years as a reminder of the correct way to handle this situation.

I expect you to be honor-bound to set forth your views boldly and without reservations until a decision is made. Thereafter your task is to support that decision with all out energy and make it work.

General Shoup USMC
Commandant of the Marine Corps
4 January 1960

Initiating or recommending change depends largely on the leadership style of the boss. Some bosses reserve all decisions for themselves. There can be many reasons for this. The experience level of subordinates or their track records may preclude delegation of the decision-making process until they can be better trained. The boss may have previous experience with subordinate decisions that gives cause for some reservation. Some bosses cannot make themselves let go initially for fear of losing control. Others believe bosses are paid to make decisions. Thankfully, leaders at all levels are moving away from these positions. This move must be made to support the implementation of TQM.

More leaders are allowing subordinates to make decisions because they believe decisions should be made at the lowest level possible to support performance improvements. They believe it is excellent training for subordinates and know people are more enthusiastic and committed to their own decisions. These leaders allow the situation to dictate who makes the decision.

Some deciding factors include the significance of change as determined by cost and scope, and the potential for interference with other groups. For example, a policy change for one group such as flex time would then require action by union, personnel, department, and other groups. Organizational policy often is the determinant as to who can make decisions. Nowhere is this more of a factor than it is in government organizations. Few workers have the authority to make decisions of any consequence. Contrary to what many believe, the military delegates such authority as a way of doing business. Leaders must have both confidence and courage to make decisions and implement change. This courage is based on knowledge of their people's capabilities and their level of training. Within a military environment that level of knowledge is known because individuals must prove their capabilities before they are advanced.

There are many other factors that impact on the leader's ability to handle change in a manner that is to her advantage. The leader's ability to sell both up and down the chain will greatly influence her ability to manage change. It also will determine how effective she is at overcoming the objectives that crop up. She must persist on her quest for support until such time as she receives a definite "no" from above. The leader must conscientiously work to develop rapport throughout the chain of command. Leaders willingly accept the risks attending their position, risks that include their boss' rejection, their subordinates' disfavor, and the possibility of a serious error.

The Change Leader

The change leader tends to think of change in the terms of the benefits that can accrue for all those involved. This requires identification of potential benefits and how they can be incorporated into established plans. This must be balanced against organization needs for profit, growth, and stability.

Change leadership involves the constant demonstration of *genuine* positive mental attitude and enthusiasm coupled with a take charge–can do attitude. Change leaders are doers with a great deal of commitment. They must be empathetic to the needs of their people so they can maintain the support of these people who are vital to the quality process.

Leaders must maintain a high personal energy level so they can channel the energy that is generated with change. Energy is generated by fear, enthusiasm, and ambition. Fear must be controlled. Ongoing concern for the work force and solid communications will alleviate much of the fear. It is important to work out any problems that arise. The leader can't let anything get in the way of his team's performance improvement efforts.

These were the defensive actions taken by leaders. The offensive side of his job requires that he drive the plans that were developed; he cannot allow this plan to unfold. All elements must be tracked and monitored. New ideas and opportunities are incorporated into the plan as they present themselves. The leader focuses activity, coordinating the team's efforts and the assets and resources that are available for use. Success is continually communicated back to the troops and up the chain so that everyone knows their efforts are paying off in performance. The performance management system becomes a leadership tool driving the quest for continuous improvement as the leader learns to use all the tools in the toolbox.

The leader maintains continuous vigilance so that problems and areas that waste time, assets, and talent can be tackled as they arise. Leaders see obstacles as challenges or opportunities to excel. The team is accustomed to solving these problems in a timely manner. It is important that the leader look beyond planned goals for hidden challenges. Hidden challenges and new technical requirements may require direction changes or additional resources. Additional personnel needs may arise. These teams will uncover organizational barriers which the chain of command must eliminate. No task is more important for organization leaders. To overlook any of these important areas is to invite team problems with a corresponding loss of commitment.

The change leader must develop new ways of thinking about change. Each person has personal ideals and fundamental truths that will guide the change activity. Those truths must be based in personal beliefs and ideals, organizational philosophies, and the needs of all personnel involved.

Many find a change planning questionnaire valuable as they undertake the initiation of the TQM process. A sample follows.

1. What is the situation, policy, process, or procedure that requires change?

2. How did this situation develop?

3. What factors are involved in maintaining this situation?

4. Who wants this change to occur?

5. Why do they desire the change?

6. What are my motives for wanting this change to occur?

7. Are these motives consistent with my personal ideals, the organization's philosophies, and the personal needs of those involved?

8. Who can be counted on to support this change?

9. Why and how will they support this effort?

10. Who will probably resist this change?

11. What will be the basis for their resistance?

12. Do I have understandable plans developed that detail the steps for change?

13. Are these plans put in terms of "the real benefit to you" for those who must live with them?

14. Are the common benefits for the organization and the work force clear?

15. Is there room for expression of objections in the beginning of the process?

16. Has the possibility of conflict with current policy, process, or procedure been thought out for discussion?

17. Is there a plan to include the people involved and those interested early in the change procedure?

18. Is there a communications plan to ensure everyone is continually informed of the change situation and progress on the plans?

19. Are the required facts available to create a beneficial and workable plan?

20. Is the exact extent of the change clear to all parties involved?

21. Are the resources available and committed to produce this change?

22. Is there a reward plan for individuals and groups who must carry out and live with this change?

23. Does upper management and the executive leadership support this change?

24. Do I have the leadership skills to complete this change?

25. *Most importantly,* do I have the energy, drive, and commitment to bring about the required change?

Well-defined goals support change. They examine assumptions and values that are used to justify the change, ensuring there is a clear idea of the exact nature of change. Consensus is important for change. This can be achieved by securing input from the involved parties and where possible, including this input in the goal action plan. The goals and strategies are presented in a positive manner so they can win approval by all levels of the chain.

Impact statements play an important part in change. What may appear to be a small change can have broad implications which affect diverse groups. All must understand there will be unanticipated problems and consequences. The statement should answer the following questions.

1. What individuals and groups will be impacted?

2. How severe will this impact be?

3. How will they be involved in the change?

4. How will they benefit from the change?

5. Will they gain or lose resources?

6. Will they gain or lose power, positions, or prestige?

7. What are the trade-offs for any losses?

The impact statement is used in all planning exercises. Another important checklist is one developed to critique the formalized plan on an ongoing basis.

1. Is the change developed in small steps?
2. Is there a concrete plan and goal for each step?
3. Do these plans/goals meet requirements for sound goaling procedures:
   a. Specific?
   b. Attainable?
   c. Realistic?
   d. Rewarding?
   e. Results-oriented?
   f. Time bound?
4. Is the plan personal?
5. Is the plan and its goals adjusted as objectives are expanded or completed and situations arise?
6. Is the plan a dynamic, ongoing vehicle that maintains commitment, enthusiasm, and motivation?
7. Is the communications plan producing desirable results?
8. When gaps are discovered in the plan, are they promptly diagnosed and fixed?
9. Are the required resources available?
10. Are there specific measures for tracking progress?

Implementing and Managing Change

Many separate factors are considered when changes are in the works. These will support the change and secure participation thereby reducing resistance. These are presented in outline format for easy review.

1. Determine the need that may come from:
   a. New customer demands.
   b. New competitors.
   c. New technology.
   d. New market trends.
   e. Management perception.
   f. Investor concerns.

    g. Work force input.

    h. Quality team input.

    i. New governmental regulations.

2. Define the change.

    a. What is required in this change?

    b. What is the potential scope of change?

    c. What are reasonable limits of the change?

    d. What are the time limitations?

    e. What are the asset requirements?

    f. What will be the customer concerns?

    g. What will be the vendor concerns?

    h. What rules, etc., govern the process to be changed?

3. Gather information simultaneous and in partnership with factor number 4.

    a. Convey that we are open to suggestion.

    b. Who knows what about this proposal?

    c. What assets will be available?

    d. What resources will be required?

    e. How does the time frame impact on the current schedule?

    f. How will we maintain what we have while we make changes?

4. Secure participation.

    a. Prepare the leadership team.

    b. Ask for volunteers.

    c. Develop quality teams.

    d. Notify vendors.

    e. Prepare customers.

    f. Sell the plan based on the "real benefit to you."

5. Develop *tentative* plans.

    a. Audit to determine the current situation.

    b. Analyze the results.

    c. Benchmark the competition.

    d. Survey the customer.

    e. Appraise and query vendors.

    f. Cultivate inputs.

    g. Form teams.

    h. Develop commitment.

6. Analyze potential problems and reactions.

    a. Problems will be varied.

    b. Solutions can cover the spectrum.

    c. Reactions will be mixed: for, against, and neutral.

    d. Remain open to change.

    e. Brainstorm.

7. Making a go/no-go decision.

    a. Is change desired?

    b. Are resources and assets available?

    c. Is it worth the price?

    d. Can it be accomplished?

    e. Will it benefit the organization?

    f. Will employees support it?

    g. Will customers use it?

    h. Will it support the goal?

8. Establish timetables.

    a. What can be accomplished by when?

    b. What are the various team schedules?

    c. What are the individual schedules?

    d. Are the schedules compatible with current demands?

    e. If not, what has to give?

    f. Speed may be as important a decision as the go/no-go decision.

9. Solve problems and concerns.

    a. Are our leaders ready?

    b. If not, what do they need to get ready?

    c. What is in our way?

    d. How can it be removed, bypassed, or overcome?

e. Who is in our way? People derail change far more often than do technical problems.

f. How can we overcome their fears, objections, and resistance?

g. Will change acceptance be achieved or will some level of force be required?

10. Implement the change.

   a. Requires continuous evaluation:

      (1) Is our plan satisfactory?

      (2) Are we on schedule?

      (3) How is the resistance being handled?

   b. Has organizational structure been modified to accept change?

   c. Has required training been held?

   d. Is there active participation?

   e. Do our people understand the change?

   f. Are we ready for change?

   g. Are the vendors ready to support change?

   h. Are the customers ready to support change?

   i. Does the change conform to rules and requirements?

   j. Are questions being answered?

   k. Should the decision be reconsidered?

   l. Can the timetable be modified?

11. Work out any problems/overcome customer hesitancies.

   a. How does the customer view the change?

   b. Are customers buying the product or service?

   c. Does quality meet expectation?

   d. Is production sufficient?

   e. Can the vendors keep pace?

   f. What are the problems?

   g. What is being done to overcome them?

   h. Will they interfere with results or schedules?

   i. What resistance has been encountered?

    j. How is it being overcome?

    k. Is additional training required?

    l. Does it help us reach the goal?

12. Maintain performance.

    a. How can we prevent backsliding on gains?

    b. How will momentum be maintained?

    c. Are further changes necessary?

    d. Are we prepared to make changes?

    e. Do we have the assets?

    f. Are our people capable?

13. Evaluate success.

    a. Were objectives met?

    b. Did results exceed expectations?

    c. Was the product or service accepted?

    d. Is recognition deserved?

    e. Are rewards due?

    f. What did we learn?

    g. What would we do differently?

14. System changes.

    a. Are changes required with rules, regulations, procedures, standards, and the like?

    b. Has change responsibility been assigned?

    c. Are the changes being made?

    d. Are both organizational and personal needs considered in the changes?

15. The next step.

    a. What's our new goal?

    b. Does it meet customer need?

    c. Does it meet our need as determined by the goal?

    d. Does it meet the needs of employees?

    e. Does it meet vendor need?

Keys to Successful Change

There must be empathy for those involved. It is important for leaders to place themselves in the shoes of workers, vendors, and customers. They must endeavor to see all sides of the issue. Consider each person individually: will he reject or resent the change, or will he accept and welcome change?

The leader must know each worker individually. Leaders should be knowledgeable of personal data such as marital status, children, education, skills, likes and dislikes, and goals and ambitions. Leaders must be empathetic. Empathy is a learned trait. People will know when you care about them and their needs and will respond accordingly. Learn the backgrounds of a couple of new people each month. One possible way is helping them keep their resumé current. This shows interest and keeps you knowledgeable. Communications is an important part of successful change. It is suggested you review Volume I, Chapters 12 and 13 on the subject of communications as you embark on change.

Participation is vital and must be encouraged whenever possible. Participative and delegative leadership allows more thought and knowledge to be brought to bear on the change. People buy in to change because they had a part in the action. Both participation and delegation must be managed. The limits of authority and any areas managers reserves for themselves should be known at the onset.

Become a Change Leader

Change leadership is important and a simple process, but this does not make it easy. Habits are built over time, and they are not easily changed. Habits have become the preferred way we do things and handle situations.

It is of utmost importance that leaders be willing to change themselves. One cannot demand of others that which one will not do. Self-change requires a concerted effort. It begins with an honest self-appraisal that is difficult at best, but extremely important for leadership success. Once the appraisal is complete, leaders should create personal visions of what they will become, understand what it will take to fulfill that vision, then become the vision. This requires goals and goal achievement that lead to the ultimate goal.

Leaders must prepare themselves for change. Outline your assets and resources. Plan to meet important needs first. Admit those needs and create a personal action plan to meet the change requirements. Integrate change gradually; you didn't become you overnight. Obtain training as the need becomes apparent and seek feedback from others on how you're progressing.

Make your organization into a change leader. Set the personal example by dealing with all the issues, including human, organizational, and technical issues. Allow and support free-flowing information. Help remove information blocks and ensure communications are complete and correct. Never support gossip in any fashion.

Once again, be a visionary leader. Paint the picture for change success and then live the painting. Always exhibit enthusiasm, a positive mental attitude, caring, and empathy.

Summary

1. Change is required to meet competition, technological advances, training requirements, rules and regulations, and consumer demands. These changes will meet resistance for many different reasons.

2. Change is a balance between the stable environment and the need to implement TQM. Change can be painful while it provides many improvements.

3. There are four times change can most readily be made by the leader: when the leader is new on the job, receives new training, has new technology, or when outside pressures demand change.

4. Leaders must learn to implement change they deem necessary, change suggested from above their level, and change demanded from above their level.

5. There are all kinds of reaction to change. Some individuals will resist, some will accept, and others will have mixed reactions.

6. There is a standard process that supports the implementation of change. Some of the key requirements for change are leadership, empathy, and solid communications.

7. It is important that each leader become a change leader. This requires self-analysis and the will to change those things requiring change.

Bibliography

Basil, D. C. and Cook, C. W. *The Management of Change,* New York: McGraw-Hill, 1974.

Bennet, T. R., III. *Planning for Change,* Washington, D.C.: Leadership Resources, 1961.

Carnegie, D. *Managing Through People,* New York: Simon and Schuster, 1975.

Conner, D. R. and Patterson, R. *Building Commitment to Organizational Change,* Atlanta, GA: O. D. Resources, 1981.

Dakziel, M. M. and Schrooner, S. C. *Changing Ways,* New York: AMACOM, 1988.

Fritz, R. *The Path of Least Resistance*, New York: Fawcett Book Group, 1989.

Grossman, L. *The Change Agent*, New York: AMACOM, 1974.

Kirkpatrick, D. L. *How to Manage Change Effectively*, San Francisco: Jossey-Bass Publishers, 1985.

Martel, L. *Mastering Change*, New York: Simon and Schuster, 1986.

Morgan, G. *Ruling the Waves of Change*, San Francisco: Jossey-Bass, 1988.

Odiorne, G. *The Change Registers*, Englewood Cliffs, NJ: Prentice-Hall, 1981.

CHAPTER 12

The Customer Defined

Times are changing. Customers in the United States are demanding quality, variety, convenience, customization, and quality follow-up service. American organizations are becoming increasingly aware of the demand for quality goods and services, and with that awareness comes a certain dedication to produce what the customer wants.

American car makers stand as examples for many manufacturers. They are tuning into the market and trying to produce what the customer desires. General Motors invested billions of dollars in quality systems and training over the last few years in their efforts to produce quality vehicles. Their success is evident. Buick was voted one of the 10 best vehicles in 1990 while the Cadillac division won the coveted Malcolm Baldrige National Quality Award. This is a tremendous achievement that is a tribute to every person who serves on the GM team. This quality consciousness should continue to improve vehicle quality which increases value—more quality for a given cost.

General Motors doesn't stand alone in this attention to quality improvement. Ford Motor Company jumped on the quality bandwagon before General Motors, and many within the auto industry quite openly stated Ford led all American auto makers in quality vehicles a few years back. Chrysler should not be slighted, either. It has invested heavily in quality, safety, style, and more.

Chrysler seems attuned to the need of the American consumer, its customer and sole reason for being in business. It produced the first mini-vans and offered a vehicle that allows Chrysler to lead sales in that vehicle class. It installs airbags on its vehicles produced in America. Additionally,

Lee Iacocca is as outstanding in the marketing end of the business as he has been innovative.

Americans couldn't be happier with this success. Many people, myself included, have remained with American manufacturers even though we realized that for a period of time "made in America" vehicles were not built to the quality levels achieved by many of the foreign competitors. It cost more for a lower-quality product which meant the value was lower. I stayed with American manufacturers out of loyalty because I would feel guilty placing my American flag in the window of a foreign-made vehicle.

It would be easy to point the finger of blame solely at American automakers. After all, they neglected the needs and wants of the American consumer as they continued to produce large gas guzzlers where there was more profit when the American consumer wanted smaller, more efficient, and higher quality vehicles. But that accusation would be unfair to some degree. American automakers have been playing on an unlevel playing field. Just the tax differential between an American vehicle and an import can run $1,000 on vehicles of equal value. This impacts heavily on the American automaker's ability to compete in terms of cost per vehicle.

Shouldn't Americans return to the American automakers now that their quality is on the upswing? Certainly the value of these vehicles as determined by quality received at a given vehicle cost is high and increasing. It would seem that American manufacturers would regain market share with so much going their way.

Unfortunately, it won't be that easy. The most important aspect of their business—*service*—still requires work. The best value won't sell without strong attention paid to quality customer service. Service is more than Mr. Goodwrench providing 29-minute oil changes. One American automaker recently lost a customer who had owned eight of its vehicles in a row, at a time when the quality of its vehicles was significantly improving. How could that be?

This customer purchased a new vehicle from one dealership. There was a safety-related problem with the vehicle, and this customer sought warranty repairs at a dealership closer to his home. The dealer refused service because the vehicle was not purchased there. A subsequent letter was written to the CEO of that organization. The return letter explained that the automaker didn't own the individual dealership and the dealer could reject such work if he so decided. Quality vehicles won't retain this customer. In fact, the person recently purchased two vehicles from another American manufacturer because of this situation.

Another service situation deals with vehicles. A customer purchased a new dual-cab truck. The quality was high, and this person was extremely happy with the vehicle. One small problem occurred with a fastener on the sliding seat. It was plastic and kept coming out. The person wrote the manufacturer a complimentary letter explaining the problem and offering a suggestion. He received a form letter back that didn't address the problem or thank him for the suggestion; another case where an opportunity to resell a customer was lost.

Quality customer service, both internal and external, has been a long overlooked part of doing business. In fact, the customer has been ignored by all types of organizations over the past several years. Businesses aren't the only culprits. Try to work a problem through a governmental organization. Renewing a driver's license can become a major hurdle at times. How well are schools meeting the needs of their customers—the students? By most measurements the answer must be, "They aren't."

Customer service is reflective of quality of product and service and directly reflects how well the organization treats its own employees. People tend to treat customers the same way the organization treats them. This creates problems because most customers do not separate the service they receive from the product or service they purchase. When they are upset with the service, they also become disenchanted with the product.

There is a great need for a quality customer service program that makes every person in the organization aware of the quality customer service (QCS) need. This need must be accompanied by the management drive and enthusiasm to provide the motivation for successful implementation of a long-term program that provides customer service equal to or exceeding the product or service quality that is rendered.

Defining QCS

Just who are the customers and how do they fit into QCS? One of Juran's theses is that every person in an organization is a user, supplier, customer, and processor. We are users or customers who receive unfinished information and products. When our part of the process is completed, we become suppliers and pass the product, service, or information on to another customer.

With this in mind, it becomes necessary to define terms. The following definitions are combinations of those presented in many different works.

1. *Quality*–The dictionary definition is high grade or great excellence.

    There are two determinants of quality: factual quality and perceived quality. Factual quality is achieved through first-time excellence in the production of products and services. This requires *effectiveness*—doing the right things; *efficiency*—doing things correctly; and *timeliness*—completing them on time.

    Perceived quality is the way our customer perceives our people, products, and services. It is achieved by satisfying the customers' needs with the desired product, which meets their expectations for that product in terms the customer establishes. It also means treating every customer with integrity, courtesy, and respect.

Quality also is defined in many other ways, some of which were presented in earlier chapters. One of these standard definitions is conformance to requirements.

2. *Customer*–The quality definition for customer is anyone who receives a product or service from a supplier. The implications of this definition include:

   a. The ultimate customer is outside of the company with the available resources to buy a particular product or service.

   b. A particular worker's primary customer may be the employee at the next desk or work station.

   c. We are all customers and suppliers at various times linked together in a chain that ultimately leads to the external customer or end user.

3. *Supplier*–The quality definition of any supplier is any person providing information, product, or service. The implications of this include the following.

   a. The customer we supply may be either internal or external.

   b. We are all suppliers at one time or another.

   c. Supplying some commodity is what earns our paycheck.

4. *User*–The quality definition is any person or organization that ultimately puts goods or services to the use for which they were designed and produced. This implies there may be intermediate users of the product, service, or information who use the information or add value to it.

5. *Service*–An act of assistance, the supplying or supplier of products, goods, information, or service.

6. *Competitive*–Superior in the attributes the customer places value on in comparison to any other similar product or service offered in the marketplace.

7. *On time*–Meeting the mutually agreed-upon date established by the supplier and the customer.

A few additional comments on quality and quality customer service are in order. The customer/supplier chain is only as strong as the weakest link. Each link provides the opportunity for the addition of problematic situations that determine the overall quality of the product, service, or customer service.

Therefore, any link in the chain has the capability of being the determining factor in the buying decision the customer makes between our product and a competitor's.

Interdependency in this customer/supplier chain mandates that every supplier provides the exact product or service the customer requires. Assumptions are out—the exact need must be known. This requires each supplier to be in direct communication with the customer asking them, "Hey, what do you want and why do you want it that way?" Management must then collect these requirements so the process can be effectively and efficiently aligned to produce those things that are wanted and needed.

Like TQM, QCS is a long-term way of life, not a here today, gone tomorrow process that is discontinued when business picks up or market share increases. Quality service is not always easy, but it is the correct way to do business. Quality involves auditing and critical assessment of work process, attitudes, skills, training, commitment, and other factors that put people on the defensive. This realization is important so that quality assessment may be handled in a positive manner that encourages support rather than hostility.

QCS and the External Customer

Americans have grown cynical concerning the claims of some American advertisers. Too many firms have taken advantage of their customers with quality claims that could not be substantiated. For too long the focus has been on a one-time sale rather than on the development of long-time repeat business. This concept of sales must be replaced by emerging ideas of customer-focused efforts.

This old way of doing business was to produce a product or service that would generate a certain level of income and profit. This product was then packaged in a slick wrapper in the form of an attractive package for products and an appealing brochure for services. There are many examples where the cost of packaging is more than the cost of the product and still more examples if you add the cost of advertising. Check your local stores for examples.

The next step was to plan and execute a well-oiled advertising campaign to *create* a need for the product or service. This concept is market creation rather than market identification. Mass media advertising is a key to success with this scenario. Quality service and need were less important factors than advertising.

The current QCS trend is a reversal that actually is a return to the pre-1960s in many ways. Market research identifies a need. Customer desires and expectations are researched and then a product or service is developed and provided to meet these needs, desires, and expectations. A sales strategy is developed to market the product or service. Ford's Taurus serves as an excellent example. It was designed and built to customer specifications and desires as they were determined by various customer surveys and questionnaires with dealer, service, and sales inputs. By all standards, it is a high-quality automobile rated well by those who judge vehicles, and is an excellent seller now being imported by the Japanese.

In this example, the Ford Motor Company recognized a key fact: customer satisfaction is achieved by producing exactly what the customer wants, when it is wanted, at a price deemed affordable by those who would purchase the product. The customer is always right. Some of the customer's current perceptions concerning quality and service may be incorrect but his viewpoints must be respected for what they are—perceptions of the individual who will be paying for the product or service. The product or service being offered may be quality, but if the customer does not perceive it to be quality or does not like it, the customer isn't going to buy it.

Customers vote on quality through their buying decisions. The product or service may be of high quality by any standard, produced on time, at a reasonable price, in eye-pleasing colors and fabrics, but the customer may not perceive it as quality or desirable. It matters not that procedures attest to the quality and desirability of the particular product; it is the customers' perceptions that have validity. Since the customers have the money we want and need, they will determine perceived quality. That is what gives them all of the votes. It is proper that customers make these decisions because they earned the money to pay for the product or service.

Quality goods or services may be difficult at times to explain, but customers know perceived quality when they see it. At times they make mistakes, but this is another one of their rights because they pay for all the mistakes they make. The implementation of QCS, quality programs, and the TQM process allows us to say we are managing quality. This does not mean we can say quality has been achieved because the customer makes the determination.

The Malcolm Baldrige award program is important to American quality progress, but winning the award does not mean the products produced by those organizations will be certifiable as quality. Once again, the customer makes that decision. In all likelihood, however, when an organization has a well-led program managing quality and quality service, especially those who are good enough to be in the running for the Baldrige award, its customers will perceive it has quality products and services.

This does not mean the customer will buy those quality products. Customers are always making BI decisions. The question becomes, are they *buy* as in take home, or *bye* as in good-bye decisions. Customers expect service. This adds to our definition of quality. It now becomes "quality is conformance to specifications, which means meeting customer expectations." Perceived quality is most important in the final analysis because it ensures customer satisfaction.

This has many implications. Some people are satisfied with products the rest of us think are junk. There are many implications for the value of QCS in this. Quality service is not an extra, it is expected. The highest priority of any business team or organization is to meet or exceed customer expectations of quality through superb QCS.

The Internal Customer

Just as the external customer must be satisfied, the internal customer must receive the product or service required for effective operation. Process effectiveness, continuous process improvement, and employee satisfaction ultimately depend on the level to which the internal customer is satisfied.

Several years ago, a computer programmer designed a program that would tie proposal efforts, cost estimates, job tracking system, billing process, and reporting efforts into one system. Each of these individual processes used much of the same data in one way or another, but each required individual entry for data common to other processes. Such a system would reduce time, eliminate many areas for mistakes, and save a considerable amount of money each month.

The programmer was provided charts to show how the processes were interrelated and asked to discuss the project with the accounting person who would use it. He then programmed the effort, completing it in rapid fashion.

However, accounting personnel hated it and wouldn't learn to use it effectively. During discussions about the problem it became immediately evident what was wrong. The programmer completed the program in the manner easiest for him which made it difficult for his customer to use. He was accustomed to doing things in that way where he was previously employed and was quite insistent on continuing operations that way.

Some discussion occurred before he realized that in the present organization the customer was right. He reprogrammed the product for ease of use and went from being the goat to the hero in a few weeks. Apparently he liked his new role, because future projects were designed for user-friendliness instead of for ease of programming.

Discovering the internal customer network is as simple as asking, "Who gets my work?" Once that is answered there are other questions of the customer: what do you want? How do you use it? What should be different? How can I make it easier for you?

This is nothing new; it's just plain, old, everyday, run-of-the-mill conversation. Therein lies the problem. People are not accustomed to discussing things in such terms. In QCS, they find the following questions must be asked and answered for improved service.

- What exactly do you need from me?
- Am I giving you what you need?
- What do you do to the product your receive from me?
- What can we do together to make things work better?

Employees who work with each other to this extent soon begin producing noticeable improvements. Other processes follow suit and soon the operation improves. It acts much like a neighborhood. When one person fixes up and repaints her home, it makes the neighbors look a little shabby by comparison. Soon the owners on each side invest in a little upkeep. Three houses now look good and the neighbors across the street and on each side work on their properties also. Similarly, improvements in one area of an organization prompts improvements in others and the end performance improves dramatically. The manager's role in this is to point out the improvements to everybody concerned so they want to join the movement.

Ongoing communication is essential. Work groups who labor in common processes must take time to talk the process through, determining how each group improves the process for the benefit of all. Depending on the process, these team meetings can select a particular part of the process for improvement, or they can tackle an ongoing situation they would like to fix. The decision is purely situational.

Supervisors must be on the lookout at this point. Occasionally an individual in charge of a process dominates suppliers and customers alike. These weak links prove difficult to satisfy beyond reason and don't place much effort into satisfying the customer. This becomes a situational leadership problem that must be handled as circumstances dictate.

There is no requirement for strict rules to guide these process improvement efforts. In fact, the less structure required and the more flexibility allowed, the better such efforts tend to work.

Difficulties with the QCS Concept

Many leading management writers and theorists have long recognized the connection between asserted and perceived quality. Now the rest of us must make the same connection in order to understand the importance of this concept. In education, QCS isn't determined by happy teachers; educated students make that decision. QCS in business isn't determined by managers, sales personnel, or employees, it is determined by customers, especially those who provide repeat business.

Okay, so what does that tell us? It says that although the customer perspective on quality may be suspect at times, that customer still determines quality. The buying decisions may not have anything to do with our concepts of quality, although, if we have done our homework correctly, there is every reason to believe the perceptions of both parties will be reasonably close.

An area of considerable importance in deciding this quality lies with value. All customers want the most for their money. Some haggle over costs with the supplier so they can brag about the deal they received to anyone who will listen. Other customers read every article available on the products so they are satisfied that they achieved the best value. To others, value is determined by length of product service at some given cost. Still others determine value by how others judge the choice they made. This suggests that value also is determined solely by the customer.

These concepts of QCS carry many implications. A manufacturer can have a great team that is producing excellent products at the right cost, but business suffers if it has a poor understanding of QCS. A school system can have modern facilities, a highly paid staff with excellent credentials, and winning athletic teams, but the customer will not be satisfied if the school system has a high dropout rate and produces graduates perceived to be of poor quality who have difficulty getting into college.

The same situation affects service institutions such as banks. A bank can have well-designed, modern facilities that are easily accessible, excellent tellers and customer service personnel, and competitive rates and services, but if the billing department continually screws up statements or customers' checks bounce because of bank errors, the organization will not be perceived as one that provides quality service by the customers who use it.

Organizations must come to grips with the need to train every person within the organization on the concepts of QCS. Each person must realize that the weakest link who meets the customer determines how customers perceive that organization. The valet who parks cars and the janitor who cleans the place have just as much direct impact on the customers perception of QCS as customer service personnel. The people in the human relations department have a less understood impact on QCS. Employees who have continuing paycheck and benefit problems or who receive no or minimal raises while management receives big bonuses and stockholders huge dividends will not contribute for long to quality service in any manner. Perhaps you have noticed personnel thus treated standing around complaining about the way they are treated while you waited to check in for a room or some other service. It appears to be a common problem.

Let's summarize some of the difficulties that can impact on QCS.

1. *Our wants*–We want to brag about the quality work we do or services we offer, and in turn we want to buy quality products and services. The difficulty is that the things we sometimes receive are not the same things we thought we were buying. It is upsetting when quality is expected, but junk is received.

2. *Human relations skills*–Management must ensure each person on every team in the organization is treated as good as it wants the customer treated. People treat customers much the same way they are treated. To expect anything different is not realistic.

3. *Quality by example*–Internal quality must meet or exceed expected quality of products or services for external customers. If the personnel director is called Claymore after Claymore Mines because he is anti-personnel and goes off with a bang whenever he is asked a question about the personnel program he is destroying, a certain message is sent. The same message is sent if finance produces incorrect financial data or late checks, management continually calls shots incorrectly, etc. It is a safe bet these will impact on quality service in one way or another.

4. *Implementing change*–The employee mind-set must change so every employee agrees to the fundamental truth that the organization exists and they are employed to deliver quality goods and services to customers who have the money to pay for them.

5. *Communications*–QCS is communicated to all employees so they understand the correlation between the task they perform and the product or service delivered to the customer.

6. *Indoctrination and training*–Continuous effort must be placed on quality and QCS from the initial indoctrination to the continuing training program.

7. *Continuous enthusiastic effort*–QCS is a long-term program requiring continuous process review and training for quality.

8. *QCS isn't easy and it isn't free*–If it were free and easy, there would be no quality service problems. Customers often cause problems which makes serving them difficult.

Customer Expectations

No area can possibly be more misunderstood than expectations, yet it is a critical part of defining the customer, whether internal or external to the organization. Because there are so many misconceptions in this area, it seems wise to discuss what they don't expect prior to a discussion of expectations. Several recent personal examples illustrate situations with which readers may be able to identify.

That Which Isn't Expected

A short time ago while we were having dinner with our guests, a call was received from a company noted for the book sets it sells. Because I own several of these series, I can attest to the quality of them. I had recently agreed to subscribe for another set. The caller was checking to ensure I had placed the order and I agreed I had. He then asked if I minded if he asked a few questions. I explained we were in the middle of dinner, but that seemed to be of little consequence as he replied, "I can understand that, but these questions will take only a minute to answer." My reply, "Please cancel the order and don't send anymore literature or make any more calls to this home." The service was unsatisfactory.

* * *

After a quality forum where I was a presenter, several individuals came up after the session ended. The topic quickly drifted to automobiles and then to automobile sales. At a time when American auto companies were losing market share and facing considerable red ink, their distributorships didn't seem to want to sell vehicles. A person had priced trucks at several agencies but only two had followed up. One would not quote a price up front because his company's policy was that you had to take a test drive before prices could be discussed. It was explained that an identical model was driven at another agency, but it made no difference to the salesperson. He had rules to follow and those rules precluded him from making the sale. The sales process was unsatisfactory.

* * *

We had made a major equipment purchase at an operation I managed. It worked well and we were satisfied for a few months. As time passed we received a barrage from the salesperson who made the sale wanting to know how things were going, if we had recommended her to others, and if we knew of anyone she should call. She found ways to get past the receptionist and was difficult to get off the phone, quickly becoming a pest. The person was unsatisfactory.

* * *

Every few nights we receive sales calls, often computer-generated, during the dinner hour. We refuse to listen to them longer than it takes to hear the introduction. Regardless of how good the products are, we make notes of the company and refuse to buy from them. The introduction to their service is unsatisfactory.

* * *

I enjoy hard candy. I purchased a certain brand and thoroughly enjoyed the taste. There was one problem, the paper tended to stick to the candy as if it were glued. The paper that didn't come off made its presence known because it had a terrible taste. I wrote the company a nice letter explaining the problem. A few weeks later I received a complimentary package of candy and a return letter explaining there must have been a problem with the batch I purchased. It was signed by the company president. I offered a piece to my daughter and proceeded to unwrap one myself. Mine stuck to the paper as did my daughter's. In fact, six out of the nine pieces we tried to unwrap refused to become unglued. I sent them back to show what was happening. I haven't received a reply. I haven't purchased any more of their candy either. The response was unsatisfactory.

I can't conceive of any adult who cannot identify with at least half of these examples. It suggests things for all of us who are concerned with customers and quality.

What Do They Want?

Perhaps nothing is more misunderstood about customers than their desires. Most people who deal in any way with customers have heard the following conversation and many have voiced it, some quite often: "How do you figure people out? I know the customer is always supposed to be right, but what in the world do they want? Can I be expected to give them something when I don't know what it is they want? I'm not a mind reader but it would seem like they all expect me to be."

You're not alone if you share this sentiment. People often have this feeling about their spouse or children when they are in a customer role. Is it any wonder we have doubts about what the customer wants if we have a problem understanding the needs, wants, and expectations of those closest to us.

To better understand you customers, whether internal or external, begin by placing yourself in their shoes in a similar situation. An old proverb has merit here: "Don't criticize me until you have walked a mile in my shoes." Once you have done this, the second part of the solution becomes an ample application of the golden rule.

1. *Respect*–Customers are people and all people want to be treated with respect. It is common to the human race and we expect it even when we might not deserve it. The first and most important rule in life (not just customer service) is to treat every customer with the same respect

you wish others to accord you. "Do unto others as you would have them do unto you."

2. *Fulfillment of need*–Customers expect fulfillment of need as a given. What is need? It is one of the factors in quality that must be determined by the customer-focused organization. For example, the customer needs a 1/4-inch hole in something but he cannot buy this hole. His need is met when he purchases a 1/4-inch drill bit.

3. *Value*–Customers also expect value equal to or greater than the money they have expended. That is what draws people out to shop—the expectation of finding a bargain in terms of value. In the previous example, value was received when the drill bit was competitive in price, sharp enough to make the drilling operation easy, and correctly hardened so it retained its edge.

4. *Attention*–Of equal importance is the expectation of quality attention by everyone the customer meets in the supplier organization. This includes total freedom from hassle. Customers want and deserve solutions to their problems and they want to feel great about their purchases.

5. *Efficiency*–Their time is valuable. Customers detest delay, especially when they think it is avoidable or that others received priority over them.

6. *Confidence*–They need to believe the supplier personnel and the products and services they supply will meet or exceed their needs without problems.

7. *Helpfulness*–They like assistance and service above and beyond that which would reasonably be expected.

8. *Personal interest*–They want a one-on-one caring relationship where they are the center of attention.

9. *Reliability*–The customer needs reliability and they want to know the product is dependable and the service will be forthcoming as promised.

10. *Competence*–The customer wants to feel the people they deal with know the products and services they provide and are competent to meet customer needs.

11. *Professionalism*–The customer needs professional service to feel good about the product or service in order to build a lasting relationship.

12. *Honesty*–They need to know the supplier is honest about the products and services that are promised and the results that can be expected.

The Questions

As providers of goods and services, certain questions should be formulated to assist with QCS. The following list includes some of these questions.

1. What action would be best for our customers?
2. Why is this the best action?
3. Can we provide the expected service?
4. Why is it to the customer's advantage to deal with us?
5. Why would it be to our advantage to provide the product or service?
6. Will the customer receive the expected value with our product or service?
7. What costs will be accrued by providing this service?
8. Are those costs justifiable in terms of return on investment?

Potential Errors

"Our customers swear by us, not at us." Many claim this, but how do they know. With so much at stake, it is important to examine potential problem areas that exist within organizations. Each of these is a place of customer contact that can be either highly supportive or detrimental to follow-up business. Any of them has the capacity to be the weak link that could cause customers to perceive something less than a customer-focused organization.

Figure 12.1 illustrates the provider/user–customer/supplier relationship. It serves to point all the places where potential problems lurk in order that they may be identified and prevented.

The Informal Link

The informal link covers the meetings of members from each organization that come together in a nonwork environment. These meetings also can be a source of considerable problems. Individuals who complain about their company, the product, or other members of the company can cause as many problems through informal meetings as they can in carrying out the duties of their jobs.

Off-duty comments may actually have more effect. This is the same phenomenon that governs publicity and advertisement. The same information presented in the form of a publicity release often has a great believability factor than a similar advertisement because it does not appear to be paid advertising. For the same reason, off-the-cuff comments about company people, policies, quality, or service may seem more valuable when it takes place informally where the employee is free to tell it like it is. The problem is that

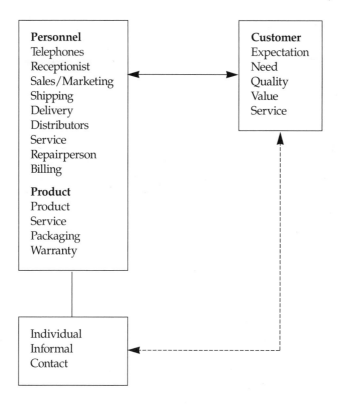

Figure 12.1   Customer/Supplier Links

the person usually isn't telling it like it is; she is blowing off steam out of some frustration and appears believable. The worst part of this situation is that the organization has a difficult time combatting the problem because it is impossible to discover until the damage is done. For that reason, employees must be solidly supportive of their organization or keep their mouths shut when away from the organization while working to change it from within. Those who cannot support the organization should leave it for a more comfortable position. Additionally, the leader who discovers a person cutting down the organization they have a duty to support should consider it as reason for immediate dismissal.

The Formal Chain

No one can tell exactly where the buying decision is made. Therefore, no customer contact can be left to chance. Slipshod effort or haphazard communications and complaining with which members of the customer organization come in contact, can prevent sales opportunities and turn hard-earned customers into shoppers for better service. Management must continually be on the lookout for any activity it would not want the customer to see or hear, regardless of whether the customer is internal or external. The situation must be discussed with the perpetrator the minute it is discovered. The ensuing conversation would cover the problem area, the possible ramifications of such actions, and the penalty for it continuing.

Most people have overheard members in provider organizations complaining on the phone, arguing among themselves, or complaining about everything from the ivory tower to the quality of their products. I personally question the person's motives for remaining a member of the organization and why the organization would allow her to remain on the payroll. When considering the current proposal or follow-up efforts with the organization, those overheard conversations immediately come to mind. Were they the truth? Was the organization trying to fool us with a smoke screen, or was it merely a disgruntled employee mouthing off?

As a manager, I was tipped off about a similar problem by one of our best customers who wanted us to provide a proposal for a certain training service. One of our engineers visiting that same customer organization on another matter was overheard discussing this training proposal with two other department heads. Although he didn't know much about the subject, he felt sufficiently confident to discuss the program in rather derogatory terms. He progressed from that point to complaining that the company should provide more support for his projects and worry less about new services such as training.

The engineer in question was a solid performer with an excellent professional future. However, that was of little consequence in this situation. When he returned from meeting with the customers, the engineer, his project engineer, and I met to discuss the situation. When confronted, he readily admitted the conversation took place. He then endeavored to explain, "Hey, I was only kidding. I didn't know all that much about that other project and probably should have kept my mouth shut. But, they asked, and I gave them my opinion. I guess I was just frustrated. Anyway, they know me and know I fire off at times. It couldn't have hurt anything."

When asked, he agreed that he knew the policy concerning conduct and customer contact. He also stated, "I don't think this case is that big of a deal." Perhaps some readers would share his views. However, his project engineer and I did not. We provided him a box, waited while he emptied his desk, retrieved his keys, and escorted him to the business office where he completed his time sheet, debriefed for security, and was escorted from the building.

This action may seem harsh and perhaps it was. However, actions such as his cannot be tolerated. How many other projects had he torpedoed? Were his actions the reason the customer hadn't expanded the project as planned? If this wasn't all that "big of a deal," what did it take to be a big deal?

His work team was happier and considerably more productive after he departed. They hadn't been satisfied with his efforts as a part of the team and felt he didn't pull his share of the load. His project engineer was ecstatic, as was the customer.

Do these kinds of problems exist in your organization? Could your internal and external customers face this same kind of situation and the same kind of service providers? Shouldn't you know if they do? Aren't harsh actions required if this sort of problem is discovered?

There are many areas in the supplier–user link where problems can easily develop between customer expectation and the service they receive. Each of these areas should be carefully reviewed and then discussed as part of internal all-hands training.

People-Related Factors

1. *Telephones*–Customers expect courtesy, warmth, and help. They need correct information, straightforward answers, and time enough to solve their problems. Potential errors include poor voice tone, rudeness, unprofessional answers, and inaccurate information. Other problem areas include professional hold, the never-ending sales message played while they're on hold, and evasiveness.

2. *Receptionist*–Customers expect neatness, courtesy, warmth, and willing assistance. They need straight answers, correct information, and solutions to their problems. They dislike snappy answers, rudeness, evasiveness, and unprofessionalism.

3. *Sales/marketing*–The customer expects appointments kept, accurate estimates, and reliable proposals. Problems occur with inaccuracies, delayed promises, proposals with loopholes, or salespeople who badger clients.

4. *Shipping*–Customers expect their orders correctly packaged and promptly shipped to the correct location by the agreed upon date. Problems occur when any of these do not occur as expected. It is extremely important to know your carrier.

5. *Delivery*–The customer expects the product to be delivered by courteous, knowledgeable workers who respect their property and equipment.

Problems occur when delivery personnel are discourteous, track mud, destroy furniture, or rough up the premises during delivery.

6. *Distributors*–The distributor is expected to be an extension of the manufacturer or service provider, committed to upholding the same policies and standing behind the product or service in the same manner. Problems occur when there is any deviation. That is why franchisers carefully select the people to whom they issue franchises.

7. *Service/repairs*–These personnel are expected to be clean, courteous, knowledgeable, and prompt. Problems occur when the provider is unkempt in any manner, difficult to work with, doesn't appear to know what he is doing, doesn't meet the agreed upon time schedule, or leaves a mess for the host to clean up.

Thing-Related Factors

1. *Product*–Customer expectations include solution to need, quality, value, on-time delivery, and proper service. Problems encountered include the wrong product, poor quality, cost different than expected, and service differences.

2. *Advertising*–Customers expect truth in advertising and clear concise information. They expect the advertised product to be there just as it was advertised. Problems are encountered by misleading ads, bait and switch, and lack of product.

3. *Billing*–Expectations include accuracy and on-time billing. Problems occur when there are mistakes or the product doesn't arrive on time.

4. *Service/warranty*–Customer expectations include timeliness and hassle-free services just as they were promised. Problems occur with delays, hassle, or difficulties getting serviced.

5. *Follow-up business*–Customers expect to be approached at reasonable intervals with additional business proposals. They expect appointments to be made. They don't expect to be continually hassled for business or walk-in calls without prior appointments.

Summary

1. CQS, like TQM, is a long-term way of life. Customer service is the responsibility of every person in every organization. It can be met only through continuous dedication to the effort.

2. Quality and QCS relate to the customer in the following manner.

   a. The customer is always right.

    b. The customer has the money.

    c. We want and need money.

    d. The customer has all the votes.

3. Recent American ideas concerning sales were to produce a product or service and sell it with slick advertising. This concept does not support the concepts of QCS and it is no longer valid. QCS concepts can be difficult because it is a new way of doing business that develops profits through quality products and services, rather than slick advertising.

4. Customer service has been defined in many ways. This is fine as long as both internal and external customers and their needs, expectations, and requirements are considered.

5. Customers have certain expectations that must be met. They expect needs fulfillment, value, and caring suppliers that will willingly meet their needs. There are potential errors that cause a variety of expectations to remain unsatisfied, generally through supplier slip-ups.

6. Customer service errors often go unrecognized because supervisors are not prepared to watch for them. Every employee must know what the QCS policies are and what happens if they are not followed. The supervisor must act promptly whenever infringements against these policies and practices are discovered.

Bibliography

Albrecht, K. and Zemke, R. *Service America,* New York: Warner Books, 1985.

Albrecht, K. and Bradford, L. J. *The Service Advantage—How to Identify and Fulfill Customer Needs,* Homewood, IL: Dow Jones-Irwin, 1990.

Davidson, W. H. and Uttal, B. *Total Customer Service—The Ultimate Weapon,* New York: Harper and Row, 1989.

Drucker, P. F. *The Frontiers of Management: Why Tomorrow's Decisions Are Being Shaped Today,* New York: E. P. Dalton, 1986.

———. *Management Tasks—Responsibilities—Practices,* New York: Harper and Row, 1974.

———. *Practice of Management,* New York: Harper and Row, 1954.

Eastman Kodak Company, *Keeping the Customer Satisfied,* Milwaukee: ASQC Quality Press, 1989.

Guaspari, J. *The Customer Connection,* New York: AMACOM, 1988.

———. *I Know It When I See It,* New York: AMACOM, 1985.

Hanan, M. and Karp, P. *Customer Satisfaction*, New York: AMACOM, 1989.

Lefevre, H. L. *Quality Service Pays*, Milwaukee: ASQC Quality Press, 1989.

Shaw, J. C. *The Service Focus—Developing Winning Game Plans for Service Companies*, Homewood, IL: Dow Jones-Irwin, 1990.

Townsend, P. L. *Commit to Quality*, New York: John Wiley and Sons, 1986.

CHAPTER 13

The Customer Served

Customer service, like quality, is difficult for the provider or supplier to determine; the main determinant is the customer. In this vein, McDonald's has been used to define what customer service is all about.

I consider myself somewhat of an expert on McDonald's restaurants having been a customer of them all over the United States. From preschool days on, our son could be sound asleep traveling in the back seat of our car and pop awake just as we arrived at a McDonald's sign. It almost seemed as if those signs were putting out hidden commands only kids could receive. I also have traveled extensively on business with a friend who loves hamburgers. John even ordered them in Paris while the rest of his family enjoyed French cuisine in all its glory. Because of this extensive exposure, I use McDonald's as a positive example.

As connoisseurs of McDonald's meals know, all of their restaurants are identical in many ways. It doesn't matter in what section of the country they are located; the race, religion, or creed of the employees; or whether it is an inner city of rural location, they are all similar. One can depend on clean facilities, common products, dependable quality, and speedy service. They couldn't have built up such a huge following if it were any other way.

Other commonalities exist. McDonald's restaurants are located where there is business and usually lots of it. That, too, is important because you can't serve customers if your location isn't accessible. Their competitors often spring up in close proximity because they know the business will be there. It always is. McDonald's also is noted for innovation. They continually come up with new offerings, some on an advertised short-term basis, but all are successful.

McDonald's know its customers. You can't serve customers if you don't know their needs and wants.

The similarity doesn't end there. In fact, that is only the beginning. McDonald's knows service. It has a training facility, Hamburger University, which is widely known for providing service concepts that work in practice—at every McDonald's location. One can depend on it. Their employees have the authority and responsibility to serve their customers, genuinely serve them.

One early morning I was considerably ahead of schedule and decided to run through one of McDonald's drive-in windows. I placed an order and proceeded to a nearby park along the river to enjoy the scenery and eat a second breakfast. I opened the bag and discovered the wrong meal. It would have been fine, too, but I decided to see how Mr. McD's folks would react if I returned it. The result should have been expected. The young lady apologized for the problem, put the correct meal in the bag accompanied by hash browns for my trouble, asked if my coffee was still hot, and bid me adieu with a smile. She didn't tell me I must have ordered incorrectly; she didn't argue about changing the order, or search for a manager to gain permission to handle the problem—she acted. That's what service is all about.

Anything less than this can cause long-term problems. McDonald's knows that and so do most other organizations bent on excellence, long-term profitability, and employee satisfaction. Yes, employee satisfaction. The employee who has permission to provide excellent on-the-spot customer service is a much happier individual. Their customers will note that fact.

This customer service did not begin in the local McDonald's. It didn't even begin at Hamburger University—it began with its founder, Ray Kroc. Customer service still begins at the top and emanates down through the organization, as it should; it is the only way customer service will ever become a way of life within an organization.

The converse also is true. Failed customer service is not an employee fault; it is a management-caused or management-allowed problem. Beginning with correct hiring procedures, training, and appraisal, followed by example from the top, every employee must be brought into the organization, trained, and retained based on their ability and willingness to serve and they must see management as examples of the way this service should work. Employees mimic their leaders whether the example they are provided is productive or harmful.

Employee retention and turnover rates make excellent barometers of both employee satisfaction and the service they provide. Those who are well-treated and satisfied are generally long-term employees and those who are not, aren't. Even those employees who leave for better jobs should have difficulty leaving if they are treated correctly. Management should hate to lose them.

This type of employee tends to provide the service customers want. Service excellence is the first ingredient in customer retention. Most of us are willing to pay a little extra for long-term service with a smile. I certainly am. In fact, one national retailer has lost my business because the firm does not know service. Apparently others feel the same way because the retailer has long-term sales problems, which are creating significant lost market share with accompanying loss in profits. Service is mandatory for success.

The Internal Problem

Problem areas within organizations can severely impact on customer service. Often, external customer focus is directly related to the way internal operations are conducted. Employees tend to treat their customers the way the organization treats them.

It is important to understand some factors that impact on QCS. One often hears people discuss constructive criticism in terms of their interpersonal dealings with others. Consider this term carefully before using it because by definition, the terms are mutually exclusive. One supports or builds up, the other tears down. It is important to go beyond personal criticism and examine system and process criticism. This can be accomplished through the use of the following process- or system-focused questions.

1. What are the objectives and standards of this department?

2. Does this team meet department objectives and standards?

3. Where do the problems lie in any area that falls short of stated objectives?

4. What are the work and quality procedures by which work is processed in this department?

5. What measurements can be taken to monitor success of these procedures?

6. When these measurements are analyzed, where do they suggest improvements can be made? Remember, a main thesis of quality programs is that quality can and must be continually analyzed and improved for program success.

Leaders, supervisors, and managers can easily get on the wrong side of their performance teams by critically assessing quality or performance incorrectly. Human resource program training is crucial. QCS requires a high degree of human relations skills. Quality (and especially the start-up of a quality program) takes time, energy, and commitment. Most people believe they are already short of time. Time management training is a must in a quality program. Quality and QCS require changes and flexibility. People fight change because they are uncomfortable with it or it is forced upon them without the people involved having an input in the matter. Studies of change agents and techniques become important.

Quality customer service is a never-ending process that must be continually improved over the life of the organization. The never-ending process is not a "quick fix, find a secret solution" type of thing. It takes perseverance and visionary leadership to maintain a long-term, continuously improving quality program. Leadership education and training are important in this situation.

Some potential problem areas follow.

1. *Communications*–All communications must be open up and down the organization, within the team, and between supplier and customer. Recognition of communications mistakes can prevent repeats. These mistakes provide guidance:

   • Advising

   • Arguing

   • Criticizing

   • Cross-examining

   • Name-calling

   • Lying

   • Coercing

   • False praising

   • Ordering

   • Threatening

   • Moralizing

   • Manipulating

   Listening is important and the correct response is mandatory. All communications should stress quality. This includes:

   • Verbal

   • Memos

   • Advertisements

   • House organs or papers

   • Bulletin boards

2. *Orientation*–Proper orientation of the work team is important. Everyone must be aware of the need for QCS and how it can be provided. QCS

and TQM should be discussed during all hiring interviews. They should be reemphasized during the initial orientation day at the organization. Team meetings should be a continual forum for the discussion of QCS.

3. *Training*–Training must continually focus on all aspects of quality. Quality service is a discussion point of most general meetings. Specific quality service training is provided to all employees on a recurring basis. Training is used to create both team work and team spirit.

4. *Employee reviews*–All employee reviews should contain mention of quality service. Annual reviews must represent the good qualities of individuals plus any less than admirable traits. Exit reviews, regardless of why the person is departing, should include questions about that person's perceptions of the organization's concern for QCS and how well it is meeting those concerns. The results of the reviews should not be a surprise to either party.

Excellent customer service should be rewarded in some way that is important to the employee; they are the internal customer and must be pleased with the organization. The question becomes how to reward employees for such excellence. The rewards section presented in Chapter 9 provides suggestions.

Customer Complaints

Customer complaints are an extremely important source of information. The complaining customer makes two points: "I want attention and respect," and "I have unsatisfied needs." It must be understood that all customer complaints may not be valid. Once this is understood, it becomes easier to have patience, a necessity for satisfactory conclusion to the complaint. Try not to argue because that increases hostility and resistance. Ask questions to ascertain the entire problem as the customer sees it. Questioning serves three functions. It gathers an outline of the problem, it provides attention to the customer, and it cools hostility. As people talk out their problem they generally see things in a more positive light. This leads to win–win solutions that are acceptable for both parties.

Complaints can be turned into additional sales. Listen. The exact complaint and the situation that caused it must be determined. Identify what the exact complaint is from the customer's perception and then deal appropriately with the complaint. Question each customer concerning her original needs that are being satisfied and any current needs that may be different from original needs. Present any new information on additional benefits or services that supports customers and their needs.

At this point it is important to check for any additional complaints and overcome these objections. Then ask for the order. In all too many cases, this part of the resale is forgotten. In fact, more initial sales are lost because the salesperson neglects to ask for the order, or when they do ask, they forget to stop talking long enough to write up the order when it is given. Sales was a big part of my career for many years. This vital step was the one most often botched. Many salespeople talk themselves out of a sale even after the customer has placed the order. They cannot shut up and meet the customer's need by accepting the order.

Let us recap the reasons why a customer buys. Customer have needs they want satisfied. Customers see you as a supplier who can meet their needs at a competitive, reasonable cost for the value delivered.

Appraising QCS

Customers' satisfaction must be continually appraised. Their needs, wants, and desires continually change. They may have desires or concerns they haven't expressed which could impact on their buying decisions. These must be ascertained. Questions that can assist with this assessment follow.

Negative

1. Are we receiving customer complaints?
2. How does customer service impact on growth?
3. Is our market share increasing?
4. How frequently do problems occur?
5. What are the problems?
6. Does one individual cause all or most of the problems?
7. When there is poor performance, what causes it?
   a. Employees unsuited for the job.
   b. No push for better service.
   c. Lack of experience.
   d. Poor supervision.
   e. Inadequate training.
   f. Poor attitude.
   g. Poor quality.
   h. Poor organizational support.
   i. Poor organizational example.

8. How do problems affect employees?
9. How do problems affect the customer?
10. How important is the customer?
11. Who is affected in addition to the customer?
12. What will happen if problems continue?
13. What is the permanent solution?
14. What will it cost?
15. Are we willing to spend the money?

Positive

1. What are we doing right?
2. How do we know we are doing it correctly?
3. Who is providing excellent customer service?
4. What are they doing to provide this service?
5. Are they helping others in their customer service needs?
6. Are they encouraged by their supervisor?
7. Are they encouraged by organizational example?
8. What customer service training are we providing all our employees?
9. To what degree is our service improving?
10. How are we measuring customer service?
11. What are the motivating factors that promote excellence in customer service?
12. Are the people who provide excellent customer service acknowledged for their efforts?

Answering the Questions

The questions posed previously must be answered if any organization is to satisfy the customers it serves. This is easier said than done. However, this puzzle can be put together through the accumulation of material from several readily available sources followed by careful analysis of the material.

1. *The customer will tell you*–Customers serve as a readily available source of information. They want products and services that meet their needs, and they want to articulate these needs to you so you can help them. In my mind, the only strange part of it all is that so few

organizations realize this about their customers or cash in on the information they willingly provide.

Information is available from the first contact made with the customer regardless of how that contact is initiated. Body language and voice are the first indicators. Customer interviews are extremely important. The answers to carefully orchestrated questions also provide a great deal of insight. The people who handle customer complaints and service personnel can play a big part in gathering this intelligence. Marketing and sales personnel provide an excellent source of information, and no group has more reason to provide solid information that will boost sales than the people involved in selling.

It is imperative that all organizations regularly bring these internal groups together and gather the information they hold. Reports from these groups are a good idea. Reports should be easily completed with a minimum investment in time. Training should be provided so these people know the kinds of information that is needed and how they can obtain it. It is also important that these people know how to seek information in a way that allows the customer to know the information is required to support them and their needs or they won't be as willing to provide it.

2. *Surveys and questionnaires*–Surveys and questionnaires can be an important part of intelligence gathering. There are all kinds of surveys ranging from the kind that are included with product warranty material to those mailed out seeking information. Numerous surveys are now completed over the telephone (much to the chagrin of many). Surveys must be carefully planned in order to collect useful information from the correct focus group in a manner that does not offend people in the process. Questionnaires also must focus on customer need in a nonoffensive way. They must be simple and should not require a substantial investment in time. Computer programs that will accept, sort, and collate the data are important if the survey will have considerable size. The results should be reported out in a manner that supports the survey's intent. The actual development of surveys and questionnaires is beyond the scope of this text. The information for this part of the survey is readily available in most libraries.

3. *Delivery notices*–Delivery notices can be effective sources of information. When regularly scheduled deliveries are a part of the normal way business is conducted, they can be developed to provide a constant source of quality and service information. The questions should be simple and must not consume a lot of time. Four or five questions are

enough. They should be positive in nature. This information should be consolidated after it is analyzed and fed back to the customer on a regular basis. With the customer's permission, this information also can be used to support other sales and marketing endeavors.

Maximizing QCS

There are warning signs of quality service problems, although these signs might not be readily apparent at first glance. Therefore, it is important to continually monitor all aspects of the operation searching for these signs. Warning signs can be visible in different ways outside of the readily visible complaint.

Contact with the customer may decrease because the customer doesn't initiate the communications and may not return yours. There may be a slowdown in orders, proposal approval, and work or service. Current projects are spread out over longer periods of time. You hear through the grapevine that the customer is experimenting with other vendors. The flow of customer information also moves more slowly.

Another indicator occurs when access to upper-level customer service managers disappears. Personal and work contacts are pushed lower in the organization because upper management doesn't have time. When upper-level contact is available, it doesn't have the same meaning that was previously attached to such meetings.

Some indicators are much more abrupt. Contract terminations may be discussed. Plans for future work is scheduled for shorter terms or placed on hold for reasons other than the economy. Discussions about long-term efforts become futile because it is evident they don't consider us as a long-term supplier. The customer develops a wait and see attitude instead of planning with you and committing to new efforts. Your advice no longer seems valued as it once was.

There are general causes for these problems. Customers may perceive a difference between the value you advertised and the value they received. They may believe the bargain they struck and the products or services received are different. They may receive the agreed-upon products, but the time schedule slipped. This discrepancy causes customers to have a problem either satisfying internal needs or the needs of their customers.

All of these explanations are possibilities, but surveys find the number one reason customers remain customers or seek out other suppliers is the service, or lack thereof, that is provided. I'm not sure where the following sign originated, but I had it posted in prominent places throughout our organization.

Why Customers Quit

1% die

3% move away

5% go with other friends

9% consider competitive reasons

14% have product dissatisfaction

68% quit because of an attitude of indifference by an employee

Service with a smile is our number *one* product.

   The number one reason customers quit is not dissatisfaction with the product they receive; it's based on customer service, the way they are treated. The company with the best mousetrap might not have a path beaten to its door unless it has equally good customer service.

   We had a similar sign posted at each place where employees signed in for the day. It said:

> Are you coming to work?
>
> How will you serve our customers today?
> -
> Are you done for the day?
>
> How did you serve our customers today?

Identifying Customer Need

Most QCS writers identify three basic customer needs. These are product-, service-, and purchase-related factors. Each of these are outlined.

   Human relations factors–There is a great need for sales people to be human relations experts. Human relations and interpersonal skills are involved in every sales effort. The customers' perceptions of the desire and ability of sales personnel to serve their needs often impacts on how they value the product. A professional salesperson goes a long way toward pleasing the customer in regard to product acceptance. The poor salesperson can make any product appear less valuable.

Our customers are just like we are. They want to make easy, no hassle purchases through a cordial professional who can be depended on to take care of all the important details of the sale. How easy is it for the customer to buy from you? The easier it is, the more apt you are to get initial and return sales.

Service-related factors–Service-related factors impact in three ways. The first service factor is the service that takes place from the time the customer is made aware of the decision to buy at the purchase point. It is based on the interaction between the supplier and the customer. It is interpersonal in nature and extremely important to the purchase decision. In fact, as we just learned, most sales are based on this factor.

Warranty is the second part of any deal. Two considerations impact on the warranty: how often it has to be used and how willing the supplier stands behind it. It must be remembered that the customer wants a strong warranty that will be correctly serviced. At the same time, they want to buy a quality product or service which never requires warranty work. Care must be exercised to ensure the warranty does not become a self-fulfilling prophecy where employees who produce a product or service mistakenly believe the warranty is so good they can exercise less care in production.

Response time to service need is important and getting more important every day. Most organizations are no longer willing to have redundant and costly systems serving as backups. At the same time a system as common as a copier can seriously impact on the customer's ability to deliver goods and services. How rapidly the supplier responds and how well the problems are handled becomes increasingly important. Attitude can be a large part of how this service is perceived. Is there hassle or service with a smile? Perhaps no other group has more impact on customer perceptions after the sale than the repairperson.

Product-related factors–Value is the premier product-related factor. It is determined by the customer's purchase price in comparison to the product or service received. The supplier must successfully sell value in terms of return-on-investment or life cycle costs. The customer's perception of value must be understood in terms of cost to the customer and the profit customers can hope to make irregardless of how that customer determines profit: money, well-being, satisfaction, or whatever. The supplier must endeavor to increase the value to the customer while simultaneously improving the supplier's profit picture where possible. After all, that is why profit-based organizations are in business. Every attempt must be made to customize solutions to the exact need of the customers. The price charged for these solutions must be based on the value provided and the market.

Customers need and want quality products and services. It is the customer's perceived quality of the product or service you hope to sell. Benefits are values added, while features are physical characteristics. Benefits are what makes or breaks the sales as in, "The real benefit to you is . . . ." Reliability is important in terms of both product performance and supplier dependability.

Customer Satisfaction

Satisfying the customer may not always be an easy task, but it is crucial; it's our job calling in all of its importance. It is an ongoing evolution that is never satisfied. Complacency must be continually guarded against lest someone slip in and help themselves to our customer base.

Satisfaction is not a complex issue. It is similar to eating an elephant—one must take small bites, one bite at a time. In fact, simplicity probably is best. There is nothing complicated about service at McDonald's; its employees simply provide the service they would expect if they were the customer. McDonald's empowers its people to provide that service as the way of doing business, not as an exception. Since it is the way they always do business, it becomes habit and easily repeatable. There are fewer risks, less data, and simple strategies. Planning is much easier and system simplicity allows for easier continuation because everyone knows the plan and how it is to be carried out.

Estimates of any kind must be conservative. This pertains to both product and service value plus the additional benefit the customer receives for dealing with your organization in particular. If there is no particular value you have over your competitors, perhaps it is time to think through your operation. Changes may be long overdue. This keeps the customer from expecting more than can be delivered.

Remember, customers may tend to see more than we think we promise. They are looking for value and wish to find it in your product. If they didn't think it was there and they couldn't justify the purchase to themselves they would either forgo buying it or buy it somewhere else. Sound communications are extremely important so that the exact terms of the transaction are understood. Unsatisfied expectations lead to dissatisfied customers, reduced follow-on sales, and sales returns.

Satisfaction is monitored as an ongoing process in terms of progress toward the goal through satisfied customers internal and external to the organization. Emerging problems must be spotted and overcome. The evolving opportunities that occur because of the service provided are exploited as they arise. Direction toward the goal must be maintained, but the course taken might require change to take advantage of the circumstances that arise. This is much like a ship at sea. The ultimate destination won't change but the course at any given time might change to take advantage of the sea, dodge a storm, or make the ride a little easier.

A QCS Management Plan

QCS demands commitment and customer focus from the top to bottom in the chain of command and in every operation throughout the organization. Nothing less will suffice. This requires planning with the customer and not just for them. Customers want to have a say in what they purchase. Planning strategies begin with the desire to meet customer needs and are followed by efforts to provide added value above that point. Need is the expectation; true customer satisfaction comes from the value added above that basic need.

Management must carefully guide the plan to ensure goals, objectives, and priorities are met. These include operational, financial, sales, and customer service goals. Customer satisfaction enters into every detail of the planning with strategies developed that build a win–win partnership. This can gain access to customer decision-making managers and customer-supplied proprietary information which further supports your efforts to serve the customer. Both parties must perceive a solid partnership, that is, working together in this relationship. As a supplier, you must be customer smart, market smart, human relations smart, and dedicated to QCS.

Bring the customer into all possible planning efforts as early as possible and on a continual basis. Secure knowledge of customer needs from all possible sources by discovering what customers believe it will take to meet their needs. With that knowledge, plan to meet or exceed these needs for success.

All involved parties must work together to solve each customer's problems and meet each customer's needs. This effort is supported by continuous feedback. Where possible, provide networking and added-value type services. They cost little and provide for a feeling of true teamwork. Continually search for ways to ensure your customers know you are on their team working energetically to support their success and congratulate every customer on the successes they achieve in their business endeavors. If this sounds like public relations you really are into this QCS program.

Success must be carefully monitored. Perhaps no monitoring procedure is easier and has more validity than asking the customer. Customers often pinpoint satisfiers and dissatisfiers and tell exactly how they impact. This vital information can allow plan changes, new program development, new product design, and other services long before competitors become aware of a need or a market.

Professionalism remains a key factor. Providing service by itself is not enough. Customers must see the service and know that it supports them, that its sole purpose is to satisfy the customer. Anything less appears to be an advertising gimmick which reduces effectiveness.

Every employee must become a human relations expert of sorts. Getting along with people, the customers and suppliers of our lives, becomes increasingly important in organizational dynamics. Human relations ensures customer relations and customer service.

Customer Relations

Individual relations with others is essential for effective customer service. It matters not whether the customer is internal or external; the way customers are treated will be a measure of your success.

Organizations are measured by the people who represent them. It isn't important who the people are, what their jobs within the organization are, or how professionally they can complete assignments—if they cannot success-fully work with customers they quickly become a major liability. One never knows who a customer or potential customer may encounter. That is why QCS training is important for all employees.

In many ways this section is a recap of other sections. Communications is especially important in our relationships with others. Volume I, Chapter 13 should be reviewed as a part of this study. Listening skills are helpful in our efforts to satisfy the customer.

Volume I, Chapter 17 contains considerable information that proves invalu-able in customer relations. At times, customers can be difficult to work with, especially those customers who believe they have been wronged.

A better understanding of people is in order, which prompts some basic concepts concerning individual needs. People are ethnocentric and want others to notice them. Attention is important to them. They also want to be needed and appreciated. Self-esteem is valuable to this concept. To think well of others and treat others with respect, you must think well of yourself. This requires individuals to know who they are, to look inside and see themselves, and to appreciate the person they are. Now would be a good time to make a list of your strengths and the things you like about yourself. It can greatly assist in your efforts to improve yourself and your efforts with customers.

Trust also is important. People want to work with others they can trust. Track record is most important for successful, ongoing customer relations. Once trust is developed, a major plateau is achieved toward long-term, mutu-ally beneficial relationships.

A great many human relations skills are important in respect to dealing with customers. Some of the most important follow.

1. Look for ways to be agreeable. This does not mean you have to agree with the customer on everything. Learn to disagree without being dis-agreeable. However, when you must disagree, cushion it so that you do not turn them off. Remember the concepts of win–win relationships.

2. Ask others for their help and opinions when working with them. Not only will people respect you more, but often they will sell themselves on you and your products.

3. Seek out the positive aspects of others and build on them. It is important to share the things you may have in common.

4. Thank people for their efforts on your behalf. Show your appreciation as a matter of routine.

5. Learn people's names at first meetings. Write them down and then use them correctly thereafter.

6. Be prompt in your dealings with others. Be on time for meetings. Always return calls and correspondence promptly. Immediately send thank-you notes where appropriate.

7. Learn to empathize with others. Understand their feelings and positions even when you cannot agree with them.

8. Learn to be a problem solver. It will be greatly appreciated. People will look forward to your assistance. Be sure to tell them how you are going to help them and then carry through with it.

9. Consider all others as important people. Their stations in life should have little to do with the respect you give them.

10. Avoid open anger at all times. Many situations in customer relations can be trying. However, when you blow your cool, you lose. Control your emotions and come out a winner.

11. Be assertive in your work with others. Take charge of your life and your actions.

12. Learn to use the telephone correctly. Always smile before answering it. Be polite and cordial while striving to produce a warmth in your voice that tells the caller they are important to you. Now would be a good time to reread the telephone section in Volume I, Chapter 12.

13. Never promise anything you can't deliver. It is better to admit it up front when you cannot provide some needed goods or service.

14. Never rely on company policy to settle a complaint. Few things turn off a customer more than "I'm sorry but that's company policy."

15. Never be too busy to serve the customer. The service counts as much or more than the products involved. Remember, it is our job calling us when the customer is in need. Nothing can be more important than that.

Questions Concerning Your Customers

1. Do you learn everything possible about your organization, its products and services, its people, and its capabilities so that you can better serve your customers?

2. Do you always represent your organization well, speaking highly of it, its people, and its goods and services?

3. Do you refrain from unflattering discussions about your competitors, their people, and their products?

4. Do you carefully research your customers, learning all you can about their needs so you can best match your organization's products, services, people, and capabilities to their needs?

5. Do you have a motto such as, "The customer comes first?" Is the motto readily apparent to both internal and external customers?

6. Do you respect your customers, and their needs, placing them first in the decision-making processes?

7. Do you always help your customers, make the decision that is most beneficial to them?

8. Do you work hard for your customers, and does it show up in substantial repeat business?

9. Do you readily steer potential customers to someone else if you cannot help them?

10. Are you actively working to become a human relations expert so that you can continually improve on the service you provide others?

11. Can you disagree without being disagreeable?

12. Do you avoid conflict with customers regardless of their actions?

13. Do you willingly work past quitting time to best serve your customers?

14. Do you refrain from negative and unflattering discussions about your customers?

There are many other questions each of us should be continually asking ourselves as we strive to improve our customer service capabilities and actions. This list provides a foundation for further study in this area.

Summary

1. QCS, like quality itself, is customer-determined. It is a simple procedure complicated by ignoring customer needs and expectations.

2. Solid proverbs for providing customer service are, "Walk a mile in my shoes," and the golden rule. Treating others as you desire treatment as a customer goes a long way toward defining customer service requirements.

3. The QCS process features open communications, an orientation to customer service, training, employee reviews, continuing feedback, and a rewards strategy.

4. Dealing with a customer complaint begins with the discovery of the basis for the complaint, the determination of validity, and a plan for recovery.

5. Organizations must continually appraise their QCS. This determines how well you are doing compared to your plan and the customer's need.

6. Maximize customer satisfaction through needs assessment and a teamwork effort to meet these needs. The QCS plan involves a commitment with organizational strategies from the top down that meet the customer needs on time and with a genuine smile.

Bibliography

Albrecht, K. and Zemke, R. *Service America*, New York: Warner Books, 1985.

Albrecht, K. and Bradford, L. J. *The Service Advantage—How to Identify and Fulfill Customer Needs,* Homewood, IL: Dow Jones-Irwin, 1990.

Davidson, W. H. and Uttal, B. *Total Customer Service—The Ultimate Weapon,* New York: Harper and Row, 1989.

Drucker, P. F. *The Frontiers of Management: Why Tomorrow's Decisions Are Being Shaped Today,* New York: E. P. Dalton, 1986.

———. *Management Tasks—Responsibilities—Practices,* New York: Harper and Row, 1974.

———. *Practice of Management,* New York: Harper and Row, 1954.

Eastman Kodak Company, *Keeping the Customer Satisfied,* Milwaukee: ASQC Quality Press, 1989.

Guaspari, J. *I Know It When I See It,* New York: AMACOM, 1985.

Guaspari, J. *The Customer Connection,* New York: AMACOM, 1988.

Hanan, M. and Karp, P. *Customer Satisfaction,* New York: AMACOM, 1989.

Lefevre, H. L. *Quality Service Pays,* Milwaukee: ASQC Quality Press, 1989.

Shaw, J. C. *The Service Focus—Developing Winning Game Plans for Service Companies,* Homewood, IL: Dow Jones-Irwin, 1990.

Townsend, P. L. *Commit to Quality,* New York: John Wiley and Sons, 1986.

CHAPTER 14

Time Management

Many people might initially question what time management has to do with quality. A simple question provides insight into the connection: "Why isn't there ever time to do things right, but there is always time to do them over?" There is a good chance projects aren't completed correctly because insufficient time and effort was utilized in their production, and there isn't enough time to do them over, but there also is no choice. The customer won't accept poor quality, at least not for long.

A high-quality, productive environment depends on wise time utilization. There isn't time to waste with the installation of a TQM process. Performance improvements will use all the time available and cry for more. Fortunately, much of the time required is available within the system in the form of waste of one sort or another and much of it can be retrieved for productive efforts.

Definition: Time management is getting the things done that must be accomplished in the amount of time available using the available assets with the end result being a quality product or service.

This definition suggests one must know or do the following:

1. The task at hand must be known by those who must accomplish it.

2. The time available to complete these tasks must be known.

3. Task priorities must be established.

4. The assets available that can be utilized must be known by those who will complete the task.

5. The end result must be a quality product or service.

This chapter presents the methods by which this can be accomplished. Some people believe they don't need any more time management training because they don't use their time half as well as they could right now. The human mind can solve any problem it can accurately conceive if the rest of the body will follow through. To be a good time manager, you must love life with a desire to get the most out of it accompanied by the will to return the most to life. Success demands solid time management which is the method of achieving quality, on-time production. This suggests work–goal achieving rather than busy work. It requires priorities with the first priority being effective work and the second priority being efficient efforts.

Many busy people accomplish little that carries importance in terms of progressing toward the goal. They are efficient and get a lot done that doesn't need to be done, but they are totally ineffective regarding performance. They pursue activities apart from their goals so they cannot accomplish the things important to them, their career, and their life. *Most important*, in their mind when time runs out too soon, they have not failed. There just wasn't enough time. Generally, there is not a time management problem, there is a time mismanagement problem.

This time management discussion is geared toward supervisors, managers, and other professionals who have some control over their time. Although time management is important for all employees, most employees on the work floor have little discretionary time. Their choice is between wise time use which supports performance improvement or putting in their time to get through the day. As managers invest the additional time in the workplace required by TQM, their interaction with employees will encourage wiser time use.

The Nature of Time

Time is an impartial, nonrenewable resource that treats each individual identically. Every person, supervisor or subordinate, leader or follower, receives exactly the same amount of time each and every day. This amounts to 60 seconds a minute, 60 minutes an hour, and 24 hours or 86,400 seconds a day. This time cannot be bought, sold, or saved. What you get is all you have have. The only choice with time is to invest it or waste it. The way time was used yesterday has little impact on the way we choose to use time today. Each night at midnight we begin over with the same choice: will we invest our time wisely, or will it be carelessly wasted?

Nature of Time Problem

A certain person has a 6-mile trip and must average 30 mph over the trip. With plenty of time and a new car, he averaged 20 mph the first 2 miles.

Feeling an increased sense of urgency at the 2-mile mark, he sped up to 30 mph and averaged 30 mph for the next 3 miles. How fast must he travel the last mile to average 30 mph?

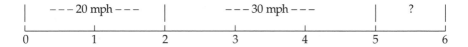

Answer: He can't make it. He has 12 minutes to make the trip because it takes 2 minutes to go each mile at 30 mph. At the 5-mile post the 12 minutes he had allowed was used up, 6 minutes to go 2 miles at 20 mph and 6 minutes to go 3 miles at 30 mph. At that point the time deadline has arrived.

This leads to the first important ingredient in time management—getting started. A good start is mandatory in all projects. Consider the operation of carrier aircraft as an example. The entire mission depends on the start—the cat shot.

Considerable time is wasted before most projects ever get started. The first step in any project is defining the project after looking it over and thinking it through. More time is wasted when it is examined, reexamined, and examined again without any action being taken. Then it is considered and reconsidered several more times, still without taking any action. *Get started!*

The longer any project is considered, the more difficult it appears. *Get started!* Once anything appears difficult, the difficulty factor provides something to worry about. Worry solves nothing and only worsens as time quickly passes without action. That is the nature of worry. *Get started!* Faked or halfhearted attempts to start generally follow. These faked attempts can be separated from genuine solution efforts. The faker's efforts are accompanied by doodles and scribbles, the worker's by problem-solving efforts. *Get started on the solution!*

When an effort is not started on time, there soon is pressure to get it done on time—not done correctly, but completed on time. Granted, the hope is that it will be done properly, but the pressure is to get it done. There is no time for course changes, improvements, or problem correction—only time to get it done. Completion is the main thrust, simply because the project was not started in time.

There is never enough time to do everything. One could live several lifetimes and not have enough time to do everything that is important. Stop and think of all the things you intend to do just as soon as you have time. Now acknowledge that you are mortal and cannot do everything that needs to be done, so there won't be time to accomplish the nice-to-do projects. This emphasizes the need to establish goals to map out our lives. Activities must be prioritized so the most important tasks are accomplished. Each choice made opens up new opportunities with new choices. Each choice also precludes other choices. Whenever low-priority, low-payoff activities are completed, they preclude activities that are more important. A time inventory should be completed to determine how time is used. The time must be estimated for completing everything that must be accomplished. Others must be made aware of our time constraints. Take care when accepting or beginning new efforts. Constantly strive to eliminate less-important activities and streamline the high-priority, high-payoff tasks. Equally important, secure the assistance of others where possible.

Where Did My Day Go?

It is difficult to know where time goes if the use of time is not planned, tracked, and evaluated. This is vital at the beginning of a time management improvement effort. The various holes allowing time to escape must be discovered and successfully plugged in order to gain the additional time required to implement TQM. Several tools follow that help provide an understanding of your personal use of time so that you may plan to use it more wisely.

Time Management Survey

The time management survey (Figure 14.1) presented is a questionnaire designed to guide thinking about your use of time. The time spent completing this survey is an introduction to the remainder of this chapter and will pay dividends in your efforts to master time utilization. Often = O, sometimes = S, rarely = R.

Time Evaluation

Time management demands that we know how our time is used or abused. It is impossible to control the unknown. It takes a concentrated effort to determine how time was used. Time management research can provide insights on how time is used. Check how you use your time. Figure 14.2 will help your efforts.

1. Set an alarm to go off at irregular intervals.

2. Stagger the time so you are surprised each time.

3. Keep a logbook and jot down what you are doing each time the buzzer goes off. List the time and activity.

4. As an option, you can fill in the spaces to make a more complete report between the bleeps.

5. At the end of a set period of time, usually two weeks, analyze what you have accomplished.

6. Write down your impressions, both positive and negative.

7. Go over the list and star periods when you performed critical tasks.

8. Redline activities that netted nothing positive.

9. Now you know where you can start cutting.

10. Value–Easy to use and takes little time.

11. Drawback–It only *works* if you are dedicated to eliminating weaknesses and ready to build on success.

O	S	R
			1. Do you choose the correct work to do?
			2. Do you complete quality work the first time?
			3. Do you have written, dated, personal and work goals?
			4. Do you prepare and prioritize *to-do* lists?
			5. Do you work your *to-do* list by priorities?
			6. Do you have effective work and quality procedures?
			7. Do you get a timely start on projects?
			8. Do you meet deadlines with time to spare?
			9. Are you on time to work, meetings, and events?
			10. Is your work complete at quitting time?
			11. Is your work space clean and organized?
			12. Can you locate things on your desk and in your files?
			13. Do you have a self-improvement plan that makes your job easier?
			14. Do you train so subordinates can accomplish more projects of greater value?
			15. Do you delegate easily?
			16. Do you empower your team?
			17. Do subordinates cooperate enthusiastically on projects?
			18. Do you plan your most important work for peak energy hours?
			19. Do you deal effectively with interruptions?
			20. Do you deal effectively with drop-in visitors?
			21. Do you deal effectively with long-winded callers?
			22. Do people know the best time to call you?
			23. Do you focus on problem prevention?
			24. Can subordinates do your work when you are absent?
			25. Do you make the best use of your time?

Figure 14.1 Time Management Survey

Time	Time Evaluation	Planning	Management Function	Operating Function	Meetings	Other
6:00						
7:00						
8:00						
8:30						
9:00						
9:30						
10:00						
10:30						
11:00						
11:30						
12:00						
12:30						
1:30						
2:00						
2:30						
3:00						
3:30						
4:00						
4:30						
5:00						
5:30						
6:00						
7:00						

Figure 14.2   Time Activity Evaluator

Again, note the word *work*. For any time management process to have a positive impact, we must be willing to work. So many folks show up for work and spend all day avoiding it.

Time Activity Evaluator

Another way to monitor time is a time activity evaluator. A sample of this form (Figure 14.3) follows.

Directions for using this evaluator.

1. Every half-hour or hour, the time utilization is marked on the evaluator sheet.

2. Approximate times are fine.

3. This log is kept for one week and then the activities are evaluated.

4. All wasted time is noted.

5. Later in this chapter time-wasters are presented along with ways to curtail or cutback on them.

Activity Log and Evaluator

Figure 14.3 is used to record activities as they are completed. The evaluation blank (Figure 14.4) is left until the end of the day. As a last effort prior to the end of the day, all activities are reviewed and evaluated. Time-wasters are noted. A *to-do* list is completed for the following day.

Comments are appropriate on these activity analysis systems. Each of these three methods will provide a sound evaluation of our work habits. All require a dedicated effort to complete. Objective analysis is mandatory and provides the payoff. Most people decline to use these systems because they point out problems with activities that are enjoyable, but should have lower priorities for accomplishment. It takes a strong desire to work and to work smarter to get any good from time and activity evaluation.

The Value of Time

Value must be assigned to everything so that one knows what it is worth. Without value, there may be little appreciation for time. Therefore, individuals must measure the value of their time. You can measure your efforts by asking yourself, "Would I be willing to pay another person my wages to accomplish what I accomplished the last hour, today, or this month?" If the answer is "no" other questions become appropriate. Do these activities add up to a better future at work? Home? Was I really willing to trade an hour of my life doing

Time	Exact Activity	Objective Evaluation

Figure 14.3 Activity Log

Start	Finish	Activity	Evaluation

Figure 14.4 Activity Evaluator

what I did the last hour? Would I do what I did the last hour if it were the last hour of my life?

A major shortcoming of many ambitious people is finding comfort in how many hours they "put in" rather than how much high payoff work is accomplished—*activity instead of accomplishment.* Each person has to decide what the payoff activity is. There generally is time to accomplish the most important things. If you decide something must be done, it will get done, but remember, "You don't find time, it isn't lost. You make time."

Continuous improvement requires that most of the available work time be used correctly. The word *most* is used because there will always be some amount of time used less than effectively, but that time can be continually reduced.

A further measure of the value of time comes from the value of the accomplishments that occur in any given amount of time. Cramming more and more activities in less and less time does not increase the value of that time; completing more quality efforts or products needed by the customer in a given amount of time does.

Effectiveness vs. Efficiency—Right vs. Wrong

There are two ways tasks can be completed: effectively and efficiently. Effectiveness is doing the right things, efficiency is doing things right. Effectiveness is the first order. It matters not how efficiently something is accomplished if it is the wrong thing to be doing with the time allotted.

An example I once heard used concerned a rider who was looking at a road map for the driver of an automobile. The driver questioned, "How are we doing?"

"Well," the navigator replied, "we're headed in the wrong direction, but we're making great time."

They weren't doing the right thing but they were doing it right—efficiency, but not effectiveness.

Tasks also can be measured in terms of right or wrong. An effective task could be in progress, but it could be accomplished the wrong way. This isn't of much value. Payoff comes from doing right things the right way. Nothing is more important in time management.

This discussion provides four ways of doing things or using time. On a grid they appear as in Figure 14.5.

The goal is to do the right things right all the time, not *most* of the time, but *all* of the time. Anything less hinders the search for performance improvement.

Priorities become extremely important in the effort to complete the right things correctly. Since there isn't enough time to do everything, choice

Right

Right things wrong	Right things right
1. Poor work the customer needs.	1. Quality work the customer needs.
2. Correct training that is handled poorly.	2. Correct training that is required for quality.
3. Working with customers, but ignoring their needs.	3. Working with customers and meeting their needs.
Wrong things wrong	**Wrong things right**
1. Poor work the customer doesn't need.	1. Quality work the customer doesn't need.
2. Incorrect training that is handled poorly.	2. Incorrect training that is handled correctly.
3. Ignoring the customers and their needs.	3. Ignoring the customers, but meeting their needs.

E
f
f
e
c
t
i
v
e
n
e
s
s

Wrong ———————————— Efficiency ———————————— Right

Figure 14.5   The Quality Grid

becomes important. The priority grid (Figure 14.6) helps in the effort to make choices between efforts with a high payoff and those with a high priority. The goal in time management is twofold: completing right things right and completing those with the highest payoff and highest priority first.

Major Time-Wasters

Earlier in this chapter it was stated that most time problems are not time management but time mismanagement problems. The following discussion on time-wasters is used to point out this problem. Recognition of these time-wasters and understanding why they occur is absolutely essential in the quest to make time for continuous performance improvement.

Individual must decide what their personal time-wasters are. Several common problems are listed, followed by methods that can be employed to alleviate these wasters. The items are provided in outline format for easy review, and they cover the areas of quality-related wasters, planned wasters, and unplanned wasters.

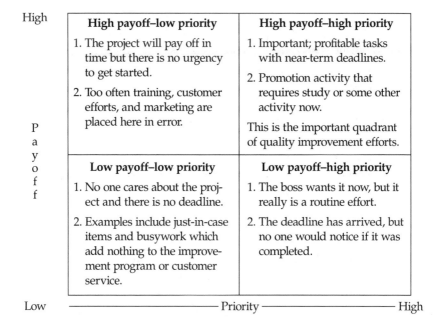

Figure 14.6   The Quality Grid

Quality-Related Time-Wasters

The first look at time-wasters covers those associated directly with quality. These must be given priority because they impact heavily on quality performance, employee morale, commitment to TQM, and the rate with which performance improvement can be accomplished.

1. *Training*–Continuous training is absolutely essential for the success of the TQM process. However, training to priority need is just as critical. Low priority, poorly planned, or training that is not used immediately is more detrimental than no training at all. It takes time away from work toward the goal and disillusions attendees. Need-based training determined by operational audit is the key. Many find the practice of buying TQM programs highly questionable because training for the TQM process should be based on and tailored to need. Certain basics are universal, but packages may not provide what is needed.

2. *Rework*–Rework is a major waste no matter how you look at it. It requires additional time; ties up production facilities, people, and equipment; costs money; frustrates people; and loses customers.

3. *Inspection*–Some inspection may be necessary in any operation. However, reliance on inspection is a time- and asset-waster. Vendor certification programs, work force self-audits at the work station, and continuous process improvement alleviate much of the need for inspection.

4. *Handling complaints*–Customer complaints, whether they are from internal or external customers, are a major time-waster when those problems generally can be prevented. The firefighter mentality creates most of these complaints because problems are not solved—they are bandaged and allowed to fester and grow.

5. *Overtime*–One of the greatest causes of overtime is poor time utilization during regular working hours. Overtime is too often a bonus achieved by misusing the normal workday. Some overtime may be required, but the cause should be known before it is finalized. Plans should be made to eliminate the causes of overtime where that is a possibility.

6. *Red tape*–Organizational structure often contains so much red tape that TQM is almost an impossible dream. Prior to instituting any policies to support TQM, the complete paperwork structure for the organization should be reviewed to get rid of redundant, outdated, unnecessary, and overzealous red tape which precludes quality instead of supporting the quest for it.

7. *Organization and reorganization*–All too frequently, the drive to begin quality is almost synonymous with a drive to reorganize. Some reorganization may be necessary, but it must be planned. Creating an entirely new quality structure outside the normal management chain of command almost always is counterproductive.

8. *Social safaris*–Much has been made of management by walking around (MBWA). It is an extremely positive action required of all leaders and managers when used to support the quest for excellence. However, there is a down side to it that also must be recognized and controlled, lest the timid abuse the practice. Many supervisors initially are unequipped to handle MBWA and go through the pretense of using the system. Their efforts turn into social safaris and employee mingling sessions, which actually hinder performance improvement instead of supporting it.

9. *Boss emulation*–Many subordinates wrongfully believe that when the boss is in, they have an obligation to be there. The boss burns the midnight oil and subordinates remain on station. Were this productive time, it would be difficult to argue against. In all too many cases it is a

wheel-spinning effort that produces little, other than frustration and upset spouses or families. People soon become bored with projects and lose interest when they spend a great deal of time in the workplace that is not constructively utilized. The boss has an obligation in the quest for excellence to ensure people leave at the end of the normal workday unless there is a demand that must be filled.

Planned Time-Wasters

There are time-wasters planned in every organization that must be hunted out and eliminated. One of our subcontractor's costs seemed abnormally high, and we decided to help its management determine the cause. Time waste was the main ingredient. They had one person who punched in and began cooking breakfast for his work group on a hot plate they had purchased to warm soup for lunch. Another spent a considerable part of each morning taking sandwich orders. Once collected, he departed for a deli where he waited while they were prepared. Another individual collected lottery tickets and other bets that were then placed during periods he was supposed to be spending with the customer. The elimination of these and a few other flagrant violations made their costs to us most competitive.

It must be understood up front that these time-wasters can occur only when management allows them. They point to a leadership problem that must be overcome.

1. *Double lunch hours*–Employees eat their lunch throughout the morning and then use their lunch period for personal chores.

2. *Checkbook Charlie*–Many organizations have individuals who balance their checkbook, pay their bills, send cards and other correspondence, make out store lists, plan for the weekend, and so forth, on company time. After all, they don't want to waste personal time on such low-priority chores. It isn't a good use of their time.

3. *Personal phone calls*–These are calls totally unrelated to any potential business. Customer/vendor relations require some level of communications that are not strictly business; however, this should not include social calls to friends and relatives.

4. *Winding down the workday*–People begin clearing their desk at 2:30 so they can be waiting in the checkout line at 3:30 to leave at 4:00.

5. *Waiting for checks*–People wait for checks, wait for training, wait for supplies, and wait to wait. Considerable waiting can be eliminated through payday training at the same time each pay period where the checks are issued at the end of the session.

6. *Business luncheons*–Some are worthwhile and produce solid business deals, working plans, and relationships while others signify an opportunity to get away from it all and lay back for a bit. Separating the reasons is not difficult; gathering the will to act is the obstacle many supervisors face.

7. *The Friday power lunch*–Many employees enjoy a Friday afternoon migration to their favorite watering hole to "belt back a few." The tendency is to overstay the lunch period and come back in a less-than-effective state at which time they begin the big wait to quitting time when they can complete the process they began at lunch. They would be less an infringement on production if they didn't bother to come back because they often bother others who want to be productive.

Environmental Time-Wasters

These time-wasters come to you and may be difficult to eliminate completely. Often others do not realize how they impact on your time. All improvements add to the amount of time available for high-priority, high-payoff activities. These external time-wasters follow along with methods to deal with the problems.

1. *The unplanned visitors*

   a. Social butterfly

   b. Office gossip

   c. Salespeople making introductory calls

   d. Mr. or Ms. Personal Problem

   e. People taking a break on you

   f. People who need your time

   g. Your boss

   Do we want to stop all unplanned visitors? The answer must be a resounding "no." They are the source of needed information. Many actually are a part of one's job. The answer lies in methods to control the problem. Plan for some interruptions. It's part of your job. Remove extra chairs from your work space. Rearrange the room so your desk faces away from the door. People are less likely to interrupt if they cannot see your face. Close your door for a planned part of each day. Handle only emergencies during this period. Be very specific about what constitutes an emergency. Become a professional if you are not already—it isn't so easy for visitors to invite themselves in to visit someone who is all business. Never entertain. Learn to say "no" and mean it. This will be covered more completely later. There are techniques for handling visitors: "I have five minutes I can spare. Can we discuss it in that time?" At five minutes announce, "Our five minutes are up. Let's schedule another session when we have the facts we need to make a decision." A second possibility can occur at the end of five minutes. "I see our five minutes are up. This is important so let's continue." When the time is up and it is desired that the person leave—stand up. If that doesn't do it, move to the door. For those who just cannot or will not take a hint, politely say, "I must get back to this project."

2. *Unnecessary phone calls*–These could be sales prospecting calls, job hunters, or someone who should be talking with someone else. Every time name lists are sold, you are bombarded with calls. Have the secretary or receptionist screen calls and take messages. Collect messages and return the required calls at your convenience. Frequent callers should be given a best time to call. Forget social small talk that accompanies most calls. When you are the caller, have an outline of questions that require answers. Learn how to get off the phone.

    a. "That's all the time I have now."

    b. "I have another call."

    c. "Excuse me, I must run for . . . ."

3. *Unorganized meetings*–Nothing wastes more time and frustrates more people than unorganized meetings. Volume III begins by dealing with this important subject. For now, the *neat* formula provides an outline for producing productive meetings:

    N Need

    E Expectation of value

    A Agenda

    T Time

4. *Socializers*–Every organization has its share of people who find a great need to use the workplace as a social club. The surprising part is that most of those involved don't recognize themselves as a problem because it has become a standard way of doing business. Some of the events socializers use are hunting stories, sports pools, family gossip, and what is happening on their favorite soap opera. There are rather simple ways this problem can be overcome.

    Begin by making certain the work assignments are at a level to keep each person constructively employed. This should be no problem with the implementation of a TQM process. There will be more than enough work that needs attention.

Delegation downward provides lower levels of management and the work force with constructive and often interesting tasks to tackle in addition to their normal efforts. Ensure goals and performance targets are established. These must be understood by each work group and become the established order of business.

There will be some flagrant abusers who must be confronted. This can be difficult because many are hesitant to confront problem-causing employees. This is one reason so many problem children feel confident in this abusive practice. Beware! Once the leader tackles this problem, many abusers will attempt to engage that leader in long-winded discussions. At times, they may switch the topic to shallow discussions of quality, but this cannot be allowed. These conversations should get to the meat of the subject, answer the questions, and proceed with business. The leader should convey a sense of urgency with the installation of TQM as if the organization's survival depends on it. It probably does.

5. *Reading material*–Reading material is an important area to review in the quest for time. Two areas are subject to review: your reading time and that of your subordinates. Your area is the first to tackle. You must free up as much time as possible and immediately establish an example for others. Question if you want every publication you now receive. Many managers receive dozens of magazines, including all the free trade publications. Of course, most are not read from cover to cover but it requires a certain amount of time to review them. Cancel those you generally don't read or give them to appropriate people. Cut out articles you want for later use. Before beginning, establish a simple file prepared to separate the subjects into appropriate subjects. You can then retrieve the material by subject to support training efforts.

Scan the material you now read to determine your need for the contents. Concentrate on the material at hand. Some would suggest a speed-reading course, although I find them of questionable value for long-term retention. Read condensed versions of material where possible. Use reports only to the extent they meet the needs of your office and the TQM process. Using reports to communicate successes of your team up the chain is considered an important need.

The second area to control is reading time by the team. Material that supports performance improvements can be considered a part of their job. Newspapers, news magazines, novels, and all such reading material that does not support the organization's efforts should be banned except for break periods. The reading policy should be made public to subordinates and each infraction confronted. It has been my experience that some will test the policy at the beginning, but the testing period doesn't last long.

6. *Travel*–Business travel can be a time-waster. The first determination should be made through the question, "Is this the best way to conduct this business or would a phone call, letter, or fax handle it just as well?" If the answer is that the trip is necessary, the time for the trip should be invested and not spent. Complete work projects while traveling. Catch up on a project you have in progress. Read a book on quality, taking notes as you go so the material can be used constructively back in the workplace.

   Commuting to work is another area that must be analyzed. Few people realize the time wasted in this daily evolution. The worker with a half-hour commute uses five hours each week traveling to the workplace. Many spend much more time. At five hours a week and a 48-week base for the work year after subtracting vacation and other time off, travel equals 240 hours annually or six 40-hour weeks annually. This time can be put to use with your self-training program through training tapes. Turn off the radio and turn on your life. You can learn things that support both your career and personal life while you travel. You also will find that traffic jams and delays are not nearly as upsetting when one is learning something of value.

   Dictate messages while traveling and commuting. *Accept* delays— they will occur. Make sure you have quality material to cover while you wait for clients to receive you. It sets a good example when they see how your time is invested while you receive information to improve performance. Say "no" to parties on business trips because these turn into all-night affairs that take time today and prevent preparation for tomorrow.

7. *Excessive paperwork*–Handle paperwork once. Make a decision on each subject possible as it comes across your desk. Write only necessary memos, letters, and reports constructed in outline format where it is appropriate. File only important material with the destruction or removal date on all material. Use data storage where possible. Let your secretary (if you have one) separate the mail. Handle mail judiciously. A good practice is to open daily mail over the trash can. Make notes on original letters and memos.

8. *Poor communications*–Chapter 12 in Volume I provides a format for effectiveness. Use these rules as a communications bible. A simple review is considered valuable here. Understand the four parts of communications and how to handle each: transmit, receive, translate, and

check for appropriate action. Organize all communications. Hasty instructions create an illusion of accomplishment, but confuse matters which prevents performance. Understand that people do not all have the same level of vocabulary. Know what you are talking about before you start talking. Give simple instructions. Ensure you understand what is communicated to you. Listen—ask questions. Forget secrecy—open up communications for effectiveness through memos, bulletin boards, media, and so forth.

9. *Duplicated efforts*–Assign responsibilities that do not overlap. When several groups want the same information from you, suggest a common format. Ensure your boss is knowledgeable of duplicated efforts for which she is responsible. Remember paperwork serves an organization—organizations are not created to serve the gods of paperwork, regardless of how it may sometimes appear.

10. *Poorly planned projects*–Chapter 7 provides a method to ensure time is properly utilized to improve performance. Three simple areas serve as a guide for planning:

    Need

    Assets

    Who, what, where, when, why, and how

11. *Conflicting priorities*–There are many ways conflicting priorities develop. The organization may have unclear plans. Your group, the customer, and others all perceive different needs. Many of these will be brought into line by a focus on TQM and QCS. Discuss priorities with all those who are involved. Compromise where it benefits all parties. Gain commitment to priorities and adhere to the set priorities of each effort.

12. *Incompetent staff*–An incompetent staff wastes more of its own time and, in turn, more of your time than any other single factor. Managers are forced to spend a great deal of time explaining to the chain and customers why performance is not what it should be. Initial steps to take include:

    • Train, it pays great dividends.

    • Hire selectively, never just to meet quotas.

    • Ensure there is a payoff for self-education.

    • Remove those who cannot or will not perform.

13. *Poor or no management plans*–Is it your responsibility? Ensure business, quality, market, and training plans are in place, relevant, updated, and used. When it isn't your responsibility, tactfully encourage such plans. Create sound plans for your level when the effort will pay off in performance.

14. *Disorganization*–This problem is difficult to correct initially because ingrained, personal, and poor habits are involved. Leaders and work teams often are swamped because of faulty or no plans. Cluttered work spaces require wasted time hunting for projects. Priority projects sit waiting because there were no *to-do* lists with priorities. Goals were not firmed on paper because of some excuse. Poor habits are excused away, "You can't teach an old dog new tricks." The correction phase of this problem is covered under many separate topics, but this outline brings the problem home and the corrections are evident. Getting started is the difficult part.

15. *Too much organization*–Again, there is a balance between disorganization and too much organization. In many case, organizations become so caught up in planning that nothing else is accomplished. These activities provide an air of accomplishment when no productive efforts are completed. The work of the day takes a back seat to planning.

    This problem occurs when completing the plans, charts, graphs, memos, and so forth, requires so much time and energy that there is nothing left for the work at hand. I was at a conference where one of the managers presented a two-hour seminar on work planning and charting using a new computer program. As a grand finale, he spread out a chart that was over 20 feet long which covered every eventuality. He proposed all program managers use it. At the end of the conference, the CEO went over our individual projects. This same manager was over both dollar and time budget with nothing from either remaining and no deliveries made. So much for the value of this plan.

    Be careful of organization. If the organization effort does not pay off in time and asset savings, plus quality and performance payoffs, it must be questioned. In planning and organizing remember KISS— Keep It Simple, Sam.

16. *Failure to say "no"*–Failing to say "no" is one of the greatest of all time-wasters, and it is a sign of weak leadership. There are many reasons why people hesitate to say "no" when it is the correct answer.

    • We don't want to hurt feelings.

    • We may change our mind.

- The situation may change.

- We owe a favor.

   However, if the question begs a "no," give it one. It is best for all parties to say it. It also is important to remember that "maybe," or "I'll think about it" are not terms synonymous with "no." Consider negotiations with children. When parents say "maybe" the parents believe they said "no" in a simple way, and the child thinks a "yes" was received even though it wasn't actually stated. The child keeps asking the questions over time and the parents keep putting her off. Nothing changes expect that time is wasted or one party or the other surrenders. Better to say "yes" in the beginning where it is possible and appropriate, and "no" when that is in order. The following list is of unknown origin and includes ways that one can say "no" in a manner that fits the situation.

- *Plain NO*–It is rewarding for both parties when presented with no emotion or excuses. It is the right thing to do.

- *There is no time NO*–"I'll have to check my schedule. I might be able to get to it the week after next."

- *Alternative NO*–"I can't do that but I could do . . . ."

- *Moral NO*–"I just would not feel right doing that."

- *Excuse NO*–"I'd love to but . . . ."

- *Decision NO*–"After considering all the factors you presented, the answer must be no."

- *Priority NO*–"I have several things to do. Some of them are: [list them]. Which do you want me to accomplish?"

- *Conditional NO*–This answer has the appearance and gentle feeling of a "yes." "I would agree to do that if you will agree to [whatever]."

- *Apologetic NO*–Easy letdown–"I'm sorry, but I have another commitment."

- *System won't let us NO*–"Have you checked the manual on that?"

- *Legal NO*–"We could go to jail for that."

- *What if . . . NO*–"What if the front office finds out?"

   These ways to say "no" serve another purpose. The leader can more easily recognize what is happening when she gets a "no" from anyone. The leader must also be aware of potential reactions to "no."

Positive	Negative
Receive less requests	You're fired
Receive new respect	People who can't say "no" get the job
Do it themselves	Others may think you're not a team player
Won't ask again	May think you don't support the organization
Find someone else	

17. *Daydreaming*–Replace daydreams with action plans.

18. *Poor delegation*–At this point in the program most leaders should be getting their feet wet in the delegation game. The following quote provides guidance:

> The best executive is the one who has sense enough to pick good men to do what he wants done and the self restraint to keep from meddling with them while they do it.
>
> Teddy Roosevelt

19. *Poor working relationships*–Working relations were covered in Volume I. Two comments serve as a review: strive for harmony, but not at the sake of quality; and practice the golden rule.

20. *Unclear goals*–See Volume III.

21. *Poor prioritization*–See Volume III.

22. *Talking too much*–Three simple steps can solve this problem.

    a. Learn to listen.

    b. Ask questions.

    c. When the sale is made, write up the order.

23. *Poor handwriting*–I once spent hours searching for a mistake caused by handwriting by mistaking a 5 for a 3. Enough said.

24. *Excessive time on enjoyable projects*–Determine who should be doing these projects or if they should be done at all. Make sure projects are worked by priority. Remember allowable level of performance (ALP). Don't create a masterpiece when it isn't required. For example, a fancy letter when a response in the margin will suffice.

25. *Spreading yourself too thin*–Complete your job first. You are paid for that. Take on additional projects only to the limit they can be accomplished correctly.

26. *Poor thought transfer*–The rules for communication apply. Listen. Speak or write to convey thought, not to impress. Check for understanding. Audit for results.

27. *Poor-self discipline*–Plan your operation. Operate your plan.

28. *Socializing*–When you feel a need to mingle, converse on work-related subjects. Remember the value of your time.

29. *Firefighting*–A continuous plan that is followed and has commitment from all who are involved prevents most fires. Most fires are caused in part by procrastination.

30. *Unfinished tasks*–Endeavor to set enough time aside to complete important tasks or portions thereof. Stick to it until completion.

Time-Waster Checklist

Reading about time-wasters and agreeing there are some in the workplace is not enough. An audit of time-wasters is an excellent way to begin their elimination. The checklist in Figure 14.7 is provided as an audit guide and doubles as the basis for an action plan to reduce the problems.

Procrastination

Procrastination is another form of time-waster, but it is a problem of significant magnitude to warrant coverage as a stand-alone topic.

Our definition: "Procrastination is the science of putting things off until you get A ROUND TUIT."

Procrastination is the greatest *work saver* ever known to man. It involves putting off until tomorrow what you have already put off until today in an effort to put things off until it is too late or it becomes unnecessary to do them. People program less work than is required for success. Then they complete less work than planned which would have made them unsuccessful in the beginning. This subpar performance causes considerable pressure. Individuals usually wind up spending more time on the job covering up for their failures than they would if they had planned and worked for success in the beginning.

Do you know why most people plan tasks for *later on?* They don't have to start right away and by the time they get *a round tuit* the work might go away. It is the immediate supervisor's job to stop procrastination. Ensure there is enough work planned to meet success and then make sure the planned work is completed each day on time. Daily checks of planned activity against completed activity prevents most procrastination. Stopping procrastination promotes success. Generally, when a person tastes success, it motivates them

The following checklist aids the identification of time-wasters that inhabit most workplaces. Check the ones that prevail in your organization. Once the audit is completed, priorities can be assigned in the effort to eliminate them.

Quality-related time-wasters

___ Training not based on need

___ Rework efforts

___ Inspection

___ Handling complaints

___ Overtime

___ Red tape

___ Organization and reorganization

___ Social safaris

___ Boss emulation

Planned time-wasters

___ Double lunch hours

___ Checkbook Charlie

___ Personal phone calls

___ Winding down the workday

___ Waiting for checks

___ Business lunches

___ Friday power lunches

Environmental time-wasters

___ Unplanned visitors

___ Unnecessary phone calls

___ Unorganized meetings

___ Socializers

___ Reading material

___ Travel

___ Excessive paperwork

___ Poor communications

___ Duplicated efforts

___ Poorly planned projects

___ Conflicting priorities

___ Incompetent staff

___ Poor or no management plans

___ Disorganization

___ Too much organization

___ Failure to say "no"

___ Daydreaming

___ Poor delegation

___ Poor working relationships

___ Unclear goals

___ Poor prioritization

___ Talking too much

___ Poor handwriting

___ Enjoyable projects

___ Spreading yourself too thin

___ Poor thought transfer

___ Poor self-discipline

___ Socializing

___ Firefighting

___ Unfinished tasks

Figure 14.7   Identifying Time-Wasters

to more success. Procrastination prevents success more than any other single problem by allowing people to defer the work until . . . .

There are several causes of procrastination:

Physical incompetence–Health keeps them from doing the job.

Ignorance–The person doesn't understand the job needs to be done, doesn't know what the deadline is, doesn't understand exactly how to do it, or maybe doesn't realize what you will do if it isn't completed.

Strategic delay–This involves planned procrastination, putting one thing off until another happens.

These three types of procrastination are not our actual problem though. The following two types are.

Dodging uncomfortable situations–This involves putting off an important or gratifying accomplishment for a minor, insignificant reason. An example might be the person who passes up the beauty of the countryside from a mountain top because he thinks he will be afraid of the heights. Slight discomfort prevents the pleasures of life or success in most endeavors. This dodging is a mental pollutant. Inconveniences become insurmountable problems that are deemed unsolvable. Any unpleasant but important activity is avoided to avoid hassle. Many performance improvement exercises remain idle because of this.

Avoid is the key here. Activity is avoided because of real or imagined reasons. For example, many pleasant activities are avoided for minor reasons. People pass up swimming because they don't like to take the required shower first. They don't mind showering, but don't want to shower before swimming. Because it is mandatory, they fight it in their minds.. Often the total resistance to the task or effort involved is the stewing about it beforehand. The longer the problem is dodged or avoided, the worse it becomes. The canoe sits on the shore because it might tip over. The person likes to swim.

Self-doubt–Self-doubt seriously impacts on performance. Self-doubt causes self putdown. It occurs when a person makes herself small in her mind and then sees herself as a negative achiever. Negative achievers tend to procrastinate because they believe they have some type of self-deficiency, which will prevent success and encourage failure. Preoccupation with supposed faults prevents creativity and productivity. The absence of creativity and productivity opens the door for procrastination.

It all begins when people doubt their ability, get down on themselves, and don't try because they think they can't. Self-doubt is relative. You can be feeling great at any one time and let a relatively minor incident upset you. Self-doubt can slip in at any point along the scale from complete confidence to utter worthlessness. This is because we all lack self-confidence at some point, such as the point of implementing TQM. The most negative self-doubter experiences some self-confidence when he is doing something he does often and knows how to do, such as telling sea stories to friends.

At some point pride tends to get into the way of accomplishment. The person fears a loss of prestige and covers for that by reminding everyone of her position. Often this is where the individual starts retreating from the task at hand and begins the career of a *workaholic*. People begin to run to avoid failure and dash past opportunity. They go for repetitive negative habits that preclude success. Increased time is wasted on relatively minor tasks. Managers don't delegate because they want it done right. All energy is used up in the pursuit of success and little is left to complete the necessary work to meet their goals.

Self-doubt and dodging often appear as a combination force. Each feeds the other retarding any advancement. The person feels helpless to turn things around.

Preventing or stopping procrastination requires strong leadership. One step to this is training to the problem using the field training method and supervision of time and activity with strict accountability for both. Plan to overcome procrastination; plan for success and follow the plan; work to destroy causes of procrastination from the start; objectively evaluate your operation; ensure timely completion of tasks that are often put off.

The value for overcoming procrastination is evident. You will have time to implement TQM and performance improvement efforts. There will be satisfaction gained from timely completion of tasks. You have time to stop and smell the roses while you gain self-acceptance with your accomplishments. This is a beginning step to success.

The first step to stopping procrastination is to closely monitor all activities. Evaluate what you complete and what you put off. Determine why you delay the things that do not get done. Are they less important or are they important but unpleasant? Cross items off where there doesn't seem to be a real need for them. If it is something mandated from above you'll need permission, of course. Get out your *to-do* list (Figure 14.8) and start. The people who procrastinate generally want to and are always allowed to. Procrastination is the single biggest cause of failure.

Gaining Control

This important topic is virtually a recap of what has been covered thus far in the chapter. Be ready to work. We don't have a time management problem, we have a time mismanagement problem. Managerial performance and quality tasks are unlimited while a managers time has definite limits. Choice through the establishment of priorities is essential. First things first.

Make decisions. Remember, the unexpected always can happen no matter how much you plan. The only thing that remains constant is the rate of change. There always will be complications. Don't let anyone discourage you. Don't be SNIOPED (subject to the negative influence of others) or afraid of change.

Things to do	Telephone calls	Appointments
	Correspondence	
		Personal

Figure 14.8   To-do List

There are a few concepts of time management that bear repeating. The first is *work—work—work—in that order.* Somebody said it well, "While it may be true that work is respectable, that doesn't seem to make it any more popular." Know what your tasks are through assignment and goal-setting. Rank the tasks in order of importance. Determine what tasks can be delegated. Determine where time can be saved by taking the correct steps now. Many people actually plan not to save time so they can *waste* time in more pleasant activities. Keep charts to track your progress on each major task. Follow up. At the end of each week, analyze your activity and time usage. Was your time used well? Why or why not? Time management takes a continual, concerted effort. It is not a sometimes thing.

Time management is a major form of self-discipline. The only way to be free for high-performance activities is through self-discipline and sound habit-forming efforts. *"Do it right often enough and you'll be free to do it automatically."* This means one must do the right things *(effectiveness)* and things right *(efficiency).* Establish goals and then plan action based on those goals. Work through simplicity, consistency, and repetition. The following must be controlled with an iron fist or you will lose what little time you now have for thinking and planning.

- Conversations (routine with little constructive meaning).
- Reading (not career-/job-related).
- Coffee and smoke breaks.
- Routine tasks.
- Windshield time–driving to work (1 hour x 5 days x 48 weeks = 240 hours or 6 weeks).

Time management consultants who observe supervisors and managers in their daily environment suggest they can save two hours daily just by controlling the first four items. *"Too much of our day is spent on* tension-relieving *rather than* goal-achieving *activities."*

Handling management tasks is an art. Many can be worked on any time up to the deadline. Plan tasks for slack periods to avoid last-minute rushes. Interruptions may occur from time to time, but the job will be in progress and will get done. You will have time to produce better product because you gave it time.

Learn to delegate. Significant emphasis has been placed on this subject but it is important enough to summarize once more. Train your relief by delegation. This does not mean dumping the dirty jobs on someone else. Manage by exception. You don't have to tell how, when, why, and how on each task when people are properly trained. This management effort will work only where there are well-trained and motivated personnel with continuous assessment of results.

Keep the boss posted on your workload. If she doesn't know the work schedule of you and your team, she can't help you or know when you are overloaded. You are dreaming if you expect your boss to sit back and admire how you grin and bear it. Chances are your reward will be increased frustration. Program ever-increasing time efficiency and effectiveness.

Ensure timely decisions. Don't defer decisions, learn to say yes or no, and handle paperwork once. Undertake better programming of activities. Consolidate tasks, screening for unnecessary work and redundancy.

Program efficient use of assets. Control the phone, use personnel wisely, secure help from outside, use sales, "I have a problem, can you help me?" and remember to work.

Some time-multipliers include:

1. Delegation.

2. Do your own work, not your subordinates.'

3. Secretary.

4. Computerized systems, reports, letters.

5. KISS.

6. Concentration.

7. Control boards with projects, dates, costs, and so forth.

8. Trained personnel.

9. Quality products, quality systems, quality personnel, quality, quality, quality.

The following is a personal audit for time leaks. Check those items that apply to you. *Be honest!*

____ Engaging in personal business before the work of the day is complete.

____ Beginning a task before thinking it through.

____ Completing tasks by hand that are better accomplished with computers.

____ Completing unproductive tasks from sheer habit.

____ Engaging in "like to do" tasks at the expense of "need to do" tasks.

____ Placing too high of a priority on low-priority tasks.

____ Allowing and condoning unproductive interruptions.

____ Making unnecessary phone calls and visits.

____ Socializing at great lengths between tasks.

____ Doing work that need not be completed.

____ Doing work that is not part of your job.

____ Doing work that should be delegated.

____ Failing to allow for crises.

____ Failing to plan on a scheduled basis with your people.

____ Failing to plan on a scheduled basis with your boss.

____ *Allowing quality that requires rework.*

Summary

Time management is extremely important for implementing TQM. Correct time utilization provides the needed time. The summary for time management is presented as a recap of time-wasters with tactics for overcoming them.

Problem Area	The Fix
1. Procrastination	Break up large tasks into manageable tasks. Plan deadlines for each smaller task and the overall project. Begin work ahead of time so the work is completed on time. Plan undesirable efforts for the beginning of the workday so you can reward yourself earlier.
2. Poor planning	Complete a daily to-do list. Rank tasks in order of importance. Complete high-priority tasks first. Plan difficult tasks for prime time so they can be completed when you are at your best.
3. Planning too much	Plan those things you must do. Delegate, say "no," and don't allow busy work.
4. Low quality work	Slow down and improve quality. Rework always takes more time than completing something correctly on the first go-around.
5. Interruptions	Have visitors and phone calls screened. Place a timer near the phone. Set it for three minutes. A lot can be accomplished in this amount of time. After that period, it is generally not business. Establish visiting hours and quiet time.
6. Poor automation	Learn to use the computer. Stop unnecessary handwork.

7. Paper clutter	Clean off your desk with the exception of the project on which you are working. Handle each piece of paper once. File it, trash it, or move it along on its way.
8. Overload of routine	Save routine tasks and handle them during nonprime time. Do these tasks in batches when you cannot do something else.
9. Indecision	Start early, gather the appropriate information, and make decisions. Realize that some risk is unavoidable. You are paid to make decisions that get today's work out today with quality.
10. Poor meeting habits	The greatest of all management time-wasters, second only to procrastination in the overall adverse impact on TQM. Schedule meetings only when there is a valid requirement. Plan an agenda and stick to it. Hold meetings before lunch and at the end of the day. Delegate meeting attendance where appropriate.

Bibliography

Azrin, N. H. and Nunn, R. G. *Habit Control in a Day*, New York: Simon and Schuster, 1977.

Bliss, E. C. *Getting Things Done*, New York: Bantam Books, 1983.

Bond, W. J. *1001 Ways to Best the Time Trap*, New York: Frederick Fell Publishers, 1982.

Crosby, P. B. *Quality Without Tears*, New York: McGraw-Hill, 1984.

Douglass, M. E. and Douglass D. N. *Manage Your Time, Manage Your Work, Manage Yourself*, New York: AMACOM, 1980.

Frank, M. O. *How to Get Your Point Across in 30 Seconds—or Less*, New York: Simon and Schuster, 1986.

Lakein, A. *How to Get Control of Your Time and Your Life*, New York: Signet, 1973.

Lee, J. W. *Hour Power*, Homewood, IL: Dow Jones-Irwin, 1980.

Rutherford, R. D. *Just in Time*, New York: John Wiley and Sons, 1981.

Scheele, A. *Skills for Success*, New York: Ballentine Books, 1979.

Sloma, R. J. *No-Nonsense Planning*, New York: The Free Press, 1984.

Smith, M. J. *When I Say No, I Feel Guilty,* New York: Bantam Books, 1980.

Webber, R. A. *Time Is Money! The Key to Managerial Success,* New York: The Free Press, 1980.

CHAPTER 15

Management Ethics

This chapter explores management ethics because these decisions generally impact in many ways on TQM. Several perspectives are viewed including the needs of the organization, its people, the customers, stockholders (where appropriate), and the United States itself. Clear-cut answers are few. Therefore, this information is presented as discussions and questions that should assist leaders and managers in their efforts to make ethical decisions.

Certain subjects will not be broached. For example, various sorts of bribes are sometimes considered a part of international business, but they have little to do with TQM so they aren't discussed. Bribing an organization's purchasing agents to accept inferior products does involve quality and the customer so it is fair game.

It is realized that some decisions will be ethically correct for all concerned, but will still be difficult to make. Firing the incompetent troublemaker is correct, but it is not easy to put a family man out in the street. Fighting a dissatisfied customer in court is correct when the problem is not a faulty product, but incorrect use of the product. Management cannot stand by and allow these situations to take place.

Those who have not served in leadership positions could easily assume that management ethics are a rather simple, cut-and-dried matter. However, those who have struggled with the trade-offs between economic, environmental, moral, political, legal, and social issues realize there are difficult decisions that must be made on a routine basis. Personal moral standards and values must be a part of all decisions. None of these items can stand by themselves without considering the other issues. That considerably compounds the decision-making process.

What's right for the organization and what's right for its people may seem worlds apart. If it's right for business is it always right for the United States? The answers are seldom black or white, right or wrong solutions.

It also suggests that stock right and wrong decisions are virtually impossible, and no attempt will be made to develop any such decisions. Rather, the issues faced by managers are discussed from different viewpoints in order to assist managers in their quest to make ethical decisions with which they can live—decisions made after carefully considering all issues.

The dilemma is quickly outlined by a commonly occurring example when mergers or acquisitions occur. Two organizations are merged into one which results in several duplicate managerial positions. The executive facing such decision finds a majority and a minority filling the two positions and one of them must go. Each person has strengths that benefit the new organization along with some weaknesses that must be considered. One of the individuals has an illness in the family that would be difficult to handle without the organization's health plan. One has a broader customer base, the other a substantial political base. One has been active in organizational training, the other in community affairs. One is closer to retirement than the other. Who stays and who goes? Can one person be used in some other position that would economically benefit the organization? Would retraining be required? Would a salary restructuring be in order?

What are the moral and social implications of turning the person out who requires the health care? Health insurance at a new organization would not pay for a preexisting condition. What are the legal ramifications concerning the Equal Employment Opportunity requirements? What are the political considerations of concern with local governmental units, the citizenry, and the people remaining with the organization? What are the economic considerations for the organization and the individuals? Which issues should take precedence and why?

How about the manufacturer who produces a product where a serious safety defect is discovered in a few products after they are on the market for some time? Should a recall be authorized that could potentially bankrupt the organization and throw everyone out of a job? If not, what if someone is killed or seriously injured because there was no recall? What would you do?

Consider white-collar crime for a moment. Is the person who embezzles large sums of money, defrauds shareholders, converts organizational assets to personal use, or pays himself an enormous salary which bankrupts the organization causing many innocent people to lose their savings less of a criminal than the person who holds up a convenience store to feed his family? How about the elected official who accepts reelection funds from unethical sources that expect favors in return? Is she any less of a criminal than the blackmail artist coercing money from someone who made a mistake and doesn't want it known.

Consider the educational system that allows a student to graduate who is not totally qualified because of a missing credit or a minor mix-up somewhere along the line. Does the trauma of repeating the senior year because of a relatively minor deficiency outweigh compliance with all educational requirements? How about the power plant spewing out pollutants to generate electricity. What are the trade-offs here? What about nuclear power? Should it be discontinued until every problem is worked out? If so, where do we get the energy to replace what we give up? Is it simply a matter of good or bad, right or wrong; or might there be some alternatives that should be explored?

All other things being equal, should the manager who saves money or the manager who keeps the customers happy be promoted? Who should be rated higher, the person completing an advanced degree or the person studying to overcome a departmental problem? Is the manager who produces short-term profit or long-term growth more valuable? Is the manager with the highest production or the best quality more important to the organization?

Is it okay to sell potentially defective goods if the buyers know what they are buying, but their organizations do not? All of these situations compound the manager's decision-making process. The solutions are not easy to come by so let's examine the process.

TQM demands addition to the study of ethics of the 1970s. Peter F. Drucker, writing in *Management: Tasks—Responsibilities—Practices,* begins with the Hippocratic oath: *primum non nocere,* or "above all, not knowingly to do harm." This is solid, golden rule common sense, but does it go far enough?

Today's organization cannot simply rely on not knowingly causing harm, rather it must be at the forefront planning, designing, and working to cause solid quality, cost-competitive goods and services for all customers while constantly striving to improve those goods and services. It also must recognize and reward people for the successes they achieve in the accomplishment of this goal. Nothing less will do for TQM and anything less may actually threaten the organization's survival.

LaRue Hosmer, writing in *The Ethics of Management,* examines this managerial dilemma and draws the following five conclusions from it.

1. "Most ethical decisions have extended consequences."

2. "Most ethical decisions have multiple alternatives."

3. "Most ethical decisions have mixed outcomes."

4. "Most ethical decisions have uncertain consequences."

5. "Most ethical decisions have personal implications."

These are interesting concepts, but what do they mean to managers? The following discussions consider the implications of each of them.

1. *"Most ethical decisions have extended consequences."* This statement means the consequences of the decision do not stop at that level of management. Instead, they migrate throughout the organization and society, impacting on many who were not involved with the initial decision. The power plant is an excellent example because all pollution affects the environment and everybody in it. Because decisions would also affect economics, they affect each person who earns a living at the plant plus all who are associated with it in other ways. Regardless of what decision is made, some person or group surely will find fault with it.

2. *"Most ethical decisions have multiple alternatives."* As mentioned earlier, those who have not been faced with the tough decisions too often believe answers to be yes or no, right or wrong, or black and white. The truth is the answers are seldom this simple. Is some power plant pollution acceptable in order to best serve energy-starved industries? Environmental groups may think any pollution is unbearable. Investors in the plant are interested in the cost of controlling pollution to various levels, and the work force wants to know how everything affects their jobs. Should it be no pollution, some pollution, or let someone else worry about pollution?

3. *"Most ethical decisions have mixed outcomes."* Too often outsiders perceive that management decisions are made over two directly opposed choices. The various economic, political, social, and legal groups often pose them this way. However, each of these various positions and others must be considered in the reality of decision-making. The strict environmentalist probably does not want his power source interrupted any more than the person willing to live with a great deal of pollution in order to receive his electricity—neither wants a power problem. What are the trade-offs between economic, environmental, and other ethical issues? It is easy to question, but difficult to answer.

4. *"Most ethical decisions have uncertain consequences."* Few can predict accurately what the outcomes will be for the decisions that must be made. Monday morning quarterbacking is easy, but it is more difficult to predict the results new technology will have over the long run. It is even more difficult to predict how the various factions will view the decisions about new technology. Consider the power plant and the radiation that is generated from transporting high-voltage, high-current electricity. What are the harmful effects of the power leakage from these transmission lines? They make your AM radio squawk; do they also make people squawk in some way? How about all the radiated energy from

the users of this energy such as radio, TV, cellular phones, electric blankets, and so forth? What are the side effects in this area? No one really knows if we are courting disaster or simply utilizing the energy source available to us.

5. *"Most ethical decisions have personal implications."* At first glance, many would believe management personnel are largely apart from the decisions they make. This is not true. The power plant management could decide to install pollutant scrubbers which clean up the air, but impact heavily on profit. The investors would begin clamoring for their scalps, and if it impacted heavily enough to require salary and benefit adjustments, the work force would certainly be upset. Those adversely affected by the pollution would be much happier about such a decision.

After this discussion the ethical dilemma should appear much more realistic for all who read this chapter. It is not easy to combine economic, environmental, social, political, and legal issues plus moral values into ethical solutions. The remainder of this chapter will be used to outline some of the ethical decisions that must be made by organizational managers.

Hiring, Firing, and Promotion

Few areas of management are more important or more prone to second guessing. Perhaps this is because of all the different human elements that are involved.

TQM requires excellent employees in every position in order to provide cost-competitive quality products and quality customer service. These employees should be hired at a salary commensurate with their potential value as determined by such things as ability, education, and experience, which will benefit the organization. Any organization will agree with these statements. The problem arises with the ethics of hiring, firing, and promotion.

Equal Employment Opportunity regulations, political considerations, and social issues are all involved. Family-owned businesses want to place family members in solid positions with a future; minority-owned businesses want to place minorities in prominent positions; and female-owned organizations want to sponsor women. The owners also want to make a profit in profit-oriented organizations and in other organizations, managers desire to provide exceptional service and benefits for the financial obligations.

The 1964 Civil Rights Act and subsequent legislation precludes discrimination based on age, race, religion, sex, national origin, or handicaps except in some carefully defined situations. That is as it should be. Shouldn't individual qualifications determine that the best person is hired for each position?

However well-intentioned these legislated acts were, they often preclude hiring the best personnel. Affirmative action programs require positive steps to locate, recruit, and hire minorities or underprivileged. The law states that all other things being equal, the minority member should be hired or promoted. In many cases this means that all other relevant things being unequal, the minority still receives the job or promotion because the organization has percentages that must be maintained for its affirmative action program. Most managers have felt the pressure to hire or promote less qualified people or to retain less qualified people to keep percentages up.

There also can be problems within minority groups. In early 1991, Paul Harvey reported on a radio broadcast that a minority-owned organization had hired all minority employees, yet was still in trouble with the law. The owner had hired Hispanic employees at a higher percentage than black employees which was out of sync with the surrounding population. The reported requirements placed on the employer to correct the problem would bankrupt the employer putting everybody involved out of work. The case was not yet settled as of the writing of this book.

In the late 1970s and early 1980s minority groups pressured Congress into forcing the military to recruit minorities to at least the same level as the American population for all positions across the total military structure. It was difficult at first, but military recruiting overcame the obstacles and hired qualified minorities at a rate exceeding the national population percentages. For minorities and poorer whites, the military is a way up the social and economic ladder.

There was no problem until the Persian Gulf War (Desert Storm). Minority groups then complained that minorities statistically made up too high a percentage of the troops employed. The news media picked up the story and gave it a good bit of time. Luckily for the military, General Colin Powell, chairman of the Joint Chiefs of Staff (himself a minority) stepped forward and said he joined for economic reasons and he believed every American should have the opportunity to serve. That took the sting out of the situation and the news services dropped a sticky issue. What would have happened if General Powell were not a minority? What if there had been heavy casualties? What is the correct policy for the military to take? Should minority enlistments be restricted?

Recent court decisions have interpreted some legislation differently, and Congress is trying to enact additional legislation to guarantee certain things for various minorities. The future of these acts is unknown at this time. Many majorities are now complaining about reverse discrimination in hiring, firing, promotion, and admission to institutions such as medical school, and so forth. Others say that professional sports, being businesses, should have majorities to the level of the population at large. No one knows how any of these situations will turn out. What is known is the situation certainly compounds decision-making for management.

Employees have rights on the job. They should be free from hassle, discrimination, bias, and harassment. This means they should not receive such treatment from management and management has an obligation to ensure they do not receive such treatment from fellow workers. Those people unwilling to work harmoniously should be removed from the workplace.

Management also has an obligation to maintain a safe working environment. This means that machines and equipment must be safe to operate, the work space must be clear of hazards, and unseen elements such as radiation, chemical hazards, or other such elements must not be present. Should there be any dangers, these must be made known to employees at the onset.

Firing people can be an equally difficult decision. Outside of contractual obligations, various acts can be at cross purposes with financial considerations which are also different from the social needs of the involved individuals and the community at large. These problems can be greatly exaggerated when there is corporate downsizing requirements for whatever reason. Last hired, first fired rules often upset gains that minorities and women have made within the organization.

At times, promotions carry their own set of problems. Promotional competence should be the main qualifier. Seniority, however, may play a large part in the decision. Racial and male/female mixes also are considerations that may be considered important. At times, they may outweigh competence as a deciding factor.

What can management do to eliminate or reduce the problems associated with this dilemma? Volumes I and II discussed these issues in various areas. Let's examine some of them here.

1. The first thing to do is to be aware of the personnel mix, pay scales and wage levels, promotional opportunities, and other such factors within the organization. These statistics should be available so that all managers can use them as they endeavor to make ethical decisions.

2. Hiring considerations are important. The first consideration should be one of the lean and mean philosophy. It may be better to use temps, overtime, and so forth, for short-term projects rather than hiring. The second step is to ensure all personnel who recruit for the organization are aware of the personnel needs to maintain a reasonable and proper employee mix. Potential openings should be widely publicized. Great pains should be taken to complete correct interviewing and hiring procedures. These are all outlined in Chapter 5.

3. All employees should benefit from solid counseling and training within the organization. They should know what is and will be available in terms of promotions and other job opportunities, educational

benefits, and training programs. All employees should be on a continuous training program which benefits them and the organization. Training, education, and other personal achievements should be recorded for use during promotion cycles so the best person stands out.

4. Unlike some, I believe in personnel performance evaluations. Truly excellent people want their performance to be recognized and evaluated. Such evaluations provide a good method of recording achievements in all areas, potential for promotion, and contributions that should be noted during considerations for promotion. These evaluations provide a way of documenting shortfalls that need to be overcome, and follow-on evaluations can document whether the individual has or has not been able to overcome the problem. Evaluations must be factual assessments and contain key informational areas that can be used for promotion or retention if they are to be of any great value.

5. Every organization should have an established procedure to handle personnel problems. Counseling should be an immediate step with counseling and butt-chewing not being considered synonymous. The deficiencies and recommended corrective action should be noted. The supervisor and individual receiving counseling both sign the counseling sheet. Copies are made for the supervisor, the individual, and the individual's permanent record. All employees should be made aware of the proper procedure to follow should they think they are being wronged. The supervisor must assist the individuals where possible in efforts to overcome the problem.

6. Firing is another matter. Individuals should have the opportunity to clean up their act. When problems persist, those employees should be removed from the work force. Often it is to their advantage to be fired. Some people hate their job for some reason, but stick with it because of the security or some other such reason. They become tied to a job they dislike because they perceive the penalty for leaving is too great. When forced to seek other employment, they often come up with work more in line with their likes and strengths.

7. Wages, salary, and other compensations are another factor that demands fairness. Wages should be based on contribution to the organization and competence on the job. Attention must be paid to the spread between compensation packages for the bottom workers and executive management. What that spread should be is beyond this work, but it should be carefully determined by each organization. Managers must question the tendency of some to give in to short-term compensation demands that could destroy the organization. Economic survival depends on fair compensation for all parties.

8. All managers should continuously strive to maintain currency with the rules, regulations, policies, laws, and so forth, that deal with this important area. It is too important to let it slide. Careers can easily be made or destroyed in this vital area.

Performance

Performance in terms of productivity and quality is vital in the quest for excellence. The organization must produce quality goods and service to remain in existence. Productivity is a major factor in the economic equation whether it be profit in business or amount of service per dollar or some other such measurement in nonprofit organizations.

Quality is important in the effort to satisfy both internal and external customers. No organization can exist for long without quality. The question is how performance becomes an ethical issue.

Many factors determine productivity: worker performance, resource utilization, process, and so forth, are included. Machines may be able to complete a task more economically with higher quality than the people who currently work the effort. The problem arises when people would become unemployed because of the change. The manager's decision must not only account for the economics and quality, but also the social and political issues of personnel layoffs.

Worker performance is an ethical issue when poor performance of any kind is tolerated by any manager. Poor performance directly impacts on the stockholders who want a profit and customers who want the best product at the correct investment level. It further impacts on the morale of the people within the organization who must work around the person or team with poor performance. It ultimately affects the individuals or team involved because their opportunities for promotion and job security are involved.

TQM improves both effectiveness and efficiency. All things being equal, more quality product can be produced quicker with less expense as the TQM process pays off. This can result in a requirement for fewer workers which could mean employees would work themselves out of a job because their efforts improved the organization. All efforts must be to retrain replaced workers for other efforts and prevent layoffs that would be caused because employees improved their job performance. This places a burden on the research and design department to come up with new products, marketing to increase sales, and so forth. How can you ensure people do not work themselves out of a job through performance improvements without negatively impacting on profit or costs?

Training is another ethical consideration. Employees must be trained to perform to the best of their ability. Their future and that of the organization depend on it. The organization deserves a payoff at least equal to the resources that were expended to provide the training. Shareholders deserve training effectiveness because profit depends on performance. The customer deserves the best product without increased costs due to training.

QCS and Customer Relations

No area of the organizational equation is more important than this. Without their customers, there would be no reason for the existence of any organization. Those organizations that refuse to recognize this factor seldom remain in existence for long. This buyer–seller or supplier–customer relationship carries legal, economical, moral, social, and often political ramifications. Therefore, its importance can not be overstated.

The supplier is legally and morally bound to provide a defect-free product or service to the customer. When the product is anything less than first line (such as in the sale of imperfect clothes or blemished tires), the seller is obligated to so note this condition. As-is sales are ethical as long as the known defects are so noted. However, a car with a known defect or a refrigerator that doesn't work cannot be sold as-is without the potential for greater problems.

Suppliers are required to provide safe products or services. In fact, suppliers may sometimes face liability if they act in a negligent manner or are not guilty of wrongful intent should they be remiss in warning customers of dangers that are involved with the operation of their product or there are design flaws of some sort.

This places the burden on the supplier. That is why new rifles have warning labels stamped in the barrels to read the directions before firing and wood stoves come with a label that reads "HOT WHILE IN OPERATION." It matters not that responsible people should know this as a given fact.

The customer has a responsibility to use products in a safe manner in the manner they were intended. In fact, their requirements are just about the reverse of the sellers. Suppliers should not share liability when the customer deliberately bypasses relays or immobilizes safety factors such as guards on power equipment. They should also be reasonably informed so they can make sound buying decisions.

This does not reduce the need for the seller to educate the buyer in certain areas. This presales education is an excellent sales tool and when followed with usage training afterward, it goes a long way toward building a solid customer base.

The supplier must recognize the customer has a right to receive a product equal to the resource that is exchanged to obtain it. Sales contracts should be a fair agreement for both parties. This precludes kickbacks for business-type deals although they are considered a part of doing business in some sectors.

Taxpayers should, on average, receive services that make their tax payments worthwhile.

Ethics demand that the customer is not deceived into buying goods or services through fraud, lies, or false advertising. Fraud exists when the person is intentionally deceived about any fact that is important in the buying decision. Lying about the product is just as bad.

Advertising ethics also require that the seller use terms more or less standard to the industry in the way industry tends to use them. Television ads that depict a person dressed like a trucker sitting in a large truck and talking out the window could reasonably be considered to suggest that the product is endorsed by truckers. If the product is not so endorsed should it be advertised in this manner?

The customer also has the right to receive the product or service that is advertised, not a similar substitute or something close to the advertised article or service. It has to be the exact item or service. Insinuations that the quality is one thing when it actually is something else also is wrong. Bait and switch tactics are definitely out. Sellers who want repeat business must be careful of tactics such as sales leaders advertised as "limited to the in-store stock only" or other such terms when there negligible amounts of these items. Would you want to drive a considerable distance for a product that is sold out when you get there? How would you feel if the salesperson told you there were only two in stock when the product was advertised?

Modern packaging can hide problems or goods other than those advertised. The customer can have recourse when this happens. Clear labeling is important on packaging so any warnings are clearly visible. Warnings for drowsiness are required on certain medications with a statement warning not to drive after using the medication.

Ingredients must now be placed on foods, beverages, and medicines so that customers can make informed decisions about the goods they purchase. This precludes hypertension sufferers from buying products heavy in salt, heart patients from buying caffeine-loaded products, and so forth.

The customer is entitled to accurate credit descriptions. A seller cannot legally deceive the buyer about the terms of the sale or the cost of credit. Sales for major purchases often require a signed disclosure statement that explains the terms in detail. Exploitation by either party is unethical at best and may be fraud. It certainly is not the basis for long-term mutually beneficial agreements.

Those providing information services are considered unethical when they provide information they know is incorrect or questionable. It is equally wrong for an organization to have a person in an advisory position when that person may not have the experience, knowledge, and training to be dispensing such advice.

There are many obligations that accompany the price. Prices advertised to be the lowest prices must indeed be the lowest. It also is illegal and unethical for sellers to cooperate with others to fix prices to some preset level.

Many companies offer better prices to large-volume buyers which limits competition in certain areas. This is a standard way of doing business, but smaller customers are now finding ways to fight back in this area. Various cooperative arrangements are used to make smaller organizations more competitive. Many smaller distributors rely more heavily on imported goods to sell in order to remain in business. Is this right for America?

The customer also has the right to expect reasonable service, no-hassle warranty work, proper set-up efforts, and any follow-up training, tuning, adjustments, and so forth, that were promised as a condition for the sale.

Lastly, customers have a right to expect respect, fair and courteous service, prompt response to need, and unbiased advice at all times, not just by sales and service personnel, but by everyone with whom they come in contact from the organization. It is due them as customers and human beings. Increasing numbers of Americans are refusing to accept anything less. It is correct that we refuse to deal with people and organizations who do not prove they want our business.

Security

Security is another ethical element. Commercial espionage and insider trading information may result in legal penalties and it certainly is unethical. Organizations must continually guard against compromise from the senior officer to the newest worker.

Background security investigations may be an employment requirement for many organizations. Companies that work with the Department of Defense share the same national security responsibilities as those people actually employed with DOD.

There also is a case for organizational security. This concerns internal formulas such as the formula for Coca-Cola which is carefully guarded. Cosmetic manufacturers have the same type internal restrictions as do many others.

There are times when organizations have security needs for certain temporary projects. One example that comes to mind is the act of preparing technical and cost proposals for the purpose of bidding on work efforts. The contents of these are carefully guarded lest they fall into the hands of competitors. Working copies are carefully shredded as the material is reworked. It is equally important that the customer guard against disclosure of such proprietary information that is supplied by a bidder.

Professionals such as doctors, lawyers, counselors, consultants, auditors, and so forth, have professional secrets. They have a professional responsibility to ensure secrecy of the client information they hold. Certain governmental agencies, such as the IRS, also receive client information that must be carefully guarded against compromise.

Joint teaming agreements for the purpose of designing, building, or producing some goods or service(s) generally have security arrangements. These are needed to ensure that technology and other secrets organizations are privy to do not migrate out of an organization without permission.

Insider information has security requirements. Many organizations have policies that must be agreed to as a condition of employment. There are laws that pertain to the use of insider information in organizations, such as the stock market or banking operations. The recent arrests, prosecutions, and jail terms for some of the perpetrators are excellent examples of what can happen to both the perpetrator and innocent investors when these rules are violated.

Community Relations

Organizations and the communities they reside in share mutual needs, benefit each other, and support each other to varying degrees. Their relationships vary accordingly. Communities and states compete for business and industry to locate within their confines through tax incentives, favorable laws, breaks on property, and relocation assistance. It is important that all incentives be above board and out in the open rather than payoffs through company officials or local politicians.

At times, a major company may control local politics and dominate the economy. There is nothing inherently wrong with this unless the company runs roughshod over the community. At times communities dictate policy to organizations that may result in their moving to other localities with more favorable climates for their existence. This is costly to all concerned parties. A caring relationship must be established through the efforts of both parties in order that the community at large, the organization, and the work force maximize the benefits they receive.

Organizations that are dominant employers have significant leverage within communities. There are cases where highly profitable companies demand unearned benefits such as out-of-line tax breaks. They acquire them through the threat to move out of the area if they are not received. Can this be considered ethical behavior?

Compensation packages also have ethical implications. Do dominant organizations have a responsibility to maintain compensation packages commensurate with the requirements of their job responsibilities? Or is it okay if they provide a compensation package that strips the best workers from other organizations? What if they can afford this compensation because they wrangle tax breaks not available to smaller employers?

Organizations often benefit communities in other ways. They provide a base for professional volunteers who will share their expertise. They often contribute heavily to local charities. Certainly the taxes they pay help the community survive.

The community and the company owe each other certain things. The community owes the company a favorable business climate in return for the jobs and taxes they provide. The company cannot be milked out of existence. On the other hand, the company owes the community safe working conditions, good labor relations, an environmentally clean operation, prompt payment of taxes, and so forth.

At times, companies will decide to relocate for whatever reason. At this juncture the company must act in good faith to minimize the detrimental effects their move will have on the host community and the surrounding areas. Some organizations provide outplacement services and retraining programs to soften the blow. Often they try to place workers at other sites or take them with to a new location. A sad point is that many moves could be prevented if the local community, the business, and the work force would work more closely as a team, aware of the needs of each other and working to best meet those needs. It must be a team effort with all parties contributing, but it seems that all to often the forces involved cut off their noses to spite their faces until it is too late for anything but relocation or a shutdown.

Labor Relations

Solid labor relations are an important part of TQM. People who are considered as plant property seldom have the will for excellence. Conversely, those who share in the rewards of TQM work the hardest to improve performance and QCS.

In the past, many companies ignored their work force. This period is gone. Skilled employees are becoming more precious and have more mobility than they previously held. It is costly to replace and retrain skilled employees. This problem will continue to grow because of the current problems within the public education system which result in ever-increasing training costs for the private sector.

Labor relations was almost a mutually exclusive statement with many organizations in the not-too-distant past. Unions and companies often saw little on which to agree. Times are changing. There is an increasing awareness that everyone must work together to survive. Many unions and companies are building closer relationships enabling them to better face the increased competition of the global market.

Unions and companies are coming to realize the costs of long-term bargaining and negotiation actions. These costs come out of profits and could be better utilized in other areas. At the same time unions must guard the rights of their members while management must guard the rights of the company and its stockholders.

Many unions realize that built-in inefficiency, discrimination, and such factors are just as harmful to their survival as it is to the companies. Many unions now provide worker training on production, safety, and quality skills that makes their organization more competitive. This can only help all concerned over the long run.

Companies also must care for employees when there is no union. It is probably more important for the company to ensure they take care of their people properly to prevent worker disruptions, unionization, and other situations that can be avoided. The work force that is cared for, recognized, and correctly compensated for its efforts will be a more productive unit.

There are many other elements requiring ethical operations. It is important that all of these issues be dealt with in a manner that tells those involved and interested outsiders that the parties concerned resolved the issues in an ethical manner after careful consideration of all aspects of the problem.

Making the Ethical Decision

Ethical decisions are not always easy ones to make. The situation is complicated when the decision-maker has a personal stake in the outcome. It becomes difficult and perhaps impossible to divorce one's personal interests from the situation. Certainly, it is much easier to make decisions when there is no personal impact. That, however, seldom happens.

Consider the purchasing agent who is shopping for the organization interested in buying several new vehicles. One extremely competitive company offers to throw in a car for the purchasing agent at a cost even lower than the one the company is getting, just for good measure. Should the agent discuss the deal with his company? Should the agent accept the car? Could it be considered a bribe? Would you turn it down? Why?

Ethical decisions are not easy to make. Management awareness is probably the best preparation for meeting the difficulties faced in making these decisions. The following discussion of these ethical factors and associated questions builds an awareness to better prepare managers for difficult decisions.

Personal values and moral standards–Managers or leaders cannot make ethical decisions without consideration of their own standards. Regardless of what those values are, they played a large part in the process that got you where you are. No decision should be made without consideration of these standards. Should the needs of the organization conflict with your standards the final decision may be one of leaving the organization for one more in line with your values. Are you prepared to do that? Can you afford it without great hardships on yourself and your family? Is leaving worth it or is a value compromise more realistic? These are all tough decisions.

Economic Issues–Economic decisions are relatively easy when they are questions of affordability or the determination of which item is the best buy. They become more difficult when they concern potential layoffs, permanent downsizing, compensation cuts, or plant closings. Should there be layoffs when increased performance results in people working themselves out of a job? Should people be required to give up a percentage of their compensation to make up for poor management decisions? If so, what is the trade-off? Many would say that what is best for the organization is the best path to take. Should management concentrate on profitability or other factors? If so, what are the other factors and what part do they play? Should small suppliers be closed out of the market for economic reasons, or is there some obligation to assist reliable, long-term suppliers in some way? Is there a moral obligation for long-time supporters?

Environmental issues–These issues are becoming increasingly important as the quality of our environment becomes more endangered through the various pollutants. Should economic or environmental issues receive top billing? Are jobs more important than environmental concerns? Should employees accept potentially harmful levels of noise or chemical pollution as the cost of a job? Should nuclear power plants be built to reduce air pollution when we have not figured out how to handle the waste effectively? Is some level of pollution okay, and if it is, what is that level? Where is the dividing line between environmental impact and economic reason?

Social issues–Our economic system is a complex one with both winners and losers. Some members of society reap a much greater reward than others. This has been the American way. Over the years some people in political circles and outside activists have tried all types of ideas to even things up. They believe that some amount of profit may actually be owed to certain groups or individuals to make up for both present and past inequities in the system which is represented as a social cost. Others disagree. Regardless of which side one chooses, many questions evolve. How does an organization compensate its community and workers for the pollution it creates? Is it proper for government to sponsor welfare systems when there are job openings available? Should government bodies take work from small businesspeople and give it to minority businesses because of past problems? What if it bankrupts the small business that develops the system or product? Should minority workers be hired or promoted over majority workers when the deciding factor is race? Should affirmative action programs push for an equal racial balance in all businesses? What about sports and minority businesses? What about women and handicapped individuals? Should social programs be allowed to impact on production and quality? If so, who decides how much?

Political issues–Political issues and considerations are playing a larger part in the operation of all organizations. By itself, this is not good or bad, although some wag said, "We have the best politicians money can buy." Realizing the problem, Congress has enacted various legislation to control contributions and the ability to influence legislators. Political action committees are still not controlled as some would wish and certainly there is cause for concern when incumbents are virtually shoe-ins for reelection. Should political help be expected because of political contributions? Is it right to seek political intercession on the behalf of your company? What if it is detrimental to another organization that is already satisfactorily providing the goods or services? What happens if your performance is not as good as the other organization, but your company would go out of business without the effort and the other company wouldn't? Should politicians work to save military bases in their congressional areas even though they are no longer needed or wanted by the military? If not, what about the loss of jobs? If so, at what cost to the United States?

Legal issues–This is a sticky area and no attempt will be made to discuss the legalities of anything. Most organizations secure legal representation to handle their needs. The difficulty is not whether things are legal or illegal, but rather what happens when something is legal but morally or socially questionable? What about the trucking company that was saved from bankruptcy by employee contributions only to have them declare bankruptcy a year later without allowing employees to buy out the company? It was legal for some American manufacturers to ask for employee wage concessions and a few months later declare large executive bonuses, but was it an ethically sound decision? Hostile takeovers are legal, but are they socially acceptable when the aim is a quick profit at the expense of the employees who built the organization?

As stated earlier, decisions are not easily made when the various ethical issues are considered. It is further complicated because no one has all the facts in most cases. When carefully considered, most issues that involve ethics also involve some aspect of TQM that further impacts on the decision.

In the end, the desire is that by asking these and other questions before the time comes to make the tough decisions (preferably as a group exercise), the choices that are made will be more ethically sound. Good luck.

Summary

1. Management ethics generally impact on the TQM process in some manner. Few decisions are made in a void or without ramifications that go beyond the borders of the decision-maker's responsibility.

2. Most occasions requiring decisions have ramifications in many different issue areas. Moral, economic, environmental, social, political, and legal issues may play a part in any decision. Seldom will one of the issues stand alone.

3. Most decisions management must make have consequences that extend far beyond the workplace. These decisions also have a high probability of affecting people beyond the vendor–producer–supplier team.

4. There are ethical responsibilities that accompany all hiring, firing, and promotion activities. There are legal, moral, social, and economic decisions that affect the individuals and the organization. These actions do not happen by themselves and they can become complicated.

5. Performance factors have ethical considerations. Should work teams be allowed to work themselves out of a job through performance improvements? What are the organizational requirements in this and other similar issues? The choices are not easy, nor are they simple.

6. Customers deserve many ethical considerations. Among these are fair and honest advertising; prompt, efficient, and courteous service; correct pricing, safe products, correct packaging; and more. American customers can no longer be taken for granted if the organization cares to survive.

7. Many aspects of security have ethical ties. This is especially evident with professional people and their obligation to keep the secrets with which they have been entrusted. Security requirements extend to many other areas that occur in most organizations.

8. Organizations do not exist in a void; they are members of some type of community. That membership requires certain behaviors in order for the organization to be considered ethical.

9. Labor relations are especially important whether or not the organization is union. The people must be properly considered and rewarded for their efforts or the organization will face rough sledding over the long run. Certainly, performance will suffer if they are not properly compensated.

10. Ethical decisions are not easily made considering the myriad of issues faced by the decision-makers in today's organizations.

Bibliography

Blanchard, K. and Peale, N. V. *The Power of Ethical Management*, New York: Fawcett Crest, 1988.

Drucker, P. F. *Management: Tasks—Responsibilities—Practices*, New York: Harper and Row, 1973.

Garrett, T. M. and Klonoski, R. J. *Business Ethics*, Englewood Cliffs, NJ: Prentice-Hall, 1986.

Hosmer, L. T. *The Ethics of Management*, Homewood, IL: Dow Jones-Irwin, 1987.

Index